Achieving QTS
Professional Studies: Primary Phase

Achieving QTS

Professional Studies:
Primary Phase

Second Edition

edited by

Kate Jacques
Rob Hyland

Learning Matters

First published in 2000 by Learning Matters Ltd.
Reprinted in 2001.
Reprinted in 2002.
Second edition published in 2003.
Reprinted in 2003.
Reprinted in 2004 (three times).

British Library Cataloguing in Publication Data
A CIP record for this book is available from the British Library.

ISBN 1 903300 60 6

Cover design by Topics – The Creative Partnership
Cover photo reproduced by permission of Educational Solutions (sales@edsol.co.uk)
Text design by Code 5 Design Associates Ltd
Project management by Deer Park Productions
Typeset by PDQ Typesetting
Printed and bound by Cromwell Press, Trowbridge, Wiltshire

Learning Matters Ltd
33 Southernhay East
Exeter EX1 1NX
Tel: 01392 215560
Email: info@learningmatters.co.uk
www.learningmatters.co.uk

CONTENTS

This book is edited by **Professor Kate Jacques** (Director of the Institute of Education at Manchester Metropolitan University) and **Rob Hyland** (educational researcher, currently working on a project for Newcastle University).

Kay Adamson (St Martin's College, Ambleside)
Robin Bundy (St Martin's College, Lancaster)
Christine Ditchfield (St Martin's College, Carlisle)
Nicky Edwards (Cumbria Local Education Authority)
Tony Ewens (St Martin's College, Lancaster)
Bernard Horsfall (St Martin's College, Lancaster)
Rob Hyland (Newcastle University)
Kate Jacques (Manchester Metropolitan University)
Kath Langley-Hamel (St Martin's College, Ambleside)
Pat Macpherson (St Martin's College, Lancaster)
Ray Potter (St Martin's College, Lancaster)
Mike Routledge (Headteacher, South Tynedale Middle School, Haltwhistle, Northumberland)
Andrew Waterson (St Martin's College, Lancaster)

This introductory chapter sets out the context for those which follow and explains how to use the book. It also seeks to place the objective of meeting national requirements for attaining Qualified Teacher Status (QTS) in a broader framework.

By the end of the chapter you should:

- *understand the overall objectives of the book;*
- *have considered some of the general requirements of becoming a teacher;*
- *understand the significance of the Standards for the Award of Qualified Teacher Status;*
- *be aware how the chapters relate to meeting the Standards for QTS.*

Becoming a primary school teacher and making a difference

If it is your intention to be a primary school teacher then you should need no convincing that this is an important, challenging and rewarding undertaking. Primary teachers have a vital position in the education system: they play a key role in the learning of nearly all children between the ages of five and eleven. Collectively and cumulatively teachers in primary schools have a significant influence over a long and important period in their pupils' development. Though they are by no means the only influence, primary schools and those who work in them can make a difference in the lives of their pupils, they lay the foundations for so much which follows. To embark upon the process of becoming a primary teacher is to undertake a serious preparation for a valuable social role.

For children, however, the felt experience of primary teachers is not one of valuable social roles or collective and cumulative influences, it is so much more immediate. For pupils at any given moment that experience is very much of Miss Oliver, Mr Abbas, Ms Jones, Mrs Rodrigues, Mr Hamilton... And when *you* are that person, then the quality of their experience – at least for the time they are with you – is very much in your hands. The majority of primary teachers have extensive responsibility for a class of pupils for an academic year and therefore *your* knowledge, skills and commitment can have a considerable effect. Individual teachers do make a difference. That is a large part of what makes teaching challenging and worthwhile.

The aims of this book

The purposes of this book are both general and specific. The overall aim is to encourage and assist you to consider a range of professional issues related to qualifying as a primary school teacher. The more specific objectives of this book are to assist you in understanding and meeting the broad professional requirements of the *Professional Standards for Qualified Teacher Status*.

Meeting the Standards for QTS

The current formal requirements for you to achieve Qualified Teacher Status (QTS) are set out in a Department for Education and Skills/Teacher Training Agency document *Qualifying to Teach: Professional Standards for Qualified Teacher Status and Requirements for Initial Training* (DfES/TTA 2002). This sets out the Secretary of State's criteria for all courses of initial teacher training (ITT). If you wish to qualify as a teacher in England (different regulations apply in Northern Ireland, Wales and Scotland), then the wording of the summary at the beginning of the circular is very clear:

> The Standards and Requirements in this document … set out:
>
> - **the Secretary of State's Standards, which must be met by trainee teachers before they can be awarded Qualified Teacher Status;**
> - **the Requirements for training providers and those who make recommendations for the award of Qualified Teacher Status.**
>
> Only those trainee teachers who have met all of the Standards will be awarded QTS.

The meaning is unambiguous: the Standards are requirements and not just desirable attributes or ideal goals.

At this stage it is important to recognise that qualifying as a primary school teacher is a demanding process, but you should not get the formal requirements out of perspective. One of the key purposes of this book, along with its companion volumes in the series, is to show you how these requirements can be met. It aims to demystify and make plain some of these demands in such a way that you recognise how they relate to effective teaching, how you might meet them and in due course demonstrate that you can do so.

The knowledge and understanding and Teaching Standards for specific subjects are covered by other books in this series. For a full list of those publications, visit the Learning Matters website at **www.learningmatters.co.uk**. It should also not be forgotten that primary teachers may teach the whole range of subjects in the primary curriculum and need to be well informed in all the areas they teach. The importance of the primary teacher's subject knowledge, and the need for the would-be teacher to develop a sound grasp of how to teach children the particular skills and concepts of the various curriculum areas, are taken as fundamental by the authors of this book. This volume, however, is concerned with professional issues which run across all subjects and indeed beyond the formal subject curriculum.

QTS and the complete teacher

At the outset it was important to make clear that meeting the government's Standards is central to qualification as a teacher: these standards are not optional – at least not if you wish to qualify! But it is also important to recognise the limitations of these formal statements of the knowledge and skills required for QTS. Underpinned as they are by statutory powers and backed by all the apparatus of official authority, they tend to give an appearance of universal agreement on what is required of teachers.

You will soon learn that there is always some disagreement amongst teachers and those who train them over just which knowledge, skills and attitudes are essential for the Newly Qualified Teacher (NQT), or indeed for the experienced teacher. The requirements of *Qualifying to Teach* are by no means the only 'standards' which we might wish to consider, nor the only version of what it might mean to be an effective beginning teacher. There has been considerable argument about the requirements for QTS (see, for example, the volume edited by Richards et al. 1998); the debate is ongoing. Nevertheless, despite all the debate about the details and how they are expressed and assessed, there is a broad consensus about the general requirements for beginning teachers. It is not merely to meet the Standards that teachers need to be able to plan appropriate work for pupils, to take account of aptitudes and needs, to assess pupils' work, to report progress, to manage the classroom, to build positive relationships with pupils and so forth: these are the core aspects of teaching. It is difficult to think of an effective teacher *unable* to do these things.

It is also important to recognise that the Standards are those for the award of Qualified Teacher Status. They are not the last word on what the skilled teacher can achieve. In 2000, the Department for Education and Employment commissioned Hay/McBer management consultants to review, research and examine the characteristics of effective teachers. They produced a model based on three factors affecting teacher expertise.

Briefly, the three identified factors which could be measured and observed are teaching skills, professional characteristics and classroom climate. The report found that it is the successful interaction of these three factors which enables some teachers to be highly effective. The report uses the language of the Standards as well as detailed descriptions of additional, quite sophisticated, ways of managing children and their learning (Hay/McBer 2000). Classrooms are not the only place where children learn, and effective teachers are in tune with children as people with lives outside school which can be used as a resource to motivate and encourage.

So while the Standards for QTS are only part of the equipment you will need to become a teacher, they are a critical part in the early stages. They provide a valuable framework for you to track your own progress and regularly self-assess your performance.

The range of professional issues covered by this book

There is no limit to the range of professional issues which might be relevant to the teacher in training. This book concentrates on the key areas which the beginning teacher needs to understand. For convenience it is divided into sections of related chapters but it is important to recognise the links between different aspects of professional knowledge and skill. The first section, *Planning and Assessment*, focuses on the planning, assessment and reporting of pupils' work; the second section, *Management, Organisation and Delivery*, looks at managing for learning; the third section, *Children and Individual Needs*, includes chapters on SEN, individual differences and equal opportunities; and the final section, *Becoming a Professional*, gives an overview of professional responsibilities outside of teaching.

Section 1 looks at the related requirements for effective planning, assessment and reporting of pupils' work. Mike Routledge (Chapter 2) explains the fundamental skills of planning lessons; this is not simply a matter of formulaic presentation but of grasping the underlying principles of organising for teaching. Nicky Edwards (Chapter 3) discusses 'differentiation' in some detail because it is fundamental to effective planning for learning when children are so different in their prior knowledge, experience and capabilities. Christine Ditchfield (Chapter 4) discusses the trinity of 'assessment, recording and reporting' (often referred to as 'A,R&R') and how important it is to chart children's progress to encourage them, to inform their parents, and to guide your subsequent teaching.

Section 2 looks at managing for learning in the classroom. It begins with a consideration of how children learn as Ray Potter (Chapter 5) outlines some of the major theories of learning. Andrew Waterson (Chapter 6) examines many of the practical issues of organising the classroom for learning. Pat Macpherson (Chapter 7) considers the climate of the classroom and the importance of promoting self-esteem of pupils to create a positive climate for learning in which all pupils are valued and are encouraged to value others. The thorny issue of discipline is always a concern for teachers in training: Robin Bundy (Chapter 8) encourages a reflective approach to examining how the classroom is functioning whilst Kate Jacques (Chapter 9) examines some possible responses to pupils' more challenging behaviour.

Section 3 looks at some broad issues which are important in all schools. Tony Ewens (Chapter 10) examines some ways in which teachers may encourage the development of spiritual, moral, social and cultural values within the classroom. Rob Hyland (Chapter 11) outlines some of the background issues as well as the legislative position with regard to equal opportunities. Pupils with Special Educational Needs are such a central concern of all primary schools today that two chapters are devoted to this topic. Bernard Horsfall (Chapter 12) outlines many of the specific requirements relating to the implementation of national policy whilst Kay Adamson and Kath Langley-Hamel consider some of the more general principles of acknowledging the range of individual differences which may be encountered in a modern primary classroom (Chapter 13).

The final section examines some of the implications of becoming a teacher. The broader professional issues here are crucial. There is a legal aspect to joining a profession and Rob Hyland (Chapter 14) sets out some of the statutory and contractual obligations you take on as a teacher. There are also broader issues involved in becoming a member of the teaching profession and Kate Jacques (Chapter 15) examines some of the commitment to professionalism which teachers should demonstrate in their work.

The chapters can be read sequentially, but individual chapters can be referred to as necessary. In any case it is important to return to some of the guidance of earlier chapters in the light of issues discussed in subsequent ones. Though the knowledge and skills of the competent teacher may be identified and classified as in the *Standards*, effective performance requires a constant synthesising of insights into different aspects of the teaching experience. Lesson planning (Chapter 2), for example, is not just the mastery of a formal organisational and presentational skill; to maximise the positive effects upon children's learning a lesson plan may have to take into account so many factors from special educational needs (Chapter 12) to health and safety (Chapter 14). You may quickly grasp the formal essentials of planning, how to set out your desired learning outcomes for pupils, your content and resources, but the insight you bring to the task will develop with experience. Learning to teach is itself a good illustration of the 'spiral curriculum' (see p. 71). You will find yourself revisiting the issues discussed in this book with progressively more understanding as you spend time in classrooms and reflect on all you see and do.

Survival, qualification and beyond

Almost inevitably, as you train to be a teacher the immediacy of so many of the demands upon you can induce an understandable preoccupation with survival! This book will help you towards meeting the Standards for attaining Qualified Teacher Status. The team of authors intends that it should illuminate many of the requirements for doing so and give you some practical guidance upon which you can act. But the book is more than a survival aid: the authors also hope that you will see these national requirements in a broader perspective, that you will be enquiring, reflective and critical. Becoming a teacher is partly about acquiring fundamental skills and knowledge but it also involves taking on professional values and standards. Not the least important aspect of a teacher's commitment is the acceptance of the need to continually develop and upgrade skills, to remain informed and keep the ideals of professional service and its broad responsibilites for children's education in mind. If the immediate aim must necessarily be to achieve qualification – to 'meet the Standards' set down for QTS – the longer-term aim must be to work towards developing the skills, knowledge and personal attributes of 'the complete teacher'.

See Chapters 14 and 15 (pp. 172 and 183) on becoming a professional.

Further reading

Cooper, H. and Hyland, R. (eds) (2000) *Children's Perceptions of Learning with Trainee Teachers*. London: Routledge Falmer. This offers some insights into the experiences of pupils working with trainee teachers in all areas of the curriculum.

DfES/TTA (2002) *Qualifying to Teach: Professional Standards for Qualified Teacher Status and Requirements for Initial Training*. London: Department for Education and Skills. This sets out the requirements for Initial Teacher Training in England; these standards which apply to all teachers are appended in this volume.

Hay/McBer (2000) *Research into Teacher Effectiveness: A Model of Teacher Effectiveness*, report by Hay/McBer to the Department for Education and Employment. The DfEE commissioned management consultants Hay/McBer to examine what makes effective teachers. They produced a model based on three levels of teacher expertise. The full report is vast, but a 70-page summary of the report is available online at the DfES website: **www.teachernet.gov.uk/_doc/1487/haymcber.doc** and a four-page summary of the 'Characteristics of an effective teacher' is available at the NUT website: **www.data.teachers.org.uk/nut/pdfs/eefective.pdf**

Pollard, A. (1997) *Reflective Teaching in the Primary School*. (3rd edn) London: Cassell. A widely used text which ecourages a thoughtful approach to learning to teach.

Richards, C., Simco, N. and Twiselton, S. (eds) (1998) *Primary Teacher Education: High Status? High Standards?* Falmer Press. This includes some critical perspectives on the standards as they originally appeared in DfEE Circular 10/97.

By the end of the chapter you should:

- *understand what the terms planning and evaluation mean;*
- *have developed an understanding of the importance of planning and evaluating within the teaching process;*
- *be able to write a lesson plan and a medium-term plan;*
- *understand the meaning of the terms desired learning outcome, assessment and differentiation and their place in the teaching process.*

This chapter addresses the following Professional Standards for QTS:

 3.1.1–3.1.5

(The Standards are reproduced in full at the back of this book.)

The teaching process

Teaching is a complex cyclical process. The diagram in Figure 2.1, adapted from a Wiltshire County Council publication in 1988, outlines the relevant stages, and the right-hand section outlines the kinds of questions teachers ask themselves as they plan each step in the cycle.

What is planning and why is it important?

> Planning is the process of thinking, consultation and developing ideas that leads to the production of plans which act as a guide for your lesson.
>
> (Hayes 1997, p. 54)

If the delivery, i.e. the teaching, is the physical manifestation of a good lesson then the foundation stones of effective teaching and learning are good plans resulting from detailed planning. Kyriacou (1998, Chapter 2) identifies five important purposes and functions of planning:

1. It allows you to think clearly and specifically about the type of learning you want to take place and to relate this to the needs of the children and the school curriculum.

2. It enables you to think about the structure, content and timing of the lesson. What will you do and how much time will you spend on each activity?

3. It reduces the amount of thinking you have to do whilst teaching the lesson. By following a plan you are less likely to get into difficulties.

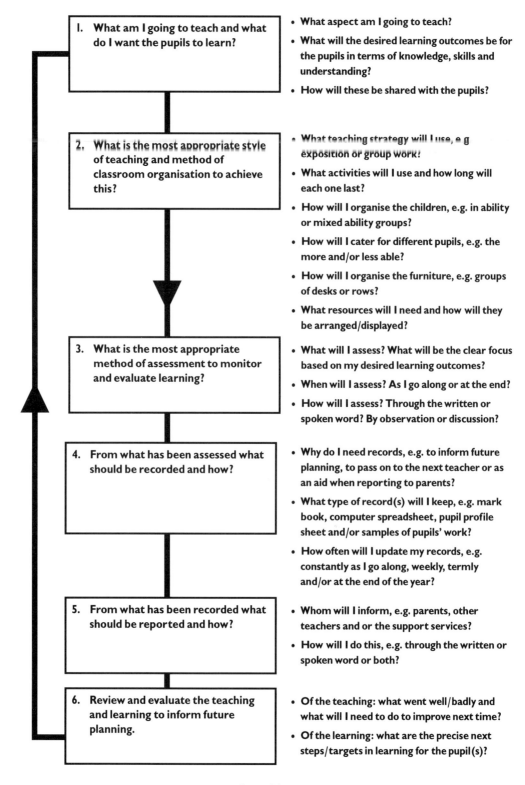

1. **What am I going to teach and what do I want the pupils to learn?**
   - What aspect am I going to teach?
   - What will the desired learning outcomes be for the pupils in terms of knowledge, skills and understanding?
   - How will these be shared with the pupils?

2. **What is the most appropriate style of teaching and method of classroom organisation to achieve this?**
   - What teaching strategy will I use, e.g. exposition or group work?
   - What activities will I use and how long will each one last?
   - How will I organise the children, e.g. in ability or mixed ability groups?
   - How will I cater for different pupils, e.g. the more and/or less able?
   - How will I organise the furniture, e.g. groups of desks or rows?
   - What resources will I need and how will they be arranged/displayed?

3. **What is the most appropriate method of assessment to monitor and evaluate learning?**
   - What will I assess? What will be the clear focus based on my desired learning outcomes?
   - When will I assess? As I go along or at the end?
   - How will I assess? Through the written or spoken word? By observation or discussion?

4. **From what has been assessed what should be recorded and how?**
   - Why do I need records, e.g. to inform future planning, to pass on to the next teacher or as an aid when reporting to parents?
   - What type of record(s) will I keep, e.g. mark book, computer spreadsheet, pupil profile sheet and/or samples of pupils' work?
   - How often will I update my records, e.g. constantly as I go along, weekly, termly and/or at the end of the year?

5. **From what has been recorded what should be reported and how?**
   - Whom will I inform, e.g. parents, other teachers and or the support services?
   - How will I do this, e.g. through the written or spoken word or both?

6. **Review and evaluate the teaching and learning to inform future planning.**
   - Of the teaching: what went well/badly and what will I need to do to improve next time?
   - Of the learning: what are the precise next steps/targets in learning for the pupil(s)?

Figure 2.1

4. It allows you to reflect on and prepare all the materials and resources that will be needed.

5. It serves as a useful record of what has been done and aids future planning.

To use your time with the pupils to best effect, you need to plan carefully for every lesson.

Levels of planning

There is a statutory requirement for every school to have a curriculum policy statement outlining the overarching principles to which all in the school will work. This is usually produced collaboratively by governors and staff. There should also be individual subject policies which make specific the school's beliefs and intent about the teaching of that subject area. Subject co-ordinators work with the whole staff to develop each policy which provides the basis for thinking when planning at individual subject or year group level.

A school's curriculum plans show how these policies are delivered. Planning operates at a variety of levels each with its own purpose. The table overleaf summarises these. The levels will make most sense if you look at them again having read the complete chapter.

Normally schools will address their long-term planning first, medium-term planning second and finally their short-term planning. However, student teachers are more likely to be required to prepare and teach an individual lesson, often to small groups of children, before moving on to planning a sequence. So let's look at this first.

Short-term planning: the individual lesson

A teacher manages a class more effectively if the lesson is thoroughly planned and structured beforehand. In devising your lesson you will need to answer certain basic questions:

How does the lesson relate to the National Curriculum?

Reference should be made to the wording or number/letter of the relevant Programme of Study (PoS). Checking these across a Key Stage is one way a school can ensure that it delivers the statutory National Curriculum.

What do you want the pupils to have learnt by the end of the lesson?

The things you want the children to learn are often referred to as the lesson objectives or desired learning outcomes (DLOs). They specify what the children will have achieved by the end of the lesson in terms of progress in their:

(a) *Knowledge* (information which is worth knowing and/or of interest).

Planning Level	What is it?	Why is it done?	Who does it?	What influences this level of planning?
Long-Term Planning (covers the whole school or key stage)	A broad framework of curriculum provision for each subject area across the school. For each year group it may: ● specify the contents to be taught; ● suggest manageable ways of organising and delivering this content e.g. sequence work into terms and/or identify possible units of work; ● identify possible links with other subjects to avoid overlap or duplication. It can also include a summary outline in the form of a curriculum map.	To ensure: ● that all statutory requirements are met etc; ● continuity and progression across the year groups; ● balance and coherence within each key stage.	Subject coordinators working with all staff.	● The school's curriculum policy statement. ● The subject's policy statement. ● National Curriculum documents ● Other government planning guidelines, e.g. NLF and NNF.

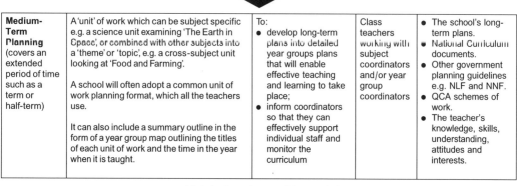

This is used to assist:

| **Medium-Term Planning**
(covers an extended period of time such as a term or half-term) | A 'unit' of work which can be subject specific e.g. a science unit examining 'The Earth in Space', or combined with other subjects into a 'theme' or 'topic', e.g. a cross-subject unit looking at 'Food and Farming'.

A school will often adopt a common unit of work planning format, which all the teachers use.

It can also include a summary outline in the form of a year group map outlining the titles of each unit of work and the time in the year when it is taught. | To:
● develop long-term plans into detailed year groups plans that will enable effective teaching and learning to take place;
● inform coordinators so that they can effectively support individual staff and monitor the curriculum | Class teachers working with subject coordinators and/or year group coordinators | ● The school's long-term plans.
● National Curriculum documents.
● Other government planning guidelines e.g. NLF and NNF.
● QCA schemes of work.
● The teacher's knowledge, skills, understanding, attitudes and interests. |

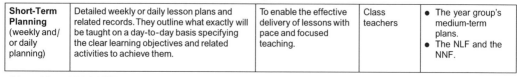

which in turn is used to assist:

| **Short-Term Planning**
(weekly and/or daily planning) | Detailed weekly or daily lesson plans and related records. They outline what exactly will be taught on a day-to-day basis specifying the clear learning objectives and related activities to achieve them. | To enable the effective delivery of lessons with pace and focused teaching. | Class teachers | ● The year group's medium-term plans.
● The NLF and the NNF. |

Adapted from SCAA (1995, p. 10)

(b) *Understanding of concepts* (generalisations which enable pupils to classify, organise and predict and to understand patterns, relationships and meanings).

(c) *Skills* (the ability to perform a task, e.g. personal and social skills like turn-taking or sharing, physical and practical skills like kicking a ball, intellectual skills like observing, identifying, sorting, classifying, hypothesising, reasoning, testing, imagining and evaluating, communication skills like speaking and listening).

For each lesson the DLOs should be limited in number (three at most) and clear (ambiguous DLOs are difficult to assess).

Using the following phrases may help you devise clear DLOs:

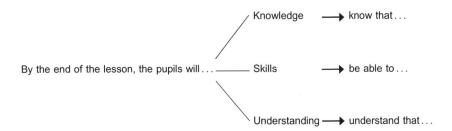

The most common mistakes are to make your DLOs too vague or to describe activities rather than outcomes.

Look at these DLOs and try to identify what is wrong with them (do not look at the revised versions underneath until after you have tried this):
In the examples above:

	English (E)	Mathematics (M)	Science (S)
The children will...	1. write a story. 2. be able to answer questions about a story.	1. sort a set of objects. 2. be able to use a calculator.	1. learn about reversible and irreversible change. 2. learn about electrical circuits.

- **El and MI describe activities.**
- **E2 and M2 are not sufficiently specific.**
- **SI and S2 are both vague and activity-based rather than outcome-based.**

These revised versions are specific and outcome-based:

	English (E)	Mathematics (M)	Science (S)
The children will...	1. be able to use a storyboard format to plan a story focusing on a sequence of events.	1. be able to sort a set of logiblocks by identifying and using the following criteria: shapes, size, thickness, colour.	1. know that some materials, e.g. eggs and bread can be changed permanently by heating, but in other materials, e.g. chocolate, water, margarine, cooling can reverse the changes.
	2. be able to make predictions about the development of the story, e.g. say what might happen next to the plot or to the character.	2. be able to use the constant function on a calculator to explore repeated addition patterns.	2. be able to predict the behaviour of, and correct common faults in, simple circuits with one battery, one bulb and one or two wires.

Practical task

Think again about DLOs. Which of these do you now think are suitable desired learning outcomes for a lesson?

- *The pupils will be able to use the terms* singular *and* plural *appropriately.*
- *The pupils will be taught about the civil war.*
- *The pupils will be able to identify adjectives in a short passage from their reading book.*
- *The pupils will play the scale of G major on the recorder.*
- *The pupils will be able to count backwards from 10 to 1.*

What will the children do?

The different types of activities you can use in your lesson(s) will be discussed later in this chapter when we look at medium term planning. The most important thing to remember at this point is that you must make sure that the activities you have planned enable you to achieve your DLOs.

In what sequence will the activities be taught and how long will you spend on each one?

The best lessons have:

(a) A whole-class introduction in which you establish your authority and stimulate the pupils' interest. From the outset the children should also be told in clear, simple terms what is expected of them and what they should have achieved by the end of the lesson, i.e. explain the lesson DLOs in 'child speak'.

(b) A variety of activities and a variation in pace of delivery. You should try to build in opportunities for whole class teaching and group, paired and/or individual work.

(c) Carefully planned transitions between different parts of the lesson. For each new activity the pupils should know exactly what they have to do and how long it should take them. This ensures they have an idea of how quickly they need to work and what you expect them to 'produce'.

(d) A clear indication of what the key teaching points are for each part of the lesson and the actions to be taken by the teacher to ensure that learning takes place, i.e. what you will do (observe, question, explain, participate).

(e) A whole-class plenary in which progress is reviewed against the stated DLOs. This is usually achieved through carefully structured questioning.

How will you differentiate, i.e. cater for children with different needs?

Children are different and therefore you will need to make yourself aware of these differences by talking to the class teacher. Cohen, Mannion and Morrison (1996, p. 89) suggest that the student teacher should consider differentiation of:

- **Time allowances and pacing.**
- **The amount, type and quality of teacher attention, prompting, support, demand and challenge.**
- **The type of language that the teacher uses and the level and order of questioning.**
- **The style of teaching.**
- **The social arrangements, groupings and working arrangements in the class.**
- **The activity type (e.g. extension, application, practice), demands, cognitive challenge and expected outcomes.**
- **Responsiveness to pupils' optimum and preferred style of learning.**
- **Interests and motivations of the pupils.**
- **Resources and resource organisation access and use.**
- **Classroom organisation, layout and uses of display.**
- **Objectives for and expectations of each pupil's behaviour.**
- **Activities, e.g. problem-solving, investigational work, desk-based work, use of IT, workshop activities.**
- **Anticipated pupils' responsiveness to different teaching styles and teacher behaviour – didactic, informal, authoritarian, *laissez faire*.**
- **Assessment and assessment requirements.**
- **Differential introductions.**
- **Student teachers' and pupils' responsiveness to different ways of organising the curriculum, e.g. through topics, through continuing and blocked work, through modules, through short projects, through flexible-learning arrangements.**
- **Expectations (social, emotional, cognitive, intellectual, physical) of pupils.**

See Chapter 3 on p. 33 for more information on differentiation.

The issue of differentiation will be discussed further in Chapter 3.

What resources will you and the children need? How will they be organised?

Classroom organisation and resources are discussed in Chapter 6. However, it is important to emphasise that in the context of a lesson the planned use of resources may include details about:

See Chapter 6 on p. 74 for more information on classroom organisation and resources.

- **the equipment and materials required (quantity and quality);**
- **their location (after you have checked to see that they are there) and/or how they will be deployed;**
- **how adult helpers will be used.**

How will I assess whether the desired learning outcomes have been achieved?

Assessments should always focus on the original DLOs. If these are not clear, detailed and explicit then it will be difficult for you to design and build in assessment strategies that will tell you whether or not the children have achieved what you wanted them to. Without this information you will be unable to gauge whether any progress has been made. The direct relationship between DLOs and assessment is illustrated below:

DLO

**The children will understand the use of pennies
to pay for goods up to the value of 5p.**

Assessment indicators:

The children can:

- **identify and name the pennies**
- **count out the coins up to 5p**
- **exchange to coins for items costing up to 5p**

Figure 2.3
Adapted from Hayes (1999, p. 177)

Assessment indicators are routed in what children:

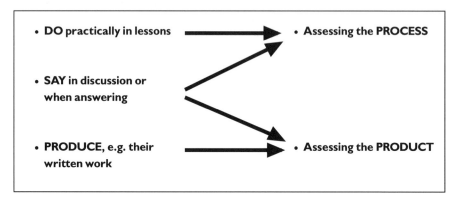

- **DO practically in lessons**   • **Assessing the PROCESS**

- **SAY in discussion or
  when answering**

- **PRODUCE, e.g. their
  written work**   • **Assessing the PRODUCT**

Figure 2.4

Practical task

Assessment wil be covered in more detail in Chapter 4. For the moment, look at the examples below and try to think of an Assessment Indicator to go with the DLO.

DLO	Assessment Indicator
To know the number bonds from one to ten.	
To be able to extract information from a dictionary.	
To understand that magnets exert a force.	
To be able to work co-operatively in a small group.	

How did the lesson go?

This is more to do with reflecting after the event than with planning before it. However, how well the children have done will dictate the starting point for the next lesson. So in that sense a careful review of the lesson is part of the planning process. The performance of the children is also closely linked to the quality of your teaching. If the children have not done well it may be because you have taught poorly.

The best teachers are constantly reflecting on their own and their children's performance in the classroom although they do not always write anything down. That is how they improve. For a student teacher keeping a written record is an important tool in facilitating your analysis and evaluation of how well the lesson went. It enables you to look back over a sequence of lessons and allows your college tutor or class teacher to see that you are learning from your successes and mistakes.

Scott-Baumann, Bloomfield and Roughton (1997, p. 171) suggest that you can use the following questions to assist you in the evaluation of your lesson:

- *What* happened?
- *What* effect did it have?
- *Why* did it happen?
- *How* can I make sense of it?
- *How* could it be different?
- *How* might I (we) have behaved differently?
- *What* would I do next time?

Some students may find it useful to have a number of even more focused questions to ask themselves:

Post Lesson Review	
Informal assessment of the children's learning	**Evaluation of your own teaching**
What did they achieve?	**What did you learn?**
• Were the learning objectives met?	• What did you do that helped or hindered the children's learning?
• How do I know?	• How do you know?
• What did they actually do?	
• What did the children learn?	**Why did this happen?**
	• Were your objectives sensible (e.g. too many, too few? Too difficult, too easy? Too structured, too vague?)
Why did this happen?	
• Did they know why they were doing what they were doing?	• Was your explanation clear?
• Did the tasks match the children's capabilities?	• Did you keep attention throughout?
• Were the children interested and involved?	• Was the content presented in manageable learning steps, in the most appropriate sequence?
• Were they able to handle the equipment safely and purposefully?	• Did you use your voice effectively?
• Did each child perform as expected?	• Was timing satisfactory?
• Were they pleased with what they achieved?	• Did the children have sufficient time to apply and practise new skills?
What 'evidence' do you have for your judgements?	• Did you help the children to articulate and organise their ideas?
• Did you see the kind of learning behaviour you anticipated?	• Were you able to make use of and build upon the children's own contributions?
• Did you see the kind of outcome or product you anticipated?	• Did you have sufficiently high expectations of all the pupils?
• Did you have any difficulty in deciding what an individual child had achieved?	

What are the implications for future planning, in terms of:

• Progression in learning?

• Your teaching skills?

Figure 2.5
Adapted from Proctor et al. (1995, p. 144)

A good tool in planning a lesson is to work to an outline plan that encompasses all the identified factors in the planning process. You may find it helpful to use the format shown in Figure 2.6.

An example lesson based on this format is shown on page 18.

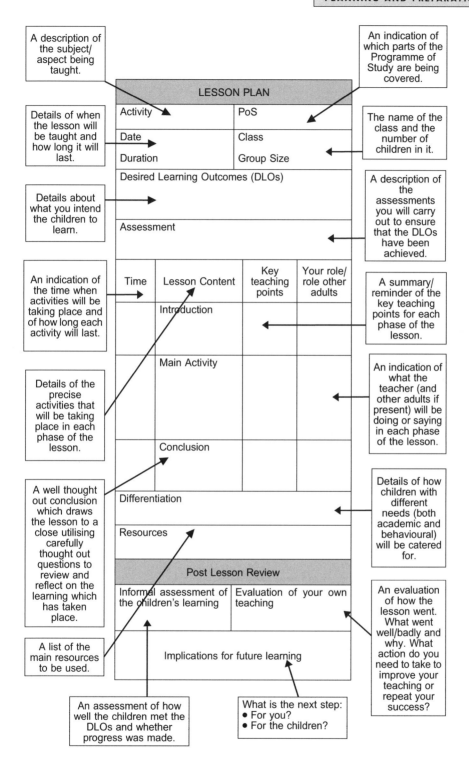

A description of the subject/ aspect being taught.

An indication of which parts of the Programme of Study are being covered.

Details of when the lesson will be taught and how long it will last.

The name of the class and the number of children in it.

Details about what you intend the children to learn.

A description of the assessments you will carry out to ensure that the DLOs have been achieved.

An indication of the time when activities will be taking place and of how long each activity will last.

A summary/ reminder of the key teaching points for each phase of the lesson.

Details of the precise activities that will be taking place in each phase of the lesson.

An indication of what the teacher (and other adults if present) will be doing or saying in each phase of the lesson.

A well thought out conclusion which draws the lesson to a close utilising carefully thought out questions to review and reflect on the learning which has taken place.

Details of how children with different needs (both academic and behavioural) will be catered for.

A list of the main resources to be used.

An evaluation of how the lesson went. What went well/badly and why. What action do you need to take to improve your teaching or repeat your success?

An assessment of how well the children met the DLOs and whether progress was made.

What is the next step:
• For you?
• For the children?

LESSON PLAN

Activity		PoS	
Date		Class	
Duration		Group Size	

Desired Learning Outcomes (DLOs)

Assessment

Time	Lesson Content	Key teaching points	Your role/ role other adults
	Introduction		
	Main Activity		
	Conclusion		

Differentiation

Resources

Post Lesson Review

Informal assessment of the children's learning	Evaluation of your own teaching

Implications for future learning

Figure 2.6

LESSON PLAN			
Activity: Investigating the properties of cuboids		**PoS:**	KS1 AT3 2a, b, c Understanding properties of shape
Date: March 2000	**Duration:** 45 minutes	**Class:** Year 2	**Group Size:** 28

Desired Learning Outcomes (DLOs): The pupils will be able to...
1. Identify cuboids through identification of shape and other properties.
2. Use everyday and specific mathematical language to describe cuboids.
3. Use properties of shape to identify and describe a cube, sphere, cone and pyramid (mentally and orally).

Assessment:
	1. Mental:	Identification of shapes through use of properties.
	2. Activities:	Tasks completed, pupils able to use everyday and mathematical language, good response to closed/open questions, ability to identify a cuboid from a collection of 3D shapes.
	3. Plenary:	Pupils able to recall properties of cuboids. Group B to count number of faces/corners.

Time	Lesson Content	Key Teaching Points	Your role/role other adults
5–10 mins	**Introduction:** Whole class mental/oral work. Children to: 1. Identify an appropriate shape and justify their choice. 2. Look at a cube, close their eyes and visualise it, can they then 'describe' it to each other.	1. Practise previous work on identification of specific solid shapes. 2. Reinforce work on language through focusing on a cube.	1. Refer to display of shapes and play 'I'm thinking of...' games e.g. a shape which rolls. 2. Pass cubes of various sizes round for checking of properties.
25–30 mins	**Main Activity:** Whole class introduction followed by group activities. Today we are going to find out about one family of shapes called cuboids. Draw a rectangle (oblong) on the board and ask for differences between that shape and the large cuboid. Each child to handle a cuboid. Compare their shape with their neighbours and talk about sameness/differences. Focus on sameness and write up children's language on board. Introduce key language to describe properties. Can the cuboid roll or slide? Show pupils a large cube. How is it the same/different from their shape? Explain that a cube is a 'special' cuboid because all the faces are the same shape and size. Group A: Paint printing to identify the faces of a cuboid (including cubes). Pupils (individually) to identify the cuboids in the display. Group B: Feely bag game to identify and describe the cuboids through touch. Refer to key language list on board. Children then to find the cuboids in the poleidoblocs and to count the number of faces/corners. Group C: Build a 'home'/robot/model using bricks (cuboids). Pairs of pupils take it in turn to use.	Key language list: solid, rectangle, square, cuboid, face, corner, edge, straight.	Set off activities. Work with groups B and C in rotation for feely bag game.
5–10 mins	**Conclusion:** Whole class plenary. Show prints: What do they tell us about faces of cuboids? Which prints were the cubes? Try to roll a cube: Why doesn't it roll? Refer to display: Individuals to identify a cuboid. How do we know they are correct? Properties of cuboids: What have we found out?		Differentiated questioning.

Differentiation: Pupils ability grouped for main activity.
Miss B. to support Anna, Najit and Sean during mental/oral section and to support Group A during main activities.

Resources: Display of and poster showing 3D shapes.   Large cube and cuboid plus a collection of various cubes and cuboids.
Junk cuboids for painting area.   Box of poleidoblocs.
Feely bag of solid shapes.   Chldren's prints.
Duplo plus other cuboid bricks/shapes.

Post Lesson Review	
Informal assessment of the children's learning: Generally sound for all groups but some confusion between 'flat' (plane) and solid shapes (2D/3D). No distinction made between cubes and other cuboids.	**Evaluation of your own teaching:**

Implications for future learning:	
Tomorrow develop theme.	Play feely bag game with group A then identify cuboids in book. Group B construction using cuboids/computer worksheet on faces/corners of cuboids. Group C sorting for cuboids...then identify cuboids in book.

Adapted from 'Sample Lesson Plans for Mathematics related to the National Numeracy Strategy', pp. 49–50, St Martin's College (2000).

Practical task

Try transferring the lesson below (planned by a group of trainee teachers) into the format on page 18. The idea is to get the children to produce a gift bag for Mother's Day. Change any aspect that you think could be improved upon. For example:

- *Is the Desired Learning Outcome sufficiently specific and clear?*
- *Is the assessment strategy appropriate? How would you assess the children?*
- *Are the teaching sequences and learning points clear?*

Activity:	Making a gift bag for Mother's Day	PoS:	Design and Technology 4b, c, d, e and f. Art 8d, e and f.
Date:	20th October	Duration:	1 hour
Year Group:	4	Number in class:	24

Desired Learning Outcomes: The pupils will:
- Know how to make a present bag from thin card following instructions.
- Be able to measure, mark out and cut the bag shape and then join it together in a permanent way.
- Know how to apply a finished design on their bags using stencils and sponges.

Activity Outline:
1. Put on art aprons and put newspaper on tables.
2. Show the children a bag made earlier. Talk about the importance of creating the best bag they can as it will be used to carry the posy of flowers they made last week, home to mum for Mothering Sunday.
3. Show the children a specially prepared instructions sheet with measurements and instructions (both written and pictorial). Point out to the children that on the instructions and pictures there will be points that the children have to show me their work before they go on to the next stage (so we do not waste lots of card!).
4. Give the children pieces of thin card, rulers, pencils and tell them to start by marking the dimensions as shown. Make sure the children show me their measured plans before they cut.
5. Keep an eye open at the point of folding the corners and show children individually if needed.
6. Put glue pots/spreaders from edge of table to centre. Allow children to stick bag together.
7. Children mark out position for holes (for string). Show me again at this stage.
8. Punch holes, measure string, thread and tie.
9. Clear the table. Put away measuring equipment and paste/spreaders.
10. Talk through the principles of stencilling again. Remind children to 'dab' paint sparingly and not to mix colours with the sponges!
11. Put on table: sponges, stencils, saucers of paints in green, red, blue and yellow.
12. Children allowed to stencil design of their choice around edges of bag and flowers in the centre.
13. Put names on insides of bags to save arguments/upset.
14. Allocate cleaning up jobs.

Conclusion:
As a group we will look at our finished bags and take pride in what we have achieved.
If there have been difficulties we will talk about improvements we could make.

My Role:
To make sure everyone knows what they are doing.
To encourage and help those who find art and design difficult.
To encourage everyone to take a pride in their work.

Timing:
Five minutes to prepare.
Five minutes for instructions.
Thirty minutes to make bags.
Ten minutes to stencil.
Five minutes clearing up.
Five minutes plenary.

Differentiation:
If anyone in the blue, red or green groups is finding the measuring difficult I will pair them with somebody who has finished that part of their work.
Non-teaching assistant will lead yellow lower ability group.

Resources checklist:

Instructions sheet	Newspaper	Scissors	Cereal boxes	Rules
Pencils	Thin Card	Glue	Spreaders	Stencils
Hole Punchers	String	Sponges	Saucers of paint, blue, green, yellow and red	

Assessment:
Bags to be completed. We will then look at the bags together at the end of the session and discuss their merits. We will consider improvements in design, fixing and decoration.

Medium-term planning: putting together a sequence of lessons/units of work

Why do schools need medium-term plans?

Some large-scale learning objectives cannot be achieved in a single lesson. They have to be covered in stages by being initiated in one lesson and developed over a series of further lessons. Each lesson will have its own desired learning outcome(s) but cumulatively they will lead the pupils towards achieving the overall goal. Medium-term planning involves teachers in putting together such a sequence of lessons.

An effective sequence is one where the different lessons are related to each other and where pupil success in the later lessons depends to a greater extent on their having mastered the earlier ones. In other words the lessons are continuous and progressive. Sequencing of lessons is an important means for securing continuity and progression within the curriculum. Lessons need to show continuity and progression or they become fragmented and pupils lose track of what is happening. Progression is the cumulative, systematic and incremental acquisition of identified knowledge, skills and understanding. Medium-term plans are a school's way of ensuring that lessons build upon prior learning and experience.

What makes a good medium-term plan?

All the teachers in a school usually plan to an agreed planning format and the outcome is referred to as a Unit of Work. There are lots of different formats:

- **The Literacy Framework approach.**
- **The Numeracy Framework approach.**
- **The Qualifications and Curriculum Authority (QCA) approaches found in their Schemes of Work.**
- **Schools' own approaches.**

An example is shown on page 30.

While the formats may vary, the best medium-term plans consistently have a detailed specification for each unit of work which sets out:

- **the learning objectives;**
- **depth of treatment and emphasis within the teaching;**
- **links and references to other units of work;**
- **suggested teaching strategies and pupil groupings;**
- **strategies for differentiating the work;**
- **a list of appropriate resources;**
- **details of specific assessment opportunities.**

Subject specific and linked units of work

Once a manageable framework of continuing and blocked work (see page 29 for an explanation of these terms) has been established, linking together, where appropriate, units of work from different subjects or aspects of the curriculum can strengthen curriculum coherence. There are three significant reasons for linking work at this level of planning.

Units can be linked when:

1. they contain common or complementary knowledge, understanding and skills, e.g. *developing reading and writing skills through work in history, or work on the water cycle in science linked with work on weather and rivers in geography;*

2. the skills acquired in one subject or aspect of the curriculum can be applied or consolidated in the context of another, e.g. *work on co-ordinates in mathematics applied to work in geography on four-figure grid references;*

3. the work in one subject or aspect of the curriculum provides a useful stimulus for work in another, e.g. *creating music from a poem, or a picture.*

In practice, these types of links are not mutually exclusive and good planning will often involve linking work from different subjects or aspects of the curriculum in more than one of these ways.

Where / how do you start?

When structuring a sequence of lessons to take into account continuity and progression consideration must be given to:

1. Establishing clear objectives for the overall unit of work.
2. Identifying the content (knowledge, skills and understanding) you wish to cover.
3. The correct sequence for teaching this content.
4. Selecting the appropriate activities to enable you to meet your teaching objectives.
5. How many teaching sessions you need to cover the activities.
6. Selecting the correct task(s) for each session to ensure you realise the purpose of that session.

The initial starting points to enable you to establish 1 and 2 are:

(a) **The school Scheme of Work**. Class teachers, year group co-ordinators and subject co-ordinators often work together to identify which parts of the Programme of Study for a particular National Curriculum subject will be taught in each year group. Most schools make use of guidance materials produced nationally to aid this process. For example: the National Numeracy and National Literacy Frameworks detail exactly what is to be taught in each year and during each term. The Numeracy Framework (Section 2.2) identifies the following key objectives for Year 1:

- **Count reliably at least 20 objects.**
- **Count on and back in ones from any small number, and in tens from and back to zero.**
- **Read, write and order numbers from 0 to at least 20; understand and use the vocabulary of comparing and ordering these numbers.**
- **Within the range 0 to 30, say the number that is 1 or 10 more or less than any given number.**
- **Understand the operation of addition, and of subtraction (as 'take away' or 'difference'), and use the related vocabulary.**
- **Know by heart all pairs of numbers with a total of 10.**
- **Use mental strategies to solve simple problems using counting, addition, subtraction, doubling and halving, explaining methods and reasoning orally.**
- **Compare two lengths, masses or capacities by direct comparison.**
- **Suggest suitable standard or uniform non-standard units and measuring equipment to estimate, then measure, a length, mass or capacity.**
- **Use everyday language to describe features of familiar 3-D and 2-D shapes.**

The framework then goes on to provide recommended yearly teaching programmes and planning grids.

(b) **The Curriculum Map.** Once the class teacher knows *what* has to be taught, s/he must decide *when* it will be taught. This is done in consultation with other teachers in their year group and the subject co-ordinator. In this way a curriculum map can be put together which provides an overview of teaching in that subject across the school. The example below is a curriculum map for science:

Year	Autumn Term		Spring Term		Summer Term	
1	Ourselves	Growing plants	Sorting and using materials	Light and dark	Pushes and pulls	Sound and hearing
2	Health and growth	Plants and animals in the local environment	Variations	Grouping and changing materials	Forces and movement	Using electricity
3	Teeth and eating	Helping plants grow well	Characteristics of materials	Rocks and soils	Magnets and soils	Light and shadow
4	Moving and growing	Habitats	Keeping warm	Solids and liquids and how they can be separated	Friction	Circuits and conductors
5	Keeping healthy	Life cycles	Gases around us	Changing state	Earth, sun and moon	Changing sounds
6	Interdependence and adaptation	Micro-organisms	More about dissolving	Reversible and irreversible changes	Balance and unbalanced forces	Changing circuits

Outline adapted from the QCA 'A scheme of work for Key Stages 1 and 2: Science' DfEE (1998)

By looking at the curriculum maps for each subject you can get an overview of the whole school curriculum. Schemes of work and curriculum maps should be available in school for you to look at.

Establishing clear objectives for the overall unit of work

Once this has been given to you there is a need to clarify what you want the children to learn and how you will achieve this. For example: in mathematics, if you were asked to teach the children about time at KSI what would you do? To begin with you would need to find out what the National Curriculum Programme of Study for mathematics specifies should be covered:

Understanding Measures
4   Pupils should be taught to:
　　a) ... compare the duration of events using a standard unit of time.

(DfEE/QCA 1999, p. 66)

This can then be converted to an overall desired learning outcome for this sequence of lessons or unit of work. Using the above example this might simply be that:

The pupils will be able to compare the duration of events using a standard unit of time.

There may be several steps to achieving this each with its own learning outcomes. The following diagram illustrates this:

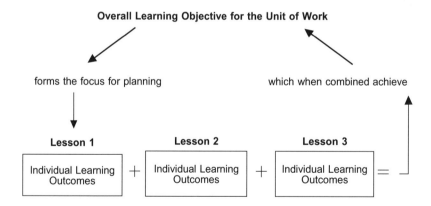

Identifying the content (knowledge, skills and understanding) you wish to cover and deciding on the correct teaching sequence

Having got your DLO the next steps are to:

1. Research the area to be taught to ensure you are well informed and your subject knowledge is sound.
2. Think up teaching ideas and activities, which will both achieve your aims and interest the children.
3. Put these into the correct teaching sequence to ensure effective learning through appropriate continuity and progression.

Your training should provide you with the subject knowledge to make a start on this and experience will hone your ability to get it right. Sequencing is often the most difficult aspect to deal with. When planning a unit, how you organise the teaching will depend on whether the knowledge, skills and/or understanding within it is:

unrelated   i.e. can be taught at any time within the unit as attainment of and progress in one part of the work is unrelated to attainment or progress in another. Units of work that are knowledge based (pass on information and facts) often fall into this category.

related   i.e. work units can be covered in any order but, because of the relationship between the content, the outcome of one cannot be independent of the other. Units that focus on understanding often fall into this category, e.g. when there is a need to understand links between different aspects of a subject or topic but the order in which you teach them is not important.

sequential i.e. the knowledge, skills and understanding form a hierarchy, completion of some of the work is a prerequisite for progress to the next part. Skill-focused units often fall into this category, e.g when a complex skill is built on a simple one.

Practical task

Let's try a sequencing activity. Can you work out the progressions for teaching TIME at KS1? It has been decided that to achieve the DLO above the children will need to be taught about the things listed below. Put these in what you think should be the correct progressive teaching sequence:

- *Number patterns in the calendar.*
- *Day, night, today, tomorrow, yesterday, days of the week.*
- *Use of arbitrary units to measure time, e.g. egg timer, sand clock.*
- *Telling the time. The half-hour, quarter hour.*
- *Events associated with time, e.g. teatime.*
- *Activities involving the passage of time: the hour.*
- *Recognition of special times on the clock face.*
- *Months of the year. Telling time: the hour.*
- *Comparisons of two intervals of time: longer, shorter.*

Did you get it right? This is the sequence suggested by Deboys and Pitt (1997, p. 5):

1. Events associated with time e.g. teatime.
2. Day, night, today, tomorrow, yesterday, days of the week.
3. Comparisons of two intervals of time: longer, shorter.
4. Recognition of special times on the clock face.
5. Use of arbitrary units to measure time, e.g. egg timer, sand clock.
6. Months of the year. Telling time: the hour.
7. Activities involving the passage of time: the hour.
8. Number patterns in the calendar.
9. Telling the time. The half-hour, quarter-hour.

Do not worry if your sequence does not match the above exactly. It should be very similar but most teachers will have differing opinions about the correct order of teaching some elements.

Selecting the appropriate activities to enable you to meet your teaching objectives

Matching appropriate tasks to selected teaching objectives is essential in order for effective learning to take place. At the start of a unit of work these may be selected in order to establish an initial body of knowledge, skill or concept. Later tasks may be to practise and consolidate the learnt material or even to apply it in a new context. Bennett et al. (1984) refer to five types of task:

- *Incremental tasks* involving the learning of new knowledge.

- *Practice tasks* where familiar knowledge is rehearsed to speed up the thinking purposes.

- *Restructuring tasks* where pupils use familiar materials but are required to discover, invent or construct new ways of looking at a problem for themselves.

- *Enrichment tasks* where pupils use familiar materials in unfamiliar contexts i.e. applying knowledge.

- *Revision tasks* where pupils restore to their working consciousness knowledge that has been learnt some time previously.

(Cohen et al. 1996, p. 88)

Let's try identifying a sequence and categorising tasks. Have a look at the summary outlines from four physical education lessons (from the *Basketball Curriculum Guide*, English Basketball Association, second edition, May 1989, section 5). The lessons are designed to introduce basketball to 9-11 year olds. Identify the correct sequence in which they would be taught. Treat them as a short unit of work and looking across the four sessions identify which (if any) tasks are: incremental, practice, restructuring, enrichment and revision.

PE1	AIM: To improve passing and receiving skills	
ACTIVITY	**TEACHING POINTS**	**ORGANISATION**
INTRODUCTION (5 minutes) Dodge and Mark	**'Dodger'**: Look and think ahead. Change space and direction to get rid of marker. **'Marker'**: Stay within touching distance and try to anticipate changes of direction.	In pairs – free space.
MAIN ACTIVITY (15 minutes) 1 2 v 1, 4 x 2 passing game.	**Passer**: Hold the ball in 2 hands. Use fake. No dribbling. Pass to signal. **Receiver**: Signal for ball with hands. Change pace and direction to make space.	In grids.
2 Circle passing drill.	Direct pass can be made to anyone in the circle. Full extension of arms towards receiver. Introduce pass and follow pass, to replace receiver.	Groups of 6 in a circle.
3 'Bull in the Ring'.	Pass can be made to anyone in the circle, except immediate neighbour. Think before you pass. Watch the 'Bull'.	Groups of 5 in a circle with one of the group stationed in the middle of the circle as the 'Bull' to try to intercept the passes. If pass intercepted replace 'Bull'.
CONCLUSION (10 minutes) 3 v 3 team passing game to score the highest number of consecutive passes.	Introduce idea of man to man defensive responsibility. Watch man and ball.	In grids.

PE 2	AIM: To emphasise passing and receiving in game situations	
ACTIVITY	**TEACHING POINTS**	**ORGANISATION**
INTRODUCTION (5 minutes) 3 v 3 passing games.	Emphasise: No dribbling. Good clear signalling. Good wrist and finger control.	Confined areas e.g. grids
MAIN ACTIVITY (15 minutes) 1 3 v 3 passing game with introduction of man to man defensive responsibilities.	No dribbling. **Defender**: Stay with man. See man and ball. Try to prevent pass by putting arm into passing lane. **Passer**: Stay cool, do not rush. Keep ball away from defender. **Receiver**: Use fake to get free. Step towards ball after fake.	Group of 6 in grids.
2 Pivoting drill to defend ball.	Stay balanced with weight on pivot foot. Opponent has to try to touch the ball. Keep ball on side of body away from opponent. Keep pivoting movements short and eyes on opponent.	In pairs: free space, similar height.
CONCLUSION (10 minutes) 3 v 3 team passing game to move the ball to a line to score.	No dribbling. Pass ahead and then move to a new position. After a score the defending team take possession from their own line.	In groups of 6. Play across a court on grid towards opponent's line.

PE3	AIM: To introduce passing and receiving	
ACTIVITY	**TEACHING POINTS**	**ORGANISATION**
INTRODUCTION (5 minutes) Running and changing direction in free space.	Head up, think and look ahead. Look for spaces and run into them. To change direction – bend knees slightly and push off with opposite leg.	Free running. Change direction on whistle.
MAIN ACTIVITY (15 minutes) 1 Passing and receiving.	**Passing**: Control with fingers of both hands. Aim for hands of partner (no lobbing). Follow through. **Receiving**: Show hands to receive. Step towards ball, catch with two hands and bring ball to chest.	Working in pairs facing each other 4 metres apart.

2 Triangle passing drill.	In 3's (4 metres apart). Introduce the idea of moving following the pass.
	
	Think of sequence:
	        Pass the ball.
	        Follow the pass to your new position.
	        Prepare to receive your next pass.
		As above but this time pass round the triangle.

CONCLUSION (10 minutes) 2 v 1 or 4 v 2 passing games – count the number of consecutive passes.	No dribbling. Move into space and signal with hands. Pass to hands.	Groups of 3 or 6 working in grids.

PE4	AIM: To develop more advanced passing and receiving skills	
ACTIVITY	**TEACHING POINTS**	**ORGANISATION**
INTRODUCTION (5 minutes) 3 v 3 team passing game 'Keep ball'.	No dribbling. Pass and move. Use fake before passing when closely guarded.	Groups of 6 in grids.
MAIN ACTIVITY (15 minutes) Continuous passing and cutting drill.	Use direct (chest to chest or overhead) and via the floor (bounce) passes. Emphasise SKID rather than BOUNCE. Use of wrist/finger snap to make overhead pass crisp and straight to target. Use of pivot step to increase passing angle. Only player with ball can pivot.	Groups of 6. After passing ball to B player A follows his/her pass and joins the team opposite. B does same, etc. OOA – – –▶ BOO◀ Groups of 6 in grids.

CONCLUSION
(10 minutes)
Game of bench ball.
	Rules: No dribbling
	        No contact
	        Scorer of goal and goalkeeper change places
	        Limit 'shooting' range
	
	Start with jump-ball
	Clean catch by player on bench = goal
	Team scored against has possession from end line.
		6 v 6 in double grid on across court etc.

Taken from English Basketball Association (1989)

The correct sequence is:

PE 3 = Lesson 1
PE 1 = Lesson 2
PE 2 = Lesson 3
PE 4 = Lesson 4

As you can see, this sequence of lessons has been very carefully thought out. If this is the first time the pupils have played basketball, then in the context of this sport the paired passing task in PE3 is incremental. However, they are likely to have been involved in paired passing in a different context and therefore the task could also be practice, enrichment or revision.

In the context of basketball the circle passing drill is practice but it is also enrichment because the skills are applied in a different context and has an element of incremental learning since it introduces a new element of pass and follow. The careful use of different activities to meet a number of different requirements does not happen by accident. Good teachers plan this type of development in order to maximise learning.

How long should a unit of work take?

Once you know the broad progressions you will need to:

1. Select which of these elements will be taught in your unit of work. In the example on page 25 a Year 1 teacher might decide to teach 1 to 5 in the Autumn Term and leave 6 to 9 until the Summer Term.

2. Decide how long you will spend on this work. This will depend on:

- **The children's ability and previous experience.**
- **The nature and difficulty of the work. A skill may need to be developed slowly over an extended period of time whilst a body of knowledge may be imparted quickly over a couple of lessons.**
- **How long you have available. Teachers are constantly having to compromise on the length of time they spend on a topic. They may well wish to spend 6 lessons on TIME but can only afford 4 because they have many other things to teach.**

As a consequence, a unit of work could be taught:

- **for two 1-hour lessons per week;**
- **for a short period every day of the week;**
- **continuously all day, e.g. a Victorian school day.**

Because of this you could be following the unit for:

- **a year;**
- **half a term;**
- **4 weeks;**
- **1, 2 or 3 days.**

In terms of time units tend to fall between two extremes:

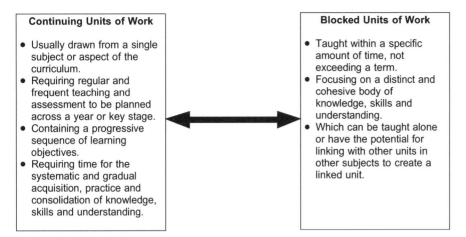

Figure 2.8

Adapted from SCAA Planning the Curriculum at Key Stage 1 and 2, pages 11, 15 and 21 (1995)

Figure 2.8 summarises the points made and provides a framework for planning a unit of work.

Now have a look at the example on page 31 and see if it meets the criteria for a good Unit of Work.

Conclusion

By way of conclusion I would draw you back to my statement near the beginning of this chapter that:

> If the delivery i.e. the teaching, is the physical manifestation of a good lesson then the foundation stones of effective teaching and learning are good plans resulting from detailed planning.

> The Office for Standards in Education (Ofsted) specifies that teaching quality should be assessed by the extent to which:

> - **Teachers have clear objectives for their lessons.**
> - **Pupils are aware of these objectives.**
> - **Teachers have a secure command of their subject.**
> - **Lessons have a suitable content.**
> - **Activities are well chosen to promote learning of that content.**
> - **Activities are presented in ways which will engage and motivate and challenge all pupils, enabling them to make progress at a suitable pace.**

> (Ofsted 1993, p. 27)

Good planning frees you from the need to hold these many complex elements in your head and is therefore something all trainees should be aspiring to.

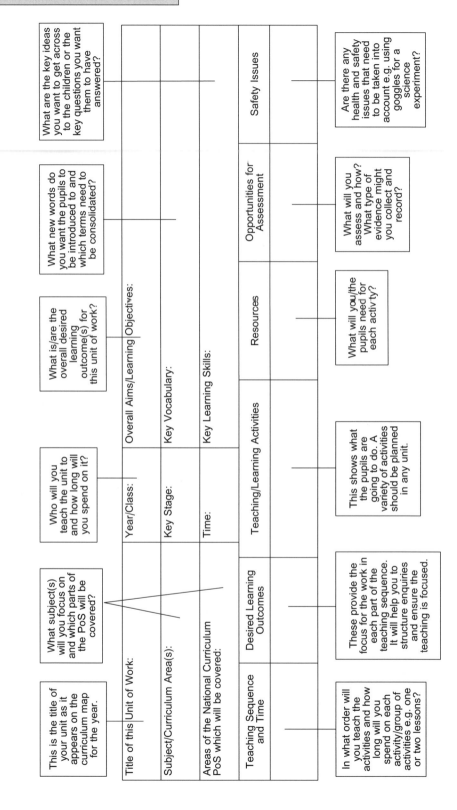

This is the title of your unit as it appears on the curriculum map for the year.

What subject(s) will you focus on and which parts of the PoS will be covered?

Who will you teach the unit to and how long will you spend on it?

What is/are the overall desired learning outcome(s) for this unit of work?

What new words do you want the pupils to be introduced to and which terms need to be consolidated?

What are the key ideas you want to get across to the children or the key questions you want them to have answered?

Title of this Unit of Work:

Overall Aims/Learning Objectives:

Subject/Curriculum Area(s):

Year/Class:

Key Stage:

Key Vocabulary:

Areas of the National Curriculum PoS which will be covered:

Time:

Key Learning Skills:

Teaching Sequence and Time

Desired Learning Outcomes

Teaching/Learning Activities

Resources

Opportunities for Assessment

Safety Issues

In what order will you teach the activities and how long will you spend on each activity/group of activities e.g. one or two lessons?

These provide the focus for the work in each part of the teaching sequence. It will help you to structure enquiries and ensure the teaching is focused.

This shows what the pupils are going to do. A variety of activities should be planned in any unit.

What will you/the pupils need for each activity?

What will you assess and how? What type of evidence might you collect and record?

Are there any health and safety issues that need to be taken into account e.g. using goggles for a science experiment?

Title of this Unit of Work: Investigating our local area. (Note: This unit is based on a village study but can be adapted for other localities.)		Year/Class: 3	Overall aims/learning objectives:	Pupils to be able to: ● Describe a range of physical and human features of their locality using appropriate geographical terms. ● Offer appropriate observations about locations and patterns in the area. ● Identify how people affect the environment and recognise ways people try to manage it for the better. ● Use a range of secondary sources and first-hand enquiry.
Subject/Curriculum Area(s): Geography		Key Stage: 2	Key Vocabulary:	hamlet village town city settlement; distance direction symbol key services; land use environment repair damage; north south east west; homes pollution shops soil; south factory valley; route buildings streams; scale transport slopes
Areas of the National Curriculum PoS which will be covered: 6a, d, e and 7a, c.		Time: 12–16 hours in the Summer Term	Key Learning/Skills:	using and interpreting secondary sources; collecting and recording evidence; making maps and plans; using ICT to handle data; using and interpreting maps; use simple fieldwork techniques

Teaching Sequence and Time	Desired Learning Outcomes In the context of the local area the pupils will:	Teaching/Learning Activities	Resources	Opportunities for Assessment	Safety Issues
1 (1 to 2 hours)	Know where the locality and school are in relation to other places.	1 Ask the children to locate the UK on a globe and then, on progressively larger scale maps, to locate region, county, village. 2 Ask the children to find the school site on a map and aerial photographs of the village. 3 Ask the children to give directions to specific points in the village, recording their directions on a map and identifying features in sequence.	Globes, atlases, aerial and ground photos, OS maps (1:10,000 or 1:25,000) and local street maps.	Discussion (questions and answers). Individual maps produced.	
2 (1 to 2 hours)	Know what the village is like in human and physical terms.	1 Help the children to match ground photographs of the main human and physical features to a base map of the village, naming features and listing questions for further research. Produce a class word bank. 2 Ask the children to study an oblique aerial photograph of the village. Ask them to use the word bank to identify the main land uses and features and then label an outline plan showing key land use boundaries. 3 Discuss with the children the layout of the settlement and reasons why it is like it is.	Aerial and ground photos. OS map (as above) and/or local street map. Outline plan of settlement based on oblique aerial view.	Class word bank displayed on wall. Outline plans labelled.	
3 (4 to 8 hours)	Know the main land uses in the village and understand why they are there.	1 Before finding out about the land use in the village, ask the children how they think land use can be recorded. 2 In the field, divide the children into pairs. Ask each pair to identify land use, e.g. houses, shops, services, farm land, within a small area of the village and mark it on a base map using a colour-coded key. 3 In class, collate the children's results and ask them to present their results using ICT, e.g. in databases, as simple graphs or simple pie charts. 4 Discuss the findings with the children and relate their findings to the land use of the village produced earlier.	Base map. Database and/or graphing software.	Pupils active, base map completed. ICT record of results. Discussion (q and a).	Ensure off-site visit is carried out in accordance with the LEA and school guidelines.
4 (1 to 2 hours)	Know what jobs people do. Understand how they get to work. Become aware of the services provided by nearby settlements.	1 With the children's help, design and conduct a class survey to identify adult jobs within and beyond the school. List the jobs and ask the children to sort them into categories and investigate where and how far people travel to work. 2 Ask the children to use a map or atlas to list three or four towns that villagers could use to buy certain goods, e.g. furniture, clothes. Ask them to use an OS map to work out how they would get to these places and to produce a map describing the route they would travel to buy a pair of trainers.	Atlases and OS maps (as above).	Class survey produced through discussion (q and a). Route maps produced.	
5 (1 to 2 hours)	Know and understand what changes have taken place in the village over time.	1 Ask the children what happened to the bridge in the village in autumn 1997 (the main recent change in the village) and consider why it happened. 2 Ask the children to study photographs of the old bridge and label problems e.g. cracking arches. Discuss with the children why these problems occurred. Discuss photographs of the 1997 bridge repairs and visit the bridge to identify improvements. 3 Discuss with the children other potential environmental concerns in the village and how they might be addressed.	Ground photos. Old newspapers.	Discussion (q and a).	

Further reading

DfEE/QCA (1999) *The National Curriculum: Handbook for Primary Teachers in England: Key Stages I and 2*. London: DfEE. This is obviously the key document setting out the primary curriculum in all subjects. This is the basis of planning and you will soon become familiar with its structure and terminology.

Hayes, D. (1997) *Success on Your Teaching Experience*. London: Hodder & Stoughton. This includes useful sections related to planning.

QCA (1999) *Early Learning Goals*. London: QCA. This is of particular importance to those focusing on teaching younger children. It sets out learning goals in nursery and reception classes before they start on the National Curriculum.

Examples of schemes of work for primary subjects and planning resources for literacy and numeracy are available on the DfES Standards site:

http://www.standards/dfes.gov.uk/schemes

Examples of lesson plans for all subjects are available on the DfES TeacherNet site:

http//www.teachernet.gov.uk

By the end of the chapter you should have:

- *increased your understanding of the term differentiation;*
- *acquired a knowledge of the different types of differentiation and their strengths and weaknesses;*
- *gained an understanding of some teaching strategies used to differentiate the curriculum in the primary classroom;*
- *learnt to select the most appropriate type of differentiation for an individual child in a particular context;*
- *developed an understanding of the relationship between assessment, planning and differentiation;*
- *become aware of the importance of differentiation in an approach to teaching and learning.*

This chapter addresses the following Professional Standards for QTS:

 3.1.1–3.1.3, 3.2.4, 3.3.4, 3.3.6

(The Standards are reproduced in full at the back of this book.)

This chapter defines differentiation in Section 1 and examines some of the factors which affect differentiation in Section 2. Section 3 looks at different types of differentiation commonly used in the classroom and Section 4 broadens its perspective, examining the relationship between assessment, differentiation and planning. The final section summarises the importance of the differentiation process for effective teaching.

What is differentiation?

Defining differentiation: a bar of soap?

> We seem to be looking for a global definition of differentiation. I don't think we can have one … it's a term that … like a bar of soap … you try and grasp it and suddenly it shoots out of your hand.
>
> (Kershner and Miles, 1996, p. 17)

Differentiation is one of those 'in' words – a buzzword for the nineties which has been pulled firmly into the millennium: it sits on the tip of every teacher's tongue and seems

Section One

to appear faithfully on every lesson plan pro-forma. It crops up daily in school during the course of the normal school day. You'll hear it muttered in curriculum planning meetings when teachers discuss medium-term (half-termly) and short-term (weekly) plans; in staff meetings and INSET sessions when teachers are developing whole school policies; in meetings with SENCOs whilst planning for pupils with SEN and in individual lesson evaluations when the teacher is evaluating how effectively (and for whom) the learning objectives of the lesson were met.

Beyond the school gates the term appears to be equally attractive to LEA advisory teachers, OFSTED inspectors and educational researchers alike. Having made its debut on the educational stage with the 1988 Education Act, differentiation quickly gained both popularity and prominence with the introduction of the National Curriculum in 1990, and rose to relative stardom, becoming a household name: a 'watchword of the early 1990s' (Kerry and Kerry, 1997). Despite its popularity, familiarity and impressive 'global' status, differentiation has proved a difficult concept to define; and trickier still to implement effectively in the classroom itself. It is such a vast (and fast growing) concept that teachers vary in their understanding of the term and this leads to significantly different classroom practices. Moss (1996) says differentiation 'is essentially about matching pupil, task and teaching method'.

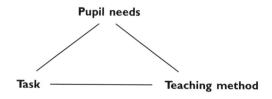

Figure 3.1

As a teacher I must make sure that the individual needs of the pupil, the specific nature of the task or activity and the way I teach are considered carefully when planning an individual lesson or series of lessons. When looking at this triangle of needs (see Figure 3.1) it becomes immediately apparent that differentiation is not a simple concept – a one-off – which can be conveniently added to a lesson plan written earlier. It is an on-going concept – an evolving process – which appears relatively simple on first inspection, but has a habit of growing and developing in complexity, alongside your teaching experiences and expertise. You develop a working definition of differentiation which expands and metamorphoses during the different stages of teaching development. It might start life in the form of a differentiated work sheet for different ability groups and gradually transform itself into an entire way of thinking and approaching the planning and delivery of the National Curriculum. Differentiation is:

> not a single event, it is a process. This process involves recognising the variety of individual needs within a class, planning to meet those needs, providing appropriate delivery and evaluating the effectiveness of the activities in order to maximise the achievements of individual students.
>
> (Dickinson and Wright 1993, p. 3)

Already the concept has changed and developed, transforming from a triangular into a rectangular process shown in Figure 3.2.

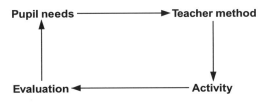

Figure 3.2

While the teacher must plan for individual needs, choose an appropriate teaching style and plan suitable learning activities, the accompanying reflective process, after the lesson has been taught, comes into its own. It is here that the teacher can analyse whether the differentiation has supported, stretched and enriched the children or challenged and motivated them by providing the best opportunity for learning. Without this evaluative process the teacher would never be sure how effective the selected differentiation was. With it the teacher is able to provide the pupils in the class with a variety of activities and approaches to learning to suit both educational and emotional needs.

Webster (1995) stresses the flexible nature of differentiation which must be understood if the teacher is to maximise learning potential of each child. Differentiation is:

> an ongoing process which needs to be planned for and is characterised by flexibility. It is the means of maximising learning for all children, by taking account of individual differences in learning style, interest, motivation and aptitude, and reflecting these variations in the classroom.
>
> (Webster 1995, p. 34)

It is a flexible approach to learning, using a wide range of teaching strategies which make learning accessible by embracing the diversity of all the pupils (Bearne 1996).

Practical task

A: Differentiation is about   **B: Differentiation is not about**

A: Differentiation is about	B: Differentiation is not about
INCLUSION	SEGREGATION
DIVERSITY	SELECTION
COLLABORATION	COMPETITION
VARIETY	UNIFORMITY
SOLUTIONS	PROBLEMS
OPTIMISM	PESSIMISM

Do these contrasting attitudes help or hinder our approaches to differentiation? Which methods of differentiation would teachers with values A and B employ in the classroom?
Adapted from Moss, 1996

Visser (1993) is concerned about the lack of understanding surrounding the term differentiation, despite its popularity. 'Differentiation has become one of the educational jargon words of the mid 1990s – used by many, understood by some, and put fully into practice by a few' (Visser, 1993, p. 4).

A lack of teacher understanding has an impact on the practical application of differentiation in the classroom. And if differentiation strategies do not meet the needs of individual pupils, then learning opportunities are lost, preventing pupils from maximising their learning potential. Teachers, then, must concentrate on gaining an in-depth understanding of differentiation. The table below details some of the key terms which are associated with differentiation which will help to clarify understanding and implications for application.

Key Terms	Meaning
• It is an on-going process	• The teacher assesses what the children can do, then plans and differentiates the curriculum accordingly. It is part of an on-going cycle of assessment, planning, differentiation and evaluation. • Process involves a continual dialogue between pupil and teacher about their learning needs (Saunders and Weston 1991).
• It is planned	• It is not an extra which is added to planning as an afterthought – it is intentional. • It can be used in medium-term planning (half-term plans) when the teacher uses different teaching/organisational strategies to meet different learning styles of the pupils in the class. • In short-term planning – weekly, daily or individual lesson plans – differentiation tailors the curriculum to specific individual learning needs (see Section 3).
• It is the teacher's responsibility	• It is important not to blame the children if they cannot understand the learning objective. • The teacher is responsible for matching the diverse needs/abilities to appropriate activities using a range of teaching styles (Convery and Coyle 1993).
• It is a flexible tool	• There are numerous different ways to differentiate learning opportunities ranging from the task set, resources used, organisation of groups and level of teacher support. See Section 4 for details.
• It values each individual	• Individual pupils, whatever their ability must feel valued. The type of differentiation must not undermine self esteem or a sense of self worth.
• It celebrates diversity	• Differentiation is a way of providing equitable access to a diverse range of pupils' needs. • It celebrates not accentuates the differences (Bearne 1996).
• It centres on entitlement	• Each individual pupil is entitled to have his or her learning needs and abilities catered for. • A teacher must provide opportunities for each pupil to have equal access to the National Curriculum (Visser 1993).
• It maximises learning potential	• Differentiation aims to maximise the learning of individual pupils. • It is the difference between where the pupil is now and where the pupil has the potential to be (Dickinson and Wright 1993).
• It is contextually embedded	• The context of the classroom plays a vital role in helping the teacher to select and use subtle and appropriate differentiation. (Kerry and Kerry 1997 p3).

Factors affecting differentiation

Section Two

Differentiation is contextually embedded

In Section I differentiation was identified as part of an ongoing process which does not occur in isolation. When a teacher is planning a lesson additional factors must be taken into consideration (see page 38). Each of these factors will affect the types of differentiation which you plan to use in the classroom. This is particularly noticeable on block placements. Factors I and 2 – pupil diversity and curriculum requirements – are beyond the control of the class teacher. The curriculum has put teachers under considerable pressure recently, as constant adaptation to educational innovations is a time-consuming and tiring occupation. Factors 3 to 5 can have a substantial impact on differentiation options and teaching strategies available to you:

- **The assessment methods used by a school might lack flexibility if they rely solely on written outcomes. Whilst you would like to use a different method of assessment – perhaps an oral presentation – you must stick to the chosen school assessment methods.**
- **There might a whole school policy for setting pupils by ability in English and mathematics. Whilst you would like to set some mixed ability problem solving group activities you might not have the opportunity to do so because of the organisational or setting policy of the school.**
- **The class you inherit during a placement will have the class teacher's behavioural and learning expectations. You might not have time (and it might not be appropriate) during your placement to set up and maintain your own behavioural expectations and standards.**

The cumulative effect of these factors can limit your opportunities of discovering which methods and approaches to differentiation are most suitable in the given context. You have to be flexible and adapt the policy of the school, trying to understand the reasoning behind the policy and practice, whatever your personal beliefs. It is important to remember that pupils learn within a unique context and each context contains elements beyond our control. It is up to us to understand that context and provide as diverse and subtle a range of differentiated opportunities as possible within it. Our own reflective, and informed approach towards teaching will prove to be the most effective tool in maximising learning opportunities.

Practical task

- *Consider your last placement in terms of the factors in the table overleaf.*
- *Which factors felt beyond your control?*
- *Think of the pupils in your last class and list 10 ways pupil diversity was evident.*
- *List the ways you catered for these differences.*

Factors for consideration	Meaning
1. Pupil diversity	• Cognitive, educational and developmental factors • Biological, gender and maturational factors • Physical, neurological, sensory motor and perceptual motor • Cultural, family, ethnic, and economic factors • Social, interpersonal, emotional, personality and motivational factors • Moral, religious and ethical factors (Moss 1996)
2. Curriculum requirements	The ever changing demands of the National Curriculum and the latest educational innovations • Curriculum 2000 • The National Literacy Strategy • The National Numeracy Strategy • National Grid for Learning
3. Assessment methods used in school	• Teachers under pressure to prepare pupils for Key Stage 1 and Key Stage 2 SATs and spend more time preparing them for SATs style assessments • Summative assessment often narrow focus – written only • Some assessment publications are unreliable – multiple choice – the data might not give a valid benchmark of added learning
4. School context	• Attitude towards differentiation can be determined by school ethos and policies – e.g. setting of pupils in maths and English/organisation of SEN • Ethos in school – valuing others and collaborative learning or winner takes all • The School Improvement Plan will prioritise the budget which might have recurring resourcing limitations for differentiation
5. Teacher style and management style	How teacher: • present tasks – diversity/quality of approach • supports pupils – praise, feedback, frameworks • sets high expectations – consistency • organises classroom – whole class/groups • organises resources – independent learning • values individuals – listens and value.

Section Three

Types of differentiation

It is hardly surprising to discover that the types of differentiation are nearly as prolific as the number of definitions. Whilst Lewis (1991) identifies 11 possible types of differentiation, Kerry and Kerry (1997) identify 15 methods and those are only for the more able learners. The table on page 39 identifies six main types of differentiation.

Considerations and implications of differentiation

In Section 1, the ambiguous nature of differentiation was uncovered: like the bar of soap, it is slippery and hard to grasp. This ambiguity must be carefully considered as it often leads to teacher misconceptions. It is possible for a teacher to define differentiation as a dividing activity where children are segregated into ability groups by their differences and taught a separate curriculum. While such an interpretation might cater for organisational needs and curriculum planning, the individual's self esteem, when labelled at the age of seven as a failure, has not been fully considered. Such an

Type of Differentiation	Examples
Input (content) Contents of the teacher contribution	• Amount of factual information/content of teacher input • Number of concepts introduced or explained • Specific vocabulary chosen • Length of time used for teacher input • Delivery of input – clear/lively etc
Resources Variety of resources to fit individual needs	• Choice of texts – layout/readability • Choice of visual resources/artefacts • Variety of writing materials – white boards/pens/paper • Organisation of classroom for ease of access to materials and for groups of pupils • Frameworks for writing/organisation
Support Additional support for pupils to enable learning outcomes to be met	• Teacher support for individual pupil • Additional adult works with a pupil or group of pupils, e.g. act as a scribe • Peer tutoring or group work where pupils assist one another • Technological support – concept keyboard, spell checkers, tape recorder, computer, CD Rom and video • Praise achievement
Task Different tasks within a specific subject area	• Series of graded tasks of increasing complexity • Separate task set for each ability group • Verbal presentation of learning • Written format – fiction/non fiction/first draft or final • Artwork/display • Choice of task • Problem-solving tasks • Use of role play and drama • Homework
Outcome Common task set but outcome of task or end product will differ from pupil to pupil	• Summative assessment – all do same test and achieve different marks, SATs or school report • Formative assessment – a piece of work marked identifying a target of the next learning step for the pupil • Answer to a question/verbal presentation • Piece of drama • Written outcome – first draft or final copy
Response Response of teacher/peers/ individual to different outcomes	• Praise for particular achievement/attitude • Setting of specific learning targets • Constructive feedback • Set clear DLOs for individuals • Individual IEPs for pupils with SEN • Using partner pupils to evaluate achievement/needs • Self assessment by pupil

Practical task

- *Which types of differentiation have you used in the classroom, when did you use it and why?*
- *Examine one of your lesson plans. What type of differentiation did you use and why?*
- *Examine one of your lesson evaluations. What does it tell you about your current approach to teaching and learning?*

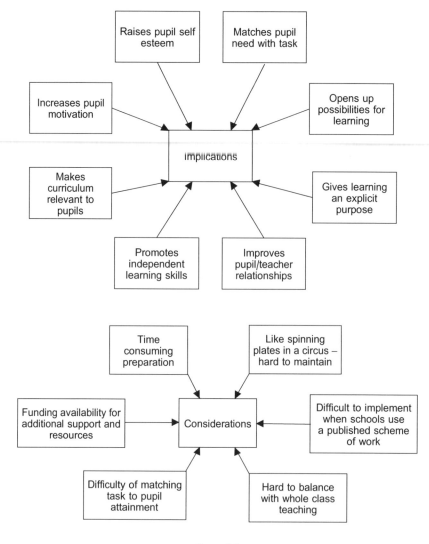

Figure 3.3

interpretation of teaching responsibility could lead to lost opportunities and children who, lacking self confidence, lack the motivation to learn. Alternatively the teacher, in trying to cater for each individual need and learning style, could get lost in a field of uncertainty over the selection of a suitable differentiation strategy. Too many strategies could be employed at once, clouding the learning objectives and clarity of teaching. Figure 3.3 looks at considerations and implications perceived by teachers when considering the notion of differentiation (Kerry and Kerry 1997).

Matching differentiation to individual needs

Matching the differentiation to individual needs is a difficult task, especially when you don't know the pupils at the start of a placement. You will feel unsure of the pupils' personal qualities, needs and levels of attainment. Similarly there will be an uncertainty

Practical task

- *Using the table on types of differentiation, consider how you might differentiate for the following children to make the outcome of their work more successful.*
- *Look at the table overleaf and see if you agree with the possible solutions suggested.*

John, age 8, has got to throw and catch a tennis ball with one hand. He says to his class teacher, 'Miss, do you need any jobs doing? I noticed the class library has got really messy' and thinks to himself: 'Maybe I can forge a note from my Mum, I hate P.E. I'm useless at it'.	**Identification of John's needs** • Lack of confidence in PE, frequent avoidance tactics • Lack of hand–eye co-ordination • Poor spatial awareness
Sarah, age 9, has been asked to write a description of a special object using adjectives. She thinks to herself, 'Quick, quick, quick one more sentence ahh, I'm the first to finish. I even beat Jane. Look, she hasn't even done a page!'	**Identification of Sarah's needs** • Rushes every piece of work – wants praise for completion • Poor listening skills • Hates re-drafting or checking work
Peter, age 5, is trying to take part in a shared reading session within the Literacy Hour. He thinks to himself, 'I'm bored I can't hear and I hope I don't get asked any questions. I wonder what's in my packed lunch?'	**Identification of Peter's needs** • Hearing impairment – intermittent • Short concentration span
Amy, age 11, must take a summative, written test on the function and structure of the muscles and the skeleton. She thinks to herself, 'Which one is the back bone? Is that one the collar bone? Oh I can't remember!'	**Identification of Amy's needs** • Very conscientious and motivated • Level 2 reading • Level 3 spelling • Confident in expressing ideas orally
Clare, age 7, must write a story about a holiday that went wrong. She thinks to herself, 'I know, we could be going on a journey in the car to France. We could break down on the motorway, then we could get stuck on the ferry. After that we could run out of petrol in a deserted country lane'.	**Identification of Clare's needs** • Quick to understand new concepts • Extensive vocabulary • Good sequencing skills

Pupil Age	Possible Problems	Possible Differentiated Solutions
John, age 8	• He will be unable to catch the small ball • He will lose even more self confidence • Hand eye co-ordination will not improve • He will develop a sudden stomach ache!	• **Resources** – larger, lighter ball with textured surface which is easier to grip • **Task** – catching with two hands or a single task given catch or throw • **Support** – teacher to partner John during paired activities to teach catching sequence

Sarah, age 8	• As Sarah has poor listening skills she might not understand the task
	• The description will lack detail with few adjectives and little evidence of checking for errors
	• Disappointment when praise is not given
	• She hates redrafting and checking words
		• **Input** –
		  a) Teacher to check through questioning that Sarah has clear understanding of task
		  b) Task can be written on white board
		• **Task** – split into several units
		  a) Sarah and partner to carry out a brain storm on adjectives and create a list
		  b) Sarah and partner to write an opening sentence using three of their adjectives
		  c) Pair to read sentence out loud and continue
		• **Resources** –
		  a) Dictionary on table
		  b) Specific word bank for piece of work
		  c) Use of computer for redrafting purposes
		• **Response** –
		  a) Teacher to make learning objectives and specific targets clear
		  b) Make success criteria of task clear

Peter, age 5	• He might not hear the teacher during the whole class input
	• He might lose interest in the session
	• He might misbehave – frustration
	• He will not gain understanding of the reading/writing objectives being taught
		• **Resource**
		  a) Classroom organisation – sit Peter where he can hear and see the teacher
		  b) Teacher to look at Peter when talking to him
		  c) Use visual aids too
		• **Support**
		  a) Check understanding with Peter quietly on a one to one

Amy, age 11	• Amy won't be able to read the questions on the exam paper and will not be able to demonstrate her subject knowledge and understanding of science • Frustration at failing • Loss of confidence and self esteem	• **Support** – ask an additional adult to read the questions and act as a scribe • **Input** – oral assessment • **Task** – Amy to prepare a presentation on the subject which will demonstrate her understanding of the subject • **Resources** – tape answers

Clare, age 9	• Will produce a good story without stretching her writing ability – won't improve
	• Become complacent
	• Get bored or lose interest
		• **Input** – introduce a more complicated story framework and ask Clare to model her story on this framework
		• **Task** – several stages
		  a) Write a plan using a structure
		  b) First draft
		  c) Check spelling and punctuation
		  d) Redraft into book
		  e) Read to audience

over the contextual factors within the school. You will not know the expectations for work and behaviour or, for example, the level of independent learning. Because of this, early attempts to differentiate, however carefully prepared, often lead to frustration and perceived failure. It is the same for experienced teachers, every September, who struggle to find effective differentiation techniques until they know the children as individuals and cater for their quirks and idiosyncrasies. The summative assessment helps, and is a starting point, but nothing beats the wealth of inside knowledge which accumulates as the teacher and the class build trust, sharing teaching and learning experiences together.

Effective matching of individual needs to an appropriate task is a subtle business, a skill which develops with the practical experience of the classroom. For this there is no substitute. The following section outlines the individual needs of five pupils. The original tasks set do not match the pupils' needs.

The big picture

The ADP (assessment, differentiation and planning) process

Section Four

In Section I differentiation was identified as an ongoing process or cycle which takes place continually in the classroom to check that individual social, emotional, physical and learning needs are being met. The process of differentiation is interwoven with both assessment and planning. In isolation each area can only function partially. Unless the teacher links the three processes, the information provided is fragmented, making it difficult to plan the delivery of the curriculum in an informed and relevant way. Figure 3.4, the ADP model, shows the relationship between the three areas of teaching.

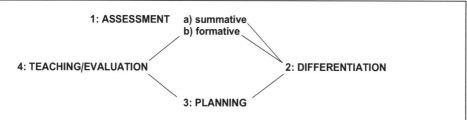

1a: Assessment (summative)
This provides the teacher with a starting point for planning. The teacher can plan what to teach because he or she knows what the children have previously learnt and which levels of attainment have been reached.

2: Differentiation
Specific types of differentiation can be chosen to meet pupil learning styles and individual needs planning is differentiated – unique to the context of each class.

3: Planning
The lesson is planned meeting the requirements of the National Curriculum and each pupil.

4: Teaching/evaluation
The lesson is taught.
Evaluation of the lesson in terms of learning environment and meeting desirable learning outcomes.

1b: Assessment (formative)
Use of formative assessment of the outcomes – the work produced to see if the differentiation has helped to maximise learning. The whole process then starts again.

Figure 3.4

ADP MODEL IN CLASSROOM USE

To clarify understanding of the ADP process, the model has been applied to a classroom situation. The ongoing cycle of assessment, differentiation and planning is followed through to show the inter-dependence of the three processes.

The cycle starts with Stage 1, Summative Assessment, where the teacher gains information about the pupils' level of attainment in speaking and listening. This helps the teacher to differentiate the planned learning in Stage 2 through resources, input, task and response. The lesson plan is written in Stage 3 and delivered in Stage 4. The evaluation which follows the lesson allows the teacher to reflect upon the teaching strategies and classroom organisation. This, combined with the formative assessment of the learning outcomes which occurs in Stage 1b, helps the teacher to plan and differentiate the next lesson successfully.

Stage 1a : Summative assessment

Key Stage 1   Age: Year 1 Class   Number in class: 29

- **Six children are working towards Level 1. They have difficulty in:**

i.   listening to others

ii. speaking audibly

iii. explaining their ideas in detail.

- **Twenty-one children have achieved Level 1. This means that they can:**

i.   listen to other people

ii. answer questions or offer ideas which are usually appropriate to the subject/ lesson

iii. speak audibly, using simple vocabulary to convey meaning, explain or extend an idea.

- **Two children have achieved Level 2. This means they can:**

i.   listen carefully to other people showing an awareness of others

ii. adapt their vocabulary and tone of voice so that it is appropriate to the context

iii. explain their ideas using relevant details.

Stage 2 : Differentiation

Resources

(a) Classroom organisation

i.   Pupils organised, sitting in a semi-circle — good view of teacher and artefacts.

ii. Each pupil can turn easily to a partner for later paired activities.

- **Eye contact helps to keep concentration and listening skills.**
- **By turning to a partner concentration and time are not lost through reorganisation.**

(b) Equipment

i.   Artefacts positioned on raised display next to teacher – easy access.

ii. Labels/vocabulary notice-board prepared with pictures of accompanying artefacts.

iii. Mini whiteboards/pens beside teacher for later paired work and activities.

- **First-hand experience of artefacts keeps interest and uses other senses in addition to sight.**
- **The labels reinforce new vocabulary.**
- **Mini whiteboards cater for children whose preferred response is not through speaking.**

Input

(a) Choice of vocabulary teacher decides to use.

(b) Type of expression teacher uses to help all the pupils listen.

(c) Use of the artefacts whilst talking to maintain interest.

(d) The amount of time taken to give the input.

- **More able pupils must be extended and the needs of the National Curriculum Speaking and Listening Programmes of study must be met.**
- **Clear speech with good intonation is a role model for the pupils and keeps them listening.**
- **Children with poor listening skills will be visually stimulated.**
- **Too much talk is hard to listen to!**

Task

(a) Verbal tasks

i.   answering of open or closed questions as an individual in a class discussion

ii. expressing an idea or opinion and justifying it in class discussion

iii. discussion in pairs most important artefact.

- **Increase pupils' confidence.**
- **Give pupils opportunities to use appropriate vocabulary.**
- **Encourage pupils to clarify their ideas and explanations when speaking.**

(b) Physical tasks

i.   coming to the front of the class to match a picture/artefact to a label

ii. match new vocabulary with pictures in pairs

iii. passing round artefacts to look at and feel them first hand

iv. jotting ideas, diagrams or pictures on a mini white board.

- **To allow for children who lacked confidence in speaking in front of the class to take part in the lesson.**

Response (outcome)

(a) Type of pupil response

i.   individual verbal response – extended or simple/use of vocabulary

ii. verbal – in pairs

iii. written

iv. diagram or picture form

- **To cater for and value individual learning style.**

(b) Verbal teacher response

i.   praise for individual contributions

ii. repetition and extension of answers given by pupils

iii. varying amount of constructive feedback

(c) Non-verbal teacher response

i.   eye contact

ii. nodding of head

iii. pointing to artefacts

(d) Time – giving pupils different amounts of time to respond

- **Increase pupils' confidence.**
- **Make individuals feel valued.**
- **Extend/ enrich pupils' understanding/thinking skills.**
- **Allow time for pupils to think for themselves and organise their thoughts into words.**

Stage 3: Short-term planning
The teacher can plan the lesson with confidence ensuring they meet both the demands of the curriculum and the individual needs of the pupils (see table on page 47).

Stage 4: Teaching/evaluation
(a) Input / Response

i.   the teacher felt confident in the class discussion and was able to react in a flexible way to pupil comments and extend their responses and confidence

ii. pupils were focused and listened during teacher input

(b) Task

i.   pupils gained confidence when chatting over possible answers in pairs before responding

ii. interested to listen to ideas of others

iii. paired activities worked well – talking/ matching pictures

Activity	PoS
• Class discussion about different types of mountaineering equipment – discovering its use in cold climates • Paired activity matching pictures to vocabulary • Paired talk to discuss most useful piece of equipment	Speaking and Listening, English 1a Clarify/explore ideas 2a To speak with confidence use relevant detail/vocabulary to express ideas 3a Extension of vocabulary
Duration 40 minutes	**Class** KS1, Y1 **Total** 29
Desirable Learning Outcomes	**Assessment**
i. Understanding and use of new vocabulary in speech ii. To speak with increasing clarity, expressing ideas/reasoning in a variety of contexts iii. Gain increasing awareness of audience as a speaker and listener	Look at learning outcomes i. Did everyone contribute individually in whole class discussion? ii. Did the matching paired activity consolidate understanding? iii. Did the paired talk increase confidence and clarify children's speech?
Differentiation	**Resources**
Teacher input Resources Tasks Response	Mountaineering equipment Labels on display Paired activity pictures and vocabulary words Small white boards and pens – one between 2

Time	Lesson content	Key teaching points	Your role/other adults
10 minutes	Introduction i. Talk cold climates re expedition ii. Show children equipment/ introduce vocabulary	Vocabulary Give clear answers – reasons/explanations	Effective role model whilst speaking Asking of open questions to promote thinking
20 minutes	Main Activity i. Label equipment as a class ii. Paired activity matching new words and pictures iii. Touching/ looking at equipment iv. Talk in pairs deciding most useful piece of equip/why?	Listen to your partner Take turns	Praise for positive learning atmosphere/ listening skills
10 minutes	Conclusion Share ideas on useful equipment Check vocabulary retention	Listen to others Speak, giving reasons for your choice	Assess if DLOs have been met

BUT

(c) Resources

i.   pupils were excited to see artefacts and found it difficult to wait their turn and tempers flared!

ii. insufficient time to use whiteboards – needs developing

(d) Organisation

i.   pupils had too long to wait to touch the artefacts

Stage Ib: Formative assessment

(a) Speaking as an individual: some children who do not usually participate in class discussions spoke when they were holding the artefacts.

(b) Speaking in a pair: the paired talking activity got all more pupils involved, talking to one another and enthusiastic to feedback verbally to the whole class.

(c) Matching pictures with new vocabulary: each pair successfully matched the artefacts with the labels.

Stage 2: Differentiation

How does the next lesson plan need to be altered to ensure that the learning opportunities are maximised?

(a) Classroom organisation

- **organise class in groups so that they can pass one artefact around a table at a time and reduce the waiting time**

(b) Task

- **use different paired tasks diagrams, notes and pictures**
- **role play using equipment in cold environment**

(c) Input

- **the length teaching input should stay the same as the children listened**
- **change in content to revise meaning of new vocabulary – play riddles where teacher gives clues and children guess which artefact it is.**

USEFUL QUESTIONS TO ASK IN EACH STAGE OF THE ADP CYCLE
Stage Ia: Summative assessment

- **What level of attainment have pupils have the pupils achieved?**
- **How were the pupils assessed?**
- **How diverse are their individual needs?**
- **Select a starting point for planning?**

Stage 2: Differentiation – selection of teaching/organisational strategies

- **Which specific individual differences must be matched to the curriculum through differentiation?**
- **Which method(s) of differentiation will it be most appropriate to use?**

Stage 3 : Planning

- **Has the plan met the curriculum requirements from the programmes of study?**
- **Has the plan catered for individual needs?**

Stage 4: Teaching the lesson

- **Have the teacher strategies been used flexibly and responsively?**
- **How did the pupils respond during the lesson?**
- **Did the differentiation enable equal access to the curriculum?**

Stage Ib: Formative assessment of learning outcomes

- **Do the outcomes reveal new information about the pupils?**
- **Do the outcomes reveal an area of subject knowledge/concept that pupils need support with?**

Stage 2: Differentiation

- **What kind of adjustments need to be made to my next lesson?**
- **What kind of differentiation – what is its purpose?**
- **How will I know if this is successful?**

Conclusion

> There are, however, wide-ranging implications if teachers are to put differentiation into practice successfully, that is, catering for the sheer diversity of children's learning needs, which Thomas describes as 'the phenomenally difficult process of making learning come alive for all children'.
>
> (McGarvey et al. 1996, p. 69–70)

Section Five

When, as an initial trainee teacher, you are suffocating with total information overload, surviving all-night planning marathons, making classroom resources which any Blue Peter presenter would be proud of and suffering from an accumulation of sleep deprivation, it might be difficult to judge whether the individual teacher really does make a difference. When the difference you make is couched in educational jargon and removed from the context of the classroom it becomes even harder to appreciate. It is hoped that this chapter will have helped you to see that differentiation is a way of making a difference to the individual pupils in your charge.

Differentiation matters because:
- **it caters for a diverse range of interests, characteristics and learning styles, celebrating 'the differing talents of children'**
- **it is child centred and considers how best to suit the learning needs to pupils**
- **it breathes life and purpose into the National Curriculum**
- **it makes every child feel valued, sensing pride in their achievements**
- **it shapes the quality of learning opportunities offered to pupils**
- **it encourages them to become involved and gain responsibility of their own learning.**

Differentiation is important because:

- the **National Curriculum requires it;**
- **OFSTED inspectors demand it;**
- **effective teaching embraces it;**
- **pupils gain curriculum entitlement through it;**
- **pupils develop a sense of value because of it;**
- **independent learning springs from it;**
- **individual learning potential is maximised by it;**
- **it brings learning to life!**

Differentiation matters because it is our job, as teachers, to make learning an intriguing and purposeful activity. We have to breathe life into (and beyond) the National Curriculum, that 2D master plan; and activate a 3D moving model which motivates and captures the learners. It is an essential teaching tool. Make sure it's on your Christmas list!

Further reading

Bearne, E. (ed.) (1996) *Differentiation and Diversity in the Primary School*. London: Routledge. The different authors in this collection of articles, edited by Eve Bearne, discuss a wide range of general issues concerning differentiation and also their application in specific areas of the primary curriculum. The chapters range from 'Hearing impaired children in the classroom' to 'Differentiation in physical education'.

McNamara, S. and Moreton, G. (1997) *Understanding Differentiation: A Teacher's Guide*. London: David Fulton. This is a very practical guide which explores different forms of differentiation and suggests how they may be implemented in the classroom.

By the end of the chapter you should:

- *appreciate the variety of purposes served by assessment;*
- *understand the terms 'formative', 'summative', 'criterion referenced' and 'base-line' assessment;*
- *understand the interconnections between planning, assessment, recording and reporting;*
- *know about the different methods of assessment;*
- *have the tools to be able to evaluate your own assessment, recording and reporting practice.*

This chapter addresses the following Professional Standards for QTS:

 3.2.1–3.2.7

(The Standards are reproduced in full at the back of this book.)

Introduction

> Promoting children's learning is a principal aim of schools. Assessment lies at the heart of this process.
>
> (DES, 1988)

Three of the six stages in the cyclical teaching process on page 8 are covered in this chapter. If you are clear about the learning outcomes set at Stage I of the process, then your assessments should let you know the degree to which they have been achieved. The case study in Section I locates assessment in the primary classroom and provides an overview of the many different forms which assessment can take. Remember that it isn't only you who will use your assessments to assist your teaching; these days it serves many different purposes in a school and these are considered in Section 2.

See Chapter 2 on p. 7 for a model of the teaching process

As a student teacher, you want to develop your assessment skills so the next sections provide practical guidance on terminology (Section 3), presenting a general model to follow (Section 4), identifying the variety of assessment methods (Section 5) and providing criteria to evaluate your practice (Section 6).

With up to 30 children in a class and all the subjects of the National Curriculum to monitor, it's important to develop records which provide an efficient means of collecting data and recording your judgements. Section 7 provides some exemplars of such records for you to evaluate. Once you have made your assessment judgements, they will need to be shared with others either through your records or through reports which are compiled using your record of assessment evidence. As a student teacher it is unlikely that you will be required to produce reports for parents but the class teacher you work with will draw on your records in creating such annual reports and these are discussed in Section 8.

Section One

What is assessment?

Every day a teacher makes a variety of assessments, some of which are planned and for a specific purpose, others of which are made spontaneously. The term 'assessment' can conjure up a picture of formal tests but in a primary classroom this is rarely the case. Assessment can take many forms but, in the end, all assessments involve collecting information and making judgements about pupils. The scenario in the following passage paints a picture of the many occasions for assessment which arise in the primary classroom.

A morning in Anytown classroom..
Veronica Pye has a class of Year 3 children. She greets individuals as they walk in to off-load bags first thing in a morning. It is a good opportunity to talk about life outside school as well as check up on where they're up to in their home-reading books. The formal day begins with literacy hour and the big book she's using provides a stimulus to look at verb tenses. She asks a lot of questions in this section of the lesson to find out how much individual children know. The questioning continues as she sits with her focus group for the day to check comprehension in their guided reading. Other groups are completing their stories about life on a pirate ship that she'll be able to take home to mark.

She's decided to use some of last year's SATs (Standard Assessment Tasks) questions in maths to get an idea of how much of the year 2 work on fractions the class can remember – it should help her to decide how she is going to group them for this topic. She's concerned that Simon is very distracted from this task today. It's not like him so she makes a mental note to have a chat before lunch. It's gym before then and the groups complete their activity by taking turns to watch each other's movements and give advice on improving the flow of the sequences they've devised.

Looking at the assessment opportunities in the above scenario, it is clear that the different dimensions of the curriculum goals of knowledge, understanding, skills and attitudes are all part of the assessment process.

Section Two

Why assess?

On a day-to-day basis, assessment provides both feedback to the teacher and pupil on what has been learned and 'feed-forward' to identify future targets for learning. In the longer term, the accumulated information from these assessment occasions informs others such as the parents, the new class teacher, the learning support teacher or the teachers in a child's new school. In these times of increasing teacher accountability, the overall class assessments will be of interest to the headteacher and the governors and feed into the overall school assessments which are ultimately available to the community at large. In effect, assessment is an informing process, but this information is used in different ways depending on the audience. The following categories might be used to identify the variety of purposes which assessment is expected to serve in a primary school:

1. **Monitoring**: The teacher checks how well individual children are getting on with their learning and is alert to any individuals who are experiencing difficulties.

2. **Diagnosis**: The teacher is using assessment to make decisions about the next stage of learning. This will support planning for differentiation described in Chapter 2. For the child who has succeeded in achieving the desired learning outcomes (DLOs) for a lesson or a topic of work, then new learning targets and related tasks need to be planned. A child who has not achieved the learning outcomes may need to have their targets modified or a different task prescribed to assist them. The classification of different types of tasks on page 13 is a helpful guide to possibilities in this respect.

See Chapter 2 on p. 7 for more information on tasks

3. **Motivation**: Positive feedback on assessment tasks is a good motivator for young learners but requires that teachers set tasks which are sufficiently challenging whilst at the same time providing a good chance of success.

4. **Grading**: It is a requirement at the end of each Key Stage that teachers link a child's achievements in the different National Curriculum subjects to a particular Attainment Target (AT) level, in effect giving a child a grade. More generally though, a teacher may want to group children by their attainment to assist differentiation by task, for example in the group activity section of the literacy hour.

See Chapter 3 on p. 33 for more information on differentiation by task

5. **Evaluation**: The post lesson review structure on page 60 demonstrates how informal assessment of children's learning can give you feedback on your own teaching and thus inform your lesson evaluation.

6. **Accountability**: The aggregation of individual pupils' grades from teacher assessments and from national tests are now used to inform the headteacher and governors about individual class performance and aggregated school grades are collected for published school performance tables. This is seen by some to increase teacher and school accountability to their communities.

Some assessment terminology

The ongoing process of classroom assessments which informs planning for learning on a day to day basis and provides feedback for lesson evaluation is categorised as **formative assessment**. The primary audiences for this assessment are the class teacher and the child. Much of it will be informal through teacher observation and oral or written feedback. Some will be formal where the child is given prior warning of an assessment such as a spelling test so that they can prepare themselves for the activity. **Summative assessment** is one which takes place at a given moment in time, often at the end of a school year or key stage. In this case, the audience includes others outside the classroom such as parents, headteacher and other teachers in classes or the school which is the child's next destination. Such assessments draw on the formative records of the class teacher together with results of SATs (the Standard Assessment Tasks/ Tests which are set nationally) and other tests to provide a picture of the child's achievement to date.

Section Three

The National Curriculum is designed to be a **criterion referenced** system of assessment, that is, criteria for performance are set in the form of attainment targets at different levels from 1-8. To reach a particular level, a child needs to meet the criteria set at that level. For example level 2 for the Art and Design Attainment Target states 'Pupils explore ideas. They investigate and use a variety of materials and processes to communicate their ideas and meanings, and design and make images and artefacts. They comment on differences in others' work, and suggest ways of improving their own (National Curriculum 2000). In fact all primary classroom assessment ought to be criterion-referenced since a teacher uses the desired learning outcomes of their lesson plans to generate assessment 'indicators' or 'criteria' on which to base their judgements.

There is a legal requirement that primary schools carry out a **base-line assessment** of all 4- to 5-year-old pupils within their first seven weeks of joining the school. The assessments cover the basic skills of speaking and listening, reading, writing, mathematical awareness and personal and social development. The idea is that, with a clear idea of a child's capabilities on entry, the school is in a better position to assess a child's progress.

Practical task

Consider your current experience of assessment for your traineeship as a teacher and identify the occasions of formative and summative assessment. What purposes do these assessments serve? Are you aware of the criteria on which assessments are made? If so, how helpful are they?

Section Four

A model for assessment

Whatever the purposes of the assessment of primary children, the process has three main stages as follows:

collecting evidence ⟶ making judgements ⟶ outcomes of judgements

The stages are the same for both summative and formative practice. In the case of informal, formative assessment during a lesson such as literacy hour, teachers will **collect evidence** by listening to children's responses, observing their activity and looking at the 'products' of activities such as written work. They will use this evidence to **make judgements** about whether pupils have achieved the learning objectives. There are many possible **outcomes of these judgements,** often linked to issues of differentiation described in Chapter 3. One outcome might be that the teacher modifies their weekly plan to take account of the fact that many children need extra practice to consolidate their understanding. Another might be that they decide to create more stretching tasks for two individuals who appear to be 'coasting'.

In the case of summative assessment, more formal tools of assessment such as the SATs may be used to **collect evidence** about a child's achievement at the end of a key stage.

The **judgements** may be made by an external marker who, on the evidence of say an English test paper, grades a child according to National Curriculum attainment levels. The **outcomes of these judgements** may have implications for the individual child, for example in the way they are grouped for English as they move to a new key stage. There are also implications for the school since the judgements made for the year group as a whole are used for accountability purposes.

Methods of assessment

Despite the myriad purposes of assessment listed earlier, a teacher's main priority for using assessment is to maximise children's learning and it is this aspect which we will explore in detail for the remainder of the chapter. Evidence for learning is provided in a variety of ways as was shown in the opening scenario. In Chapter 2 the assessment indicators were described as being rooted in what the child '**does**', '**says**' and '**produces**'. Therefore the methods of collection revolve around capturing this data by **observation**, **questioning** and **marking**. However, there is such a wealth of data that you could spend a whole day assessing an individual child and still find that there is much more to know. Therefore it is important to be very specific about the kind of evidence (the assessment criteria) you are looking for, which is why we return to the planning cycle.

When you create your plans, it is with specific learning outcomes in mind and it is evidence of these outcomes which you seek for your assessment. Thus the activities you plan arise from the learning outcomes you want to achieve and will determine the assessment method you use. Thus the curriculum, the pedagogy and the assessment are brought together in your planning and are seen as integral to each other.

If one of your desired learning outcomes for a group in your Year 2 class is 'to be able to recognise simple fractions', then your activities will be planned so that children can demonstrate this ability. You will include in your lesson plan the details of how you will manage to collect the evidence of their learning. It may be that your focus for the main activity of a numeracy lesson is this group of children. You can observe their activity and talk as they divide objects into halves and quarters to identify understandings and difficulties. You will question them individually and look at the shapes they have divided to see which tasks presented problems. You might collect physical evidence by collecting in worksheets which they have coloured to show fractions. In addition, at the end of the session you may collect evidence of learning from the other groups in the class through discussion with a classroom assistant or collection and marking of exercise books.

So far the assessment methods described are in the hands of teachers. What about the role of the child in assessing their own learning? This is a more difficult notion than it seems. Black and Wiliam (1998) point out that children do not see the difference between the ends (learning outcomes) and the means (learning activity) so they don't always know what information to extract from everything they have done to identify what they have understood. Although pupil self assessment is a challenge, there is considerable evidence to suggest that if we are to encourage children to become effective learners, then they need to understand their own thinking processes better,

Section Five

a process known as metacognition. To encourage this process, we need to be explicit about what the learning objectives are and phrase them so that they are understandable to the child. Another way of describing the process is through 'SMART targets', that is setting targets for a child which are **S**pecific, **M**easurable, **A**chievable, **R**elevant and **T**ime limited.

Thus, instead of the instruction to a child to 'work to improve your writing', a teacher might hold a more extended discussion (sometimes referred to as 'conferencing' in the literature) with the child, possibly in conjunction with a parent. Looking at the evidence of the child's writing together, they might identify strengths and weaknesses from the formative assessment comments the teacher has made on the work. Targets which could arise might be that by the Christmas holiday 'you will be able to end all sentences with a full stop' and ' you can write on lined paper with words spaced out so that your classroom partner can read it quickly'. Through this process, the child is gaining an insight into the connection between their activity in the classroom and the learning you are aiming for and is thus developing their own self-assessment skills. They are then in a better position to be able to update you on their progress towards these targets whilst at the same time being encouraged to take on more responsibility for their own learning.

Practical task

Use your own experience in the classroom to compare the possible advantages and disadvantages of the different methods of assessment described in this section as follows:

Method of assessment	Advantages	Disadvantages
Observing		
Questioning		
Marking		
Conferencing		
Pupil self assessment		

Section Six

Good practice in assessment

The word 'assessment' conjures up all kinds of emotions in people, many of them negative. If assessment is to serve the purpose of enhancing learning then we have quite a lot of re-education to do, particularly amongst parents, since many people's experience is of assessments which labelled them as failures. Taking account of the emotional effects of assessment on the learner is the key to good practice as is raising parents' awareness of how assessment can improve their child's learning.

With a criterion-referenced approach, formative assessment provides a tool to encourage children onto the next stage of learning. To do this effectively, your assessment practice should meet the following criteria:

- **recognise achievement and encourage a 'can-do' approach in the learner;**
- **provide useful feedback to the teacher and learner;**
- **be fair and reliable;**
- **be based on appropriate evidence.**

These criteria are explained in the rest of this section.

Recognise achievement and encourage a 'can-do' approach in the learner

Motivation is a key to learning and positive encouragement of children is one way of maintaining this. There is nothing more dispiriting than to be given a stack of negative feedback about all the things we've done wrong. 'Catch them being good' is not a bad discipline and is a way of encouraging positive self-esteem. All children have remarkable capabilities and it is worth identifying some of them before focusing on things they get wrong.

Provide useful feedback to the teacher and learner

If assessment is to assist the learner to improve, then the teacher needs the skills to provide useful feedback to the child. Black and Wiliam (1998) found considerable research evidence to support their conclusion that 'feedback to any pupil should be about the particular qualities of his or her work, with advice on what he or she can do to improve, and should avoid comparisons'. This was particularly pertinent with regard to research into marking written work where improvement in learning was more likely from helpful comments than by a grade or mark. Where both grades and feedback were given, the positive effects of the feedback were lost.

Be fair and reliable

This relates to the stage of the assessment process identified with 'making judgements'. With the evidence collected about a child's achievement, can we be sure that this judgement is dependable? We all know that a child's performance can be affected by all manner of personal difficulties and assessment carried out one day may reveal different capabilities to that carried out on another. For formative assessment this isn't a major problem as a teacher develops a picture of a child's capabilities over long periods of time. However, if it is the teacher's judgement which is not reliable, then we do have problems. As professionals, we need to remain alert to our own human failings and prejudices so that we maintain an appropriate level of fairness and objectivity.

Be based on appropriate evidence

This is a criterion about validity of the assessments. In the classroom, the test of validity is whether the tool for assessment is providing evidence to judge whether a child has achieved a learning outcome. For example, a worksheet in geography which gets children to identify a list of map symbols does not inform us whether a child can 'use a map to plan a route' even though knowledge of symbols will help in this skill. One of the criticisms of the science SATs tests is that although they may be a valid means of identifying a child's knowledge and understanding (Science Attainment Targets 2,3 and 4), they are not valid tests of children's investigative capabilities (Science Attainment Target 1).

Section Seven

Recording assessments

Although much formative assessment is a thinking process for you, it is also important that you keep a record of your evidence structured in such a way as to help you to plan for future learning. In addition, you will need to pass on your records to the class teacher who will take over from you so that they are fully informed about the work you have covered and the progress made. Thus the record serves a dual purpose of **monitoring** the activities the child has completed and **assessing** the quality of their responses. The grid below provides a basic structure based on our three stage model of assessment which can be applied to a variety of assessment situations.

Desirable Learning Outcomes What did I want to achieve from the activity?			
Names of Children	**Evidence**	**Judgement**	**Outcomes/Action**
	What did the child say/do/produce?	What does this tell me about the learning?	What should the child do next?

The information in the record will vary in detail depending on the period of time covered and the nature of the learning outcomes.

Practical task

Evaluate the record sheets shown on pages 59 and 60. What are the positive and negative features?

FORMATIVE/DIAGNOSTIC ASSESSMENT SHEET

Subject   Numeracy

Names	State Lesson Plan Desirable Learning Outcomes 'Knows No Bonds to 10'					Comments
	$4 + 4$ / $6/6$	$5 + 5$	$2 + 2$ / $8/8$	$3 + 3$ / $7/7$	$9 + 9$ / $1/1$	
• Jennifer	A	A	A	A	A	Orally could tell answer to question $5 +$ $= 10$ without using counting aids
x Paul	WT	WT	WT	WT	WT	Used fingers to help count on
x Aftab	WT	WT	WT	WT	A	Knew 2 without needing to use fingers to help count on
■ Susan	/	/	/	/	/	Did not understand how to proceed to find out the answer
• Sunetra	A	A	A	A	A	As above
• Mike	A	A	A	A	A	As above
• Meena	A	A	A	A	A	As above

Diagnosis to inform Future Planning

• Move on to addition to 20   A   = Achieved

x Repeat the oral lesson again using cards game   WT = Working towards

■ More practice of addition to using unifix cubes then   / = Needs repeating
onto sums using unifix which are as follows:

  $5 + \square = 10$

In addition to these teacher records of the class as a whole, many schools have developed a formative 'Record of Achievement' for each child which is described as: 'A file or folder including various assessments of the child's work, skills, abilities and personal qualities. Within the school curriculum as a whole, it gives details of achievements both inside and outside the classroom. It can also include a portfolio of samples of the child's work. A Record of Achievement, which is sometimes called a profile, forms the basis for the summary report which is needed each year' (DES 1990). This Record of Achievement can be added to by both teacher and child and provides a

CLASS ASSESSMENT NOTES

SUBJECT: Maths

CLASS: 4

UNIT TITLE/DETAILS:
Symmetry – lines of symmetry and
rotational symmetry

DATE: 15.3.99

KEY OBJECTIVES:

Do the children show clear knowledge &
understanding of terms:

a) lines of symmetry
b) rotational symmetry (Yr 6)

Can the children accurately manipulate
images to answer questions?

(Do the children need mirrors or tracing
paper which was provided only as an
option?)

DESCRIPTION OF CHILDREN'S ATTAINMENT
(The extent to which they have achieved the objectives.)

All/most pupils:

From books & observation during lesson most show basic understanding
Most clear on lines of symmetry.
Some Yr 6 not secure on rotational.
Most of the strugglers were in yellow group.

With the exception of
Andrew & some yellow group

In addition, some pupils:
Excelled – Russ (took it to a higher level by himself)
Kermuda

Other comments:
Most children used tracing paper.
Next steps: More practice for most on spotting rotational symmetry. Andrew & yellow group
extra line symmetry sheet. Russ and Kermuda problem-solving on extension sheet.

mechanism for encouraging children to celebrate their achievements and reflect on their own learning.

Reporting assessment

It is a statutory requirement that teachers report on pupils' progress at least once each year through annual reports and a meeting with parents. In fact many schools go far beyond this requirement. Parents have a right to know about their child's progress and tend to be interested in two questions. They want to know whether their child is making the progress of which they are capable. They also want to know how well their child is getting on compared with others of about the same age. As professionals, teachers are happy to answer the first question but many are more reluctant about the second since they are concerned that this information might label a child. This second question is brought into even sharper focus when the attainment levels of the National Curriculum are reported to parents at the end of a Key Stage. It could be argued that with the current arrangements which require schools to set performance targets each year for National Curriculum assessments, this process of comparing children with others in their age group is encouraged. At Key Stage 1, the percentage of children achieving level 2 is the national benchmark; at Key Stage 2, it is the percentage at level 4. These levels are therefore likely to be viewed by parents as the age group markers of 'normal' achievement with which to compare their own child.

Remember that your records will inform a class teacher's reports so it is important that they provide the necessary detail. Mitchel and Koshy (1998) identify criteria which should be met when preparing an annual report on a child to his or her parents as follows:

- **it is accessible to parents;**
- **it goes beyond generalisations;**
- **it provides a focus for home-school partnerships to address learning targets;**
- **explicit and meaningful links are made with the National Curriculum.**

Practical task

Evaluate this child's report for science using both the criteria above and any others you feel appropriate and then try to write your own.

School Science Report for Ahmed, Year 5
Ahmed has shown great enthusiasm for science this year and I can always rely on him to get on with his work. He has really enjoyed the last topic and demonstrated a lot of well developed concepts about the stars and planets. His process skills are less developed and I find that his difficulties in analysing data mean that he finds it hard to evaluate the investigations we do. He has a quiet manner and tends to take a back seat in group work. However, his writing is always neat and illustrative work is clear. He could still do much better than this as I think he could reach level 5 next year.

Conclusion

This chapter emphasises that regular ongoing assessment of pupils' progress together with summative testing are key ingredients of successful teaching and learning. Children and their parents (or carers) need to know how they are doing and are entitled to accurate information about performance. Care, however, has to be taken to ensure that assessment outcomes motivate pupils and help them progress. Handled badly, assessment activities can contribute to alienation and a cycle of underachievement. Children need to feel good about what they have achieved and confident about tackling areas needing further work. Assessment outcomes tell you what you need to work at with all children in the class.

Further reading

Black, P. (1998) *Testing: Friend or Foe? Theory and Practice of Assessment and Testing.* London: Falmer. Professor Black was the Chair of the Task Group on Assessment and Testing (TGAT) which provided the initial framework for the National Curriculum levels. This scholarly book is a very detailed look at the politics behind assessment and testing and draws on international research to demonstrate the pros and cons of assessment in practice.

Drummond, M. J. and Pollard, A. (1994) *Assessing Children's Learning.* London: David Fulton. The integral role of assessment in the planning cycle is examined and examples of good practice in the primary classroom are detailed.

Johnson, G., Hill, B. and Tunstall, P. (1992) *Primary Records of Achievement.* London: Hodder and Stoughton. Provides details and the background philosophy to the development of Records of Achievement in primary schools.

Keel, P. (1994) *Assessment in the Multi-ethnic Primary Classroom.* Stoke-on-Trent: Trentham Books. Examines the attitudes and values which as teachers we bring with us to the assessment process and the approaches which are appropriate if we are to take account of the rich diversity of children's backgrounds.

Wragg, E. C. (1997) *Assessment and Learning.* London: Routledge. A short and general text which explains the key terminology linked to assessment. Covers both primary and secondary education.

By the end of the chapter you should:

- *have an understanding of what constitutes 'learning';*
- *know that children may think about concepts in very different ways to adults;*
- *have an overview of some of the psychological theories that are applied to teaching and learning.*

This chapter addresses the following Professional Standards for QTS:

 1.2, 2.4, 3.3.3

(The Standards are reproduced in full at the back of this book.)

You will know by now from your time in school that teachers do very much more than simply teach children. You may have seen them act as accountants, social workers and even surrogate parents. Indeed, with so much going on in the modern primary classroom it is easy to forget sometimes that the fundamental task of any teacher is *to organise learning*. This chapter will help you to understand how children learn and to manage learning more effectively in the classroom. This awareness is fundamental, not only to skilful teaching, but also as an aid to behaviour management.

But firstly, it has to be admitted that human learning is highly complex and, even as we enter the new millennium, far from fully understood. Indeed it is probable that this entire book could be filled with what we don't know about learning! Take a moment to write down what you understand by *learning*.

A fairly simple but enduring psychological definition of learning is: 'Relatively permanent changes in behaviour or in potential for behaviour that result from *experience*.'

(Lefrançois 1999 p. 41)

Of course when psychologists refer to behaviour they include not only overt, that is observable, actions but also changes in thought patterns that are internal or covert. The keywords in this definition are *relatively permanent* and *experience*.

Although it is the field of psychology which has provided the clearest insights into children's learning it is worth bearing in mind that psychology is unusual in several respects. First, of course everyone is an amateur psychologist and secondly, unlike the physical sciences, people form part of their own data. Therefore we can never be too exact and many statements remain problematic.

Inevitably over the years numerous theories have been advanced to explain how children learn. Perhaps the two most widely regarded are behaviourism and cognitive approaches. Each, in its own way, has something to offer to the practising teacher and each views humans in a fundamentally different way.

Behaviourism

If you recall that learning involves a relatively permanent change in *behaviour*, then it is not surprising that for much of the twentieth century psychologists have sought to understand learning by looking at actual behaviours. The theory of behaviourism is modelled firmly on the physical sciences and, although particularly popular in America until the 1960s, it has had an enduring influence on the British primary classroom. According to behavioural theory we should seek to rid psychology of words such as mind, feeling, sensation and instead concentrate on what can be readily observed and measured. Behaviourists claim that we are what we are, not because of innate intelligence or genetic factors, but solely due to our life experiences. This suggests a just and equal view of people, a society in which literally anyone can aspire to be a doctor or a judge.

Since 'experimenting' with the human mind is ethically undesirable and rightly frowned upon, behaviourists have often gathered information from animals, particularly rats and pigeons. Although, of course, in these enlightened times the ethics of this approach may also be debatable, it has often been said that the rat is the hero of twentieth-century psychology!

One such behavioural theorist was B. F. Skinner (1968). One of his many techniques was to place a rat in a cage known as a Skinner box. A Skinner box typically contains one or more levers which an animal can press, one or more stimulus lights and one or more places in which reinforcers like food can be delivered. The animal's presses on the levers can be detected and recorded and a contingency between these presses, the state of the stimulus lights and the delivery of reinforcement can be set up. The cage may be regarded as a stimulus for behaviour and the result is that the rat moves around, initially randomly, until it accidentally depresses the lever, which results in being rewarded with a pellet of food. Not surprisingly, the rat comes to learn that the lever is associated with a reward and this can lead to frantic lever pressing. The situation may be represented diagrammatically:

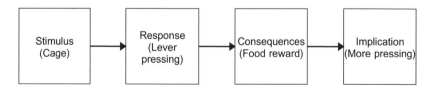

Figure 5.1a

The procedure is referred to as **operant conditioning.**

It appears that humans are also susceptible to this type of conditioning, but thankfully not involving cages. Indeed, although it is deeply unpalatable to some teachers, the classroom may be seen in some ways to resemble a giant Skinner box.

Why do you think this should be so?

It is a relatively self-contained unit where commonly there are in place reward systems which are intended to bring about certain given behaviours and eradicate others. Of course children are more intelligent than rats and classrooms are far more variable than the Skinner box but nevertheless similarities do exist.

A simple analogy is:

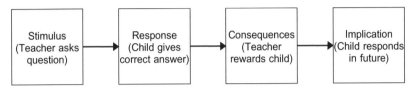

Figure 5.1b

The converse is where the child's response is met with ridicule. In this case she is unlikely to respond in the future! Classroom reward systems often include teacher praise, house points, gold stars, extra privileges, merit certificates and the like. These are collectively referred to as extrinsic (external) motivators.

But it is possible to overuse rewards systems and this can have negative consequences. In a study by Amabile (1983) children, while happily playing together, were offered certificates if they continued interacting in a similar manner. This had the rather surprising effect of not reinforcing the desired behaviour but extinguishing it. The children became less active and less creative. The reason for this may be that the children were already motivated intrinsically (internally) and needed no further en-couragement. Furthermore, they may have interpreted the adult intervention as interference; that they were being manipulated in some way and what was enjoyable became simply another adult led task.

Generally speaking, pupils do enjoy receiving external rewards but they tend not to lead to the promotion of what Lepper and Hodell (1989) describe as 'a learning culture'. Children may come to see the goal of learning not as achievement but as reward.

It is important therefore to maintain a balance between intrinsic and extrinsic motiva-tors. During the early stages of learning a new task or topic, learners need plenty of encouragement to succeed. Later, completion of the task itself and the associated satisfaction derived from it may be all the motivation that is needed.

Skinner's theories have had a major impact on schooling, particularly with regard to managing children's behaviour. Skilful teachers reward pupils on a daily basis in the hope that desired behaviours will be repeated. This theory does, however, cast the learner in a relatively passive role. It suggests 'traditional' teaching methods where the teacher is firmly in control, both of the content to be learned and of the pace of learning. Lesson content is broken down into small manageable chunks that can be reinforced when learning has occurred. It may have scant regard for the child's existing knowledge or interests and can therefore prove de-motivating for pupils.

IMPLICATIONS FOR TEACHING AND BEHAVIOUR MANAGEMENT

- **Teacher controls what is to be learned and the pace of learning.**
- **Pupils can be taught in relatively large groups.**
- **Desired learning and behaviours are rewarded, often extrinsically.**

Cognitive theories

The theory of behaviourism as outlined above might be thought of as a 'black box' approach since it makes no attempt to explain what is actually occurring in the mind. Recall that behaviourists are only interested in observable actions. Words such as understanding, thinking and memory are considered unimportant since they cannot be 'seen' – but these ideas are the very stuff of the next generation of theorists, the cognitivists.

Cognition loosely means knowing, involving information or ideas, or more precisely the kind of thought which involves perception, intuition and reasoning. Now this thinking is largely frowned upon in schools. I still recall vividly an incident from my early, somewhat tentative years of teaching.

One day, as I was working from the board, in sound behaviourist fashion, a boy at the back of the room sat silently staring out of the window. This was an unusual thing to do in that particular city so I interrupted the lesson and asked what he was doing. He responded quietly, 'Thinking'. My reply, which shames me to this day, was 'Well stop it and get on with your work!'

Jean Piaget

Piaget proved to be the most prolific and influential child development researcher and theoretician the world has ever known. His career spanned more than 60 years and his findings have proved influential to both psychologists and educationists alike. The scope of his work was wide; his theories are contained in more than 30 books and several hundred articles. Nevertheless his work is not without its critics and many researchers believe that they have discovered serious flaws in Piaget's original theories.

Piaget questioned hundreds of children aged between three and twelve using a technique he called the 'clinical method'. This involved listening to the child's answers and, where possible, pursuing the immature thoughts without distorting them. This led him to the theory that the child's adaptation to the world may be described in terms of two different ways of interacting with the environment. These he termed *assimilation* and *accommodation*. Assimilation involves the incorporation of new knowledge in existing mental structures and making a response which has previously been acquired, sometimes ignoring novel aspects of the situation, in order to make it conform to the child's existing mental system. Accommodation describes the process by which the existing mental system can be modified in order to take account of conflicting external stimuli.

A rather crude metaphor for this might be a stranger visiting a town for the first time. Initially every street and shop is new and he struggles to make sense of it all. One wrong turn may result in total confusion. He is accommodating to his new environment. Later, as roads and landmarks become more familiar, he is able to form a mental map of his surroundings and is unlikely to be perplexed by the sudden discovery of a new street or alley. He simply assimilates this to his existing mental picture.

Of course Piaget recognised that the division between the two is not always clear cut and all activity inevitably involves both assimilation and accommodation. Flavell (1985) refers to assimilation and accommodation as two sides of the same coin — both must occur together if an individual is to adapt.

Piaget developed a *stage theory* that suggests that the development of logical thinking in children can be broken down into a series of steps. Each stage derives from and builds upon the previous stage. This concept has inevitably received a great deal of attention from educators since it claims, in part, to explain the contrasts between children of differing stages which parents and teachers experience daily.

The stages are as follows:

Stage	Age
1) Sensorimotor	0-2 years
2) Pre-operational	
a. Pre-conceptual	2-4 years
b. Intuitive	4-7 years
3) Concrete operations	7-11 years
4) Formal operations	11-15 years.

The exact details of the stages may be found in any introductory educational psychology book (Child 1997; Fontana 1995; Lefrançois 1999) but the second, or pre-operational, is particularly interesting since this is a period in the child's development when many of Piaget's investigations took place.

Some of Piaget's more formal experiments involved assessing children's understanding of conservation. These varied in detail but essentially all involved presenting children with two matching sets or quantities, then manipulating one of them in some way and asking the child to compare the results. Typically children during the intuitive stage appear fooled by the transformation and answer that the amounts are now different. Piaget concluded that the child was relying on perception rather than thought and that this is one of the key differences between the thinking of children and adults. This may be true but Piaget's theories are not without their critics and other, possibly more plausible suggestions to explain this behaviour have been put forward (Bryant 1974; Donaldson 1978).

Before turning to these readings you might like to consider for yourself the profound implications of stage theory. How might this concept affect teaching?

This section has tried to give a flavour of Piaget's work with particular reference to the experiments involved during the intuitive stage of development. Piaget recognised that the stages are only approximate and that the more mature child will enter a new stage perhaps two years earlier than average. Nevertheless the stages are referred to as being *invariant*, that is, they are the same for all children. But was Piaget right? Are these stages *real*, are children younger than a certain age dominated by perception and simply incapable of logical thought or conservation? Or, are there alternative, more acceptable explanations for these phenomena?

IMPLICATIONS FOR TEACHING

Although Piaget himself was not concerned with drawing educational implications from his general theories they do provide teachers with some useful pointers:

- **First, when setting tasks for children we need to bear in mind the balance between accommodation and assimilation. For example when teaching a new concept in science we must ask how closely related this is to the child's previous learning (assimilation) or is it entirely new (accommodation).**
- **Secondly, Piaget has shown that children may think about concepts in entirely different ways to adults. His conservation investigations clearly demonstrate that children's minds are not simply the same as adults but on a smaller scale, their thinking is *qualitatively* different. Contrast this with the behaviourist view of the child's mind as simply that of an immature adult. This helps us to understand children's limitations but, importantly, should never lead teachers to set artificial boundaries for pupils.**
- **Finally, he emphasises the self-motivated, active role of the learner and the importance of meaningful interactions with the environment. This *constructivist* approach, has been developed by other cognitive psychologists.**

LEV VYGOTSKY

It is very easy to believe that Vygotsky is a contemporary theorist but in fact he died over 60 years ago. However it is only in the last 20 years or so that his writings have been translated into English (e.g. Vygotsky 1978). Unlike Piaget, Vygotsky stressed the importance of language and the role of the adult in the learning process. Naturally this has great resonance with the teaching profession.

Vygotsky describes a 'Zone of Proximal Development' or ZPD.

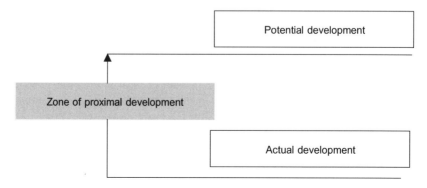

Figure 5.2

The ZPD is the gap between what the child can do independently and what might be achieved through the support of an interested adult. Imagine two pupils in your class who are working together at the computer. One is confident and takes the lead, while the other is more tentative and holds back a little. Later you discover that this is because the more assured child has a computer at home. Should we conclude that one child is simply more able? The ZPD model suggests that we are assessing the child's *actual* development rather than her potential. It is quite possible that the less confident child has equal or more potential and may, given appropriate guidance, show greater development.

The gap between actual development and potential development needs to be bridged by appropriate intervention.

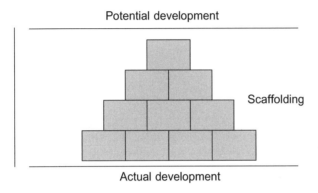

Figure 5.3

The model suggests that during the early stages of learning the teacher needs to provide a great deal of help and encouragement. But later, as the learner begins to master the technique or task, this support can be gradually withdrawn, leading towards independence.

This technique is often referred to as 'scaffolding' and may take many forms in the classroom including:

(a) providing clear and realistic objectives
(b) gaining the child's attention and focusing it on the requirements of the task
(c) providing written or actual models
(d) reducing the task to manageable subtasks
(e) drawing attention to the most relevant aspects of the task
(f) explaining procedures
(g) keeping the learner on track and motivated
(h) correcting on-task errors
(i) easing frustration associated with difficulties the child might experience.

(based on Lefrançois 1999, pp. 108, 226)

Vygotsky's model is essentially an optimistic view which suggests that instruction promotes development and that teachers can set the agenda. Contrast this with Piaget who has been interpreted as saying that it is pointless attempting to teach a child something until they are at the appropriate stage of development.

IMPLICATIONS FOR TEACHING

- **Teachers should encourage discussion in the classroom.**
- **Teaching should lead development not lag behind it.**
- **Teachers should carry out a careful diagnostic assessment of pupil abilities – know your starting point!**
- **Learning activities should be appropriately sequenced and be within the child's Zone of Proximal Development.**

Jerome Bruner

Another cognitivist theory to be discussed in this chapter is that of Jerome Bruner. In a similar way to both Piaget and Vygotsky and quite unlike Skinner, Bruner's theories view the child as an active processor of information.

According to this view, children are not simply *given* knowledge by a teacher or parent but actively *construct* their own knowledge. It follows therefore that, according to this view, pupils should not be presented with material in its final form but required to organise it for themselves, therefore schools should foster the discovery of relationships. Not surprisingly the teaching method most closely associated with this theory is known as 'discovery learning'.

Inevitably discovery learning requires far less teacher direction than some other methods but good teachers understand that teaching through discovery does not mean sending pupils away with the summary exhortation 'Discover!' No, the process of discovery must be taught and leadership given throughout. In order to emphasise the role of the teacher the term *guided discovery* is usually applied to this method.

It casts the teacher more in the role of a 'learning facilitator' – one who arranges appropriate learning experiences, guides and questions rather than merely directs. A good example might be a situation where primary school children are given an area to explore and are asked where they would establish a settlement. They are encouraged to discover that settlements need to be near rivers/harbours etc.

Advocates of this method claim that it is more motivating and increases the child's problem-solving ability.

Bruner suggests a model of children's learning. He claims that all learning should move through three set phases:

- **enactive (by doing – including motor and sensory experiences)**
- **iconic (pictorial representation)**
- **symbolic (abstract representation).**

A good example might be when teaching about electricity in science. Children should first explore making a circuit with bulbs, batteries, wires etc (enactive). When they are quite familiar with these they should be ready to draw the circuit (iconic) and only later are they introduced to the concept of the circuit diagram (abstract representation). Sadly, and all too frequently, pupils are faced with circuit diagrams and the like without having had the requisite early practical experience. Often they appear to learn but this change in behaviour is only temporary and therefore does not fit in with our earlier definition of learning that referred to 'relatively *permanent* changes in behaviour.'

The notion of re-visiting topics but at a higher and more abstract level suggests what Bruner refers to as the *spiral curriculum*. So for example a topic such as fractions might be introduced by working initially with concrete materials like cakes, wooden blocks etc. Children then move onto to other topics before returning to fractions but at a higher level, perhaps by using a pictorial representation of the blocks. Again pupils move to other topics before returning to the final abstract stage of $\frac{1}{2} + \frac{3}{4}$ etc.

IMPLICATIONS FOR TEACHING

- **Pupils should not be given information in its final form but allowed to discover relationships for themselves.**
- **Learning should begin with motor and sensory experiences and only later move to the more abstract.**
- **Topics should be first visited and later re-visited at a higher level (the spiral curriculum).**

David Ausubel

In direct contrast to Bruner's theory of discovery learning, Ausubel (1963, 1968) claims that pupils learn more speedily and easily when they receive the material in relatively final form. Ausubel sees Bruner's ideas as wasteful of the teacher's time and indeed discovery learning does take time. Of course this suggests a very different kind of classroom and a changed role for the teacher. Here we see a classroom where the teacher uses direct instruction and the pupils mainly listen. The emphasis being upon meaningful verbal learning.

Since the teacher's role is literally to *expose* the pupils to the material this method is usually known as *expository* teaching and can be seen in any primary classroom on almost any day of the week. Here the emphasis is on the teacher initially researching the topic, selecting appropriate material and sequencing the learning outcomes to make them accessible to the pupils. Since the child's role is merely to receive the information this is known as 'reception learning'.

However, Ausubel argues that there is no need for this method to lead to passive learning, nor should it encourage rote (without understanding) learning. Teachers who use this method (and we all do) must take particular care to ensure that the new material relates closely to the pupil's existing knowledge. Since it is the learner who constructs their own knowledge by creating links between the old and new material this method may also be categorised as constructivist.

IMPLICATIONS FOR TEACHING

- **Teachers should organise the material for the pupils.**
- **New learning should be related to existing knowledge.**
- **New ideas and concepts should be 'potentially meaningful' to the learner.**
- **Lessons should begin by making links to previous learning.**

Reconciling discovery and reception approaches

It may appear at first that the theories of Bruner and Ausubel are total opposites that can never be reconciled, but this is not the case. Ausubel would readily admit that discovery learning might be more appropriate, in the early years of schooling, to enhance problem solving and to establish intrinsic motivation. However, he claims that after the age of about eleven discovery learning is wasteful of time and effort. By that time most learners have sufficient background material to allow them to make their own links.

Recall that both theories are *constructivist*, learners are required to make their own sense of the material, and of course neither is behavioural. Nor should it be assumed that one method is to be preferred to the other. 'Scientific' comparisons between discovery and reception learning are full of methodological problems due to the many variables involved. For example:

- **Different criteria are often used for assessing the effectiveness of learning, e.g. speed of learning, retention, transfer, motivation.**
- **Pupils are different.**
- **Teachers are different – the same lesson may not be as effective when delivered by dissimilar teachers.**

Good teachers should of course use both methods as appropriate to the subject material and the age group of the pupils.

Conclusion

This chapter has tried to give you an overview of some of the major theories that have been applied to teaching and learning during the 20th century. Inexperienced teachers do occasionally find it difficult to perceive how these ideas can be directly applied in the classroom. This is to be expected, as it is the interplay of theory and practical application that leads to understanding. Only daily contact with pupils in a range of learning situations can help here. As you spend more time with children you will begin to make connections and realise that learning situations can frequently be seen to have a theoretical underpinning.

For now it is simply worth recalling that you are not asked to embrace one method to the exclusion of others. None is inherently superior and each has its place in the modern teacher's repertoire. The best teachers are eclectic, that is, they select the appropriate method to fit the given situation.

Finally, please do not let this chapter blind you to the fact that you will teach pupils, not theories. Children are spontaneous, often humorous, open *people* who deserve to be treated with the tolerance, respect and understanding that you would accord to any member of society.

Further reading

Child, D. (1997) *Psychology and the Teacher.* (6th edn) London: Cassell. A well-established introduction to psychology for teachers.

Donaldson, M. (1978), *Children's Minds*. London: Fontana. Widely regarded as ground-breaking. A critical examination of the work of Piaget. This book had a major impact in the education world.

Fontana, D. (1995) *Psychology for Teachers*. (3rd edn) London: Macmillan. An accessible introduction to educational psychology. Full of practical insights to aid the teacher in helping children.

Howe, M. J. A. (1999) *A Teacher's Guide to the Psychology of Learning*. (2nd edn) Oxford: Blackwell. Approaches children's learning in an interesting and accessible fashion. The suggested strategies present a stimulating challenge to all educators.

Leadbetter, J., Morris, S., Timmins, P., Knight G. and Traxson, D. (1999), *Applying Psychology in the Classroom*. London: David Fulton. Considers a range of issues for improving pupil motivation and understanding social dynamics in the classroom.

Lefrançois, G. R. (1999) *Psychology for Teaching*. (10th edn) Belmont: Wadsworth. A comprehensive introduction to educational psychological principles, written in an entertaining style.

Pollard, A. (1996) *Reflective Teaching in the Primary School: A Handbook for the Classroom.* (3rd edn) London: Cassell. Deals with most significant aspects of primary school teaching. Promotes skilful, imaginative teaching that is rewarding for both pupil and teacher.

Wood, D. (1997) *How Children Think and Learn*. (2nd edn) Oxford: Blackwell. Explores in detail the discussions surrounding how children think and learn, tracing the historical influences that have taken place over the past ten years. Wood acknowledges some of the difficulties teachers face when trying to put theory into practice in the classroom.

6 MANAGING THE CLASSROOM FOR LEARNING

ANDREW WATERSON

By the end of the chapter you should:

- *reflect on the educational approach that you wish to implement;*
- *identify those aspects of classroom management which you need to develop and strategies for achieving these;*
- *make realistic plans for implementation given the circumstances of your teaching practice;*
- *review your classroom organisation and management and plan future developments;*
- *deliver equality of opportunity for all children within the class;*
- *plan for effective learning and development of all children within your class.*

This chapter addresses the following Professional Standards for QTS:

 ## 3.3.1, 3.3.3, 3.3.7, 3.3.8

(The Standards are reproduced in full at the back of this book.)

Much of this book is concerned with the issues of what and how children learn and how teachers teach. This is fundamental to effective learning. But of equal importance is how this is realised in practice in the classroom. Primary classrooms are active, practical places where teachers and children work on tasks. This chapter addresses how, in practice, classrooms can be effectively organised.

> By organisation, it is meant the way in which the class and classroom is structured in order to facilitate learning and teaching. For such teaching and learning to succeed, classroom organisation must relate to values, aims and curriculum plans as a whole and also to practical circumstances.
>
> (Pollard 1997 p. 208)

Ofsted, in their guidance to inspectors, requires them to evaluate whether:

- **the teacher's exposition or explanation is lively, informative and well structured;**
- **any grouping by ability promotes higher standards;**
- **the teacher's use and style of questioning probes pupils' knowledge and understanding, challenges their thinking and engages all pupils;**
- **practical activity is purposeful and not stereotyped in that pupils are encouraged to think about what they are doing, what they have learned from it and how to improve their work;**
- **investigations and problem-solving activities help pupils to apply and extend their learning in new contexts;**

- the choice of pupil grouping, for example pupils working alone, in pairs or small groups or all together, achieves the objectives for teaching and learning;
- the form of organisation allows the teacher to interact efficiently with as many pupils as possible;
- the use of resources stimulates learning and sensitively reflects different groups, cultures and backgrounds.

(Ofsted 1999 p. 59)

In practice this means that you are expected to use whole class, group work or individual work as appropriate; when grouping children use effective numbers and types of group; manage your time so that you can support the children's learning; plan the children's time by setting realistic deadlines for work; make effective use of the available space and other resources; and have clear classroom routines and systems. You should use the criterion of 'fitness for purpose' when planning for effective classroom organisation and management (Alexander et al. 1992).

Every school and every teacher has a set of ideas, values and beliefs that they bring to the classroom. It is this ideology which commonly determines how, in practice, the classroom is organised and managed. If the classroom is laid out formally with children seated in rows and the teacher using didactic, instructional approaches such as whole class teaching and teacher set learning objectives, we might suspect that the teacher (or school) favours a traditional educational ideology. If, on the other hand, when we enter a classroom we see children working collaboratively in groups, involved in setting their own learning targets and devising their own approaches to tasks, we might suspect that a more progressive approach is favoured. These are not two opposite or even alternative perspectives; they merely represent two points on a multidimensional scale upon which the whole gamut of educational ideas, values and beliefs are represented. A key aim of this chapter will be to enable you effectively and realistically to realise your favoured ideology in practice. You should remember that there isn't always a direct relationship between a teacher's beliefs and what happens in the classroom in practice and that effective teachers utilise a range of teaching styles in their classrooms matched to the requirements of the curriculum and the needs of the children.

Planning for classroom organisation and management

Reflective action planning is a widely used and effective method of personal professional development. You may well be required to keep a reflective log of your development during your course of initial teacher training so that you can complete the Career Entry Profile before qualifying as a teacher.

Teaching practice contains many of the elements of reflective action planning and this chapter will support the construction of personal development and action plans which in turn will support the compilation of a reflective log.

Reflective action planning can be represented in terms of a cyclical process as shown in Figure 6.1 below.

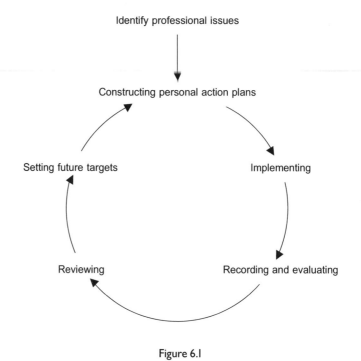

Identify professional issues

Constructing personal action plans

Setting future targets

Implementing

Reviewing

Recording and evaluating

Figure 6.1

Before, during and after teaching practice you will need to do the following.

- *Identify professional issues:* **you need to consider your strengths and weaknesses as a teacher and identify areas for development. You will need to prioritise these so that you work on the most important issues first.**
- *Constructing personal action plans:* **you will need to plan targets and tasks for each of the professional issues that you have identified.**
- *Implementing:* **this is where you implement your plans during the teaching practice.**
- *Recording and evaluating:* **how successful was your plan? Did you achieve your target?**
- *Reviewing:* **at the end of the practice, with your mentor you should review the progress you have made.**
- *Setting future targets:* **you will need to set clear targets for your own future professional development either for your next teaching practice or for the Career Entry Profile.**

So you need to begin by identifying professional issues in terms of classroom management and organisation and then move on to identifying areas for further development.

Identifying professional issues

What classroom environment do you want to create and how do you want the children to use it?

Effective classroom environments contain a number of common features:

- **They empower, stimulate and motivate children to learn effectively.**
- **They are workable and realistic given the available resources. Resources in this context include space, time, materials, learning resources and support staff as well as the personal and professional resources you bring to the classroom. That is, the classroom organisation needs to be realistic given your current professional capabilities.**
- **They support children in taking responsibility for their own learning.**
- **They reflect theoretical perspectives that you judge effectively promote learning. (For example, Bruner's view of learning as a social process would be reflected in the use of collaborative groupwork.)**
- **They enable all groups of children to obtain equality of opportunity in the classroom.**
- **They support the provision of programmes which are suitably differentiated to meet the needs of individual children.**

 See Chapter 5 on p. 63 for discussion of models of learning.

Where are you now?

 See Chapter 11 on p. 133 for information on equality of opportunity.

What is the current organisation and management of the classroom, its strengths and weaknesses and how does this relate to your ideas, values, beliefs and capabilities?

To develop effective classroom management you will need to review the current system in use within the class together with your own experience and abilities. You will need to consider the following questions:

- **What are the current systems of classroom management being used?**
- **Are the children used to working in groups? Are they used to working independently?**
- **How is the classroom laid out?**
- **What resources are available e.g. display boards, display materials, computers and software, reference books, pupil creative and investigative practical equipment and materials?**
- **What is the class timetable? How much flexibility is available to change and adapt this? How much time is actually available?**
- **What classroom and behaviour management skills do you have now?**
- **What classroom management skills will you need to develop?**
- **How much of your preferred strategy are you going to be able to put into practice within the available period of a school experience?**

 See Chapter 3 on p. 33 for information on differentiation.

Practical task

Reflect on a recent visit to a school. Answer as many of the questions in 'Where are you now?' as you can. Think about the implications of your answers in terms of how you might prepare for a future teaching practice.

Constructing personal action plans:

What kind of class organisation is going to help you achieve this?

The three most commonly utilised systems of class organisation are whole-class work, group work and individual work.

Whole-class work involves all children within the class undertaking the same activity leading to similar outcomes. The teacher commonly leads whole-class work although s/he may invite children to lead some aspects such as feedback on their work activities at the end of the lesson.

Teacher activities include:

- **introducing learning and contexts;**
- **explanation;**
- **instruction;**
- **questioning;**
- **demonstration;**
- **recapitulation;**
- **summarising;**
- **reinforcing learning.**

Children are often relatively passive in whole-class work. Their activities include:

- **listening and watching;**
- **answering questions;**
- **giving examples;**
- **reporting back;**
- **reflecting and evaluating on their work.**

The management of whole-class work is relatively easy as each activity is distinct and separate and occurs consecutively. Two examples of whole-class work are: (i) the beginning of a lesson where a teacher introduces the focus of the learning and the context in which it takes place; and (ii) the conclusion or plenary at the end of a lesson where the teacher and children summarise the learning. Teachers also use whole-class teaching for certain curriculum areas such as story, music and physical education. In Early Years and Key Stage I classes children often sit in a specific area such as the 'carpet' during whole-class work.

Group work involves children being arranged in groups of between 2 and 8 and seated around a shared workspace. There are several different activities that can be undertaken within group work and these are discussed in more detail below. These range from children sitting at the same table working individually on their own activities (essentially individual work) to all the children in a group working collaboratively towards a common outcome. The emphasis here is much more on the children's rather than the teacher's activities.

Group work tasks involve children in:

- **initiating an activity;**
- **seeking information and opinions;**
- **giving information and opinions;**
- **elaborating on ideas and concepts;**
- **co-ordinating a group's activity;**
- **summarising the learning outcomes.**

Collaborative activities include:

- **encouraging;**
- **allowing others to speak;**
- **setting standards;**
- **accepting others' decisions;**
- **expressing group feelings.**

(Bennett and Dunne 1992)

The management of group work can be relatively difficult as each activity may be made up of a series of interacting elements which occur concurrently. You will need to adopt a range of roles depending on the type of group work taking place. Your time will frequently be split between supporting groups and supporting individuals and a key issue here is the level of teacher support each group requires: in practice, most groups will need to work independently of you if group work is to remain manageable. Effective group work has been found to enhance the quality of pupil/teacher interactions.

Examples of group work include: children working individually on mathematics with differentiated work being supplied to high, middle and low attainment groups; children co-operating within a group to produce a newspaper by carrying out different tasks which build to a whole group outcome; children working collaboratively in a group to investigate the properties of different kinds of electrical switches.

Individual work involves children working on their own on tasks which have individual outcomes. By carrying out individual work children learn independence and autonomy. Individual work can include a range of children's activities such as:

- **writing;**
- **drawing;**
- **investigating;**
- **planning;**
- **redrafting;**
- **evaluating etc.**

By far the commonest activity involves a child with a paper-based task working on his or her own. The management of individual work is moderately difficult as each activity is individual and different and all these occur concurrently. Teachers spend much of their time monitoring each child's work individually and interactions with children are frequently short. Learners needing support may have to wait for the teacher's attention and this often involves queuing. Individual work needs to be carefully managed if both the children's time and your time is to be used effectively. For this reason, tasks need to be designed so that children are able to work independently for most of their time

The strengths and weaknesses of each of these class organisations are summarised below:

Class Organisation	Strengths	Weaknesses
Whole-class Work	More time is spent in whole class discussion. Interactions are more direct and efficient. More opportunity to stimulate children's thinking by exploring ideas, asking questions and sharing problems. Creative work is recognised and supported. Teacher's time is used efficiently. Very effective in some curriculum areas.	Difficult to meet every child's needs. Difficult to ensure that all children participate. Children often remain passive.
Group Work	Can support differentiated learning. In appropriate groupings children of all attainment levels make good progress e.g. mixed attainment. Children learn social and affective skills. Can support progressive, developmental and egalitarian ideologies. Teacher's time is used effectively when group work is appropriately structured.	It may be difficult to keep children on task as groups are often seen as being about friendship and fun. Monitoring of groups can be difficult, especially of collaboration. Children of middle and low attainment when grouped together make little progress. Children grouped by ability can become demotivated. Children have to be taught groupwork skills.
Individual Work	All children can work on tasks differentiated to meet their needs. Children learn to work independently and autonomously. The outcome of a task is unambiguously achieved by one child.	The same teaching point may need to be made on different occasions to different children. During monitoring and support there is a lot of movement either by the teacher or each child. Limited time is spent with each child. More time is spent monitoring work than developing understanding. Children often experience work cards or work sheets rather like a 'correspondence course'.

Sources: Pollard, 1997; Bennett and Dunne, 1992; McNamara 1994, Reason, 1993.

Reflect on your recent experience in a school. Draw up a table with three columns using the following headings: 'Whole Class', 'Group Work', and 'Individual Work'. In each column list activities that you have seen which effectively used each of these three types of organisation.

Group work

Group work, because of its much greater complexity, requires more detailed consideration. It has been the subject of a great deal of enquiry and research, much of this due to its prominence within classrooms espousing a progressive ideological perspective. Whatever the ideological perspective, group work needs to be effectively organised and managed. Bennett and Dunne describe this in the following passage:

> A management system which allows for a whole class to be working in groups at the same time and on the same task is one that we would want to encourage and develop. This does not mean that it is the only way in which groups should function; nor does it mean that it is the only management system that should be adopted. However, for that part of the curriculum which lends itself to co-operative group work, it is a system which enables teachers to focus clearly on the content of the task, and to be specifically prepared for the kinds of materials, questions, problems, and so on which emerge from that one task. This, in turn, means that they are likely to be better prepared to cope with pupil demands. It is also a system which is designed to ease the complexities of management and is most likely to give teachers time for observation and assessment.
>
> (Bennett and Dunne 1992, p. 110)

Their review of empirical research found improvements in academic, social and affective performance in group work which involved co-operative working within the group and a limited curriculum focus to the tasks being carried out within the class. Where a wider range of curriculum activities is utilised, learning has been found to be less effective (Mortimore et al. 1988; Alexander et al. 1992).

Bennett and Dunne have identified six 'grouping variants' which are commonly found in classrooms. 'Grouping variants' are the different strategies and ways of working that teachers use to organise and manage groups. These are set out in the table on page 83. In all of these variants children commonly sit in groups of between two (pairs) and eight around a table or group of tables.

Planning group work

Group size

Group size has been found to be an important element in terms of effective classroom management (Bennett and Dunne 1992). Primary classrooms commonly have between four and six children seated in a group round a table. The optimum group size is reckoned to be four. Groups containing three or five children have the tendency to fragment resulting in splits within the group structure or individual children being isolated. Groups of four children have six lines of communication – that is there are six different possible pairings within a group of four; this effectively promotes high learning potential between group members. Groups of five or more clearly have considerably more lines of communication and this can result in some children having a more limited number of interactions.

Where children are younger, teachers have found that they are often more secure working in pairs. Groups of four can then be formed by two pairs joining together.

Criteria for forming classroom groups

Bearing in mind the importance of 'fitness for purpose', you will need to determine the most appropriate grouping to meet the requirements of the curriculum and the learning of the children. A series of common organisational criteria for forming class-room groups are listed below together with a description of their utility and possible drawbacks:

- **Age groupings: These can be useful for some activities, though because of the spread of ability, achievement and interest, etc., they can sometimes be counterproductive when it comes to teaching some subjects.**

- **Single attainment groups (single ability groups): These are useful for well-defined tasks which fit the ability of the children. However, they can be divisive if used permanently. Children who are low attainers may lack the group work skills to collaborate effectively.**

- **Mixed attainment groups (mixed ability groups): Mixed attainment groupings are frequently very effective in promoting and supporting learning. Advantages include the avoidance of negative labelling of students; students working with peers of other abilities and social background promoting mutual respect, understanding and tolerance; competition being replaced by co-operation; the avoidance of errors of selection.**

- **Interest groups: Grouping children by interest is always useful and has definite social advantages when there are differences between children such as social class or ethnic origin.**

- **Friendship groups: One of the commonest forms of grouping, these go down well with the children and are a valuable means of social education. However, you must bear in mind the needs of children who do not easily form friends.**

- **Convenience groups: These are used for organisational rather than primarily educational purposes. For example, children may be assigned to groups within physical education according to alphabetical order of their first name as a method of randomising groupings.**

- **Gender groups: Single sex groupings are only permissible where this does not prevent all children having equal access to the curriculum.**

(Adapted from Cohen et al. 1996)

Grouping Variant	Task Format	Task Outcome	Advantages	Disadvantages	Examples
1: Individuals work on individual tasks.	Individual tasks.	Individual.	Simplifies organisational management.	Low quality pupil to pupil talk.	Each child working at their own pace through a text book.
2: Individuals work on a common task.	Common task.	Individual.	Simplifies organisational management. Promotes co-operative learning.	Low quality pupil to pupil talk. Often confusion between pupil co-operation and cheating.	Creative writing, mathematics exercises.
3: Individuals work on a common task with co-operation.	Common task with co-operation.	Individual.	Simplifies organisational management. Promotes co-operative learning. Talk can influence outcome.	Unusual for any real change in children's working or learning.	Creative writing, mathematics exercises.
4: Jigsaw task.	Task divided into parts. Group members work on different parts of same task.	Group outcome achieved when all parts of 'jigsaw' completed.	Co-operation and individual accountability built in. All group members must work and contribute.	Task incomplete if one member does not complete task.	Producing newspaper. Investigating the properties of materials.
5: Collaborative group work.	Group work co-operatively and collaboratively on a common task.	Single outcome for whole group.	Activities of group have to be co-ordinated. Group leader may emerge.	Each member's contribution is undefined.	Problem-solving activities. Discussion task.
6: Collaborative group work with expert groups.	As variant 5 but with roles more closely defined. All groups work on similar, related topics. Each group member assigned to an expert team which receives specialised tuition.	Single outcome for whole group.	Each member acts as a tutor to the rest of group in expert field. Activities of group have to be co-ordinated. Group leader may emerge. Each member's contribution more closely defined.	The group's learning is dependent on the 'cascade' from the teacher via the expert group.	Problem-solving activities.

Adapted from Bennett and Dunne 1992

Practical task

List the advantages and disadvantages of each of the group organisations listed on page 82.

Managing effective group work

Several authors (Kagan 1988; Reid et al. 1989; Bennett and Dunne 1992) stress the importance of effective management of group work. Beginning teachers' lesson plans are often characterised by children being set to work in groups without the necessary supporting framework for the children to be able to work effectively. Group work can easily become an opportunity for children to socialise rather than carry out assignments. It is important that you plan:

1. tasks that contain a suitable cognitive challenge
2. tasks that make appropriate social demands
3. a range of activities including group work which support the children's capability of working in groups
4. activities which promote the development of group work skills.

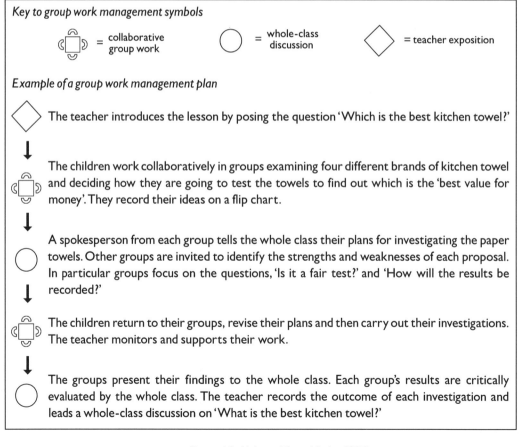

Key to group work management symbols

⬚ = collaborative group work   ◯ = whole-class discussion   ◇ = teacher exposition

Example of a group work management plan

◇ The teacher introduces the lesson by posing the question 'Which is the best kitchen towel?'

⬚ The children work collaboratively in groups examining four different brands of kitchen towel and deciding how they are going to test the towels to find out which is the 'best value for money'. They record their ideas on a flip chart.

◯ A spokesperson from each group tells the whole class their plans for investigating the paper towels. Other groups are invited to identify the strengths and weaknesses of each proposal. In particular groups focus on the questions, 'Is it a fair test?' and 'How will the results be recorded?'

⬚ The children return to their groups, revise their plans and then carry out their investigations. The teacher monitors and supports their work.

◯ The groups present their findings to the whole class. Each group's results are critically evaluated by the whole class. The teacher records the outcome of each investigation and leads a whole-class discussion on 'What is the best kitchen towel?'

Figure 6.2 (Adapted from Harlen 1985)

If children are to work successfully in groups then the tasks must be planned so that they are appropriately introduced and sustained. Reid et al. (1989) and Harlen (1985) propose similar models involving a combination of whole-class instruction, whole-class discussion and collaborative group work. Each part of the learning programme is designed to support the completion of collaborative group work with groups working independently from the teacher. The role of teacher instruction and whole-class discussion are clearly identified.

An example is shown in Figure 6.2. It is an example of a system of management for a scientific investigation into questions such as 'Which is the best kitchen towel?' The same framework could equally well be used for the management of a number of other groupwork activities.

Group work skills and their development

If group work is to be successful then children must develop the necessary skills to carry this out effectively. Bennett and Dunne (1992) identify the following key areas for the development of group work skills.

1. Co-operation
Training tasks should be designed to promote activities that require children to:

- **carry out the roles of co-ordinator, data gatherer, secretary and evaluator as appropriate;**
- **develop the key skills of conciseness, listening, reflecting and everyone contributing;**
- **take turns at talking;**
- **interview and question each other;**
- **describe accurately;**
- **edit and summarise where appropriate;**
- **negotiate a common agreement;**
- **support other group members to achieve an outcome.**

2. Self-monitoring and self-evaluation skills
There are four aspects to the self-evaluation of group work:

- **The group evaluates the whole group process.**
- **Group members evaluate each other's behaviours and contributions.**
- **Individuals evaluate themselves in the context of the group.**
- **Final presentations are evaluated by other groups and the teacher.**

Areas for evaluation include:

- **taking turns;**
- **praising others;**
- **helping others;**
- **participation;**
- **developing understanding;**
- **facilitating participation;**

- listening;
- reinforcing;
- paying attention;
- questioning;
- observing and monitoring others in the group;
- observing and monitoring the group.

What kind of classroom layout is going to help you achieve this?

Having decided what class organisations you wish to employ, you will now need to consider how you can set out the classroom to most effectively promote these. If you are likely to be utilising only a limited range of class organisations then selecting a layout that effectively supports these may well be straightforward. Where you intend to use a range of class organisations, that is not just a mixture of whole-class, group and individual work but also different types of activities from different curriculum areas as part of these, you may need to consider which classroom layout gives most flexibility.

Alexander et al. (1989) describe four classroom layouts that they have observed in Leeds primary schools. The first (Figure 6.3) shows a classroom set out to support group work with no areas specifically designated for particular curriculum activities. You might arrange your classroom like this if you wanted to carry out a range of group work activities which focused around one subject area at a time.

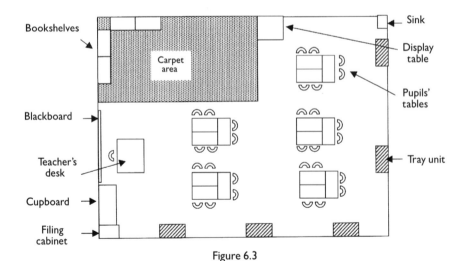

Figure 6.3

The second classroom layout (Figure 6.4) is again designed for group work as the basis of the classroom's organisation but here there are two permanent curriculum areas within the room: a reading corner and a music corner. Reading corners are common elements of many classrooms and are designed to support literacy across the curriculum. Music areas are much less common and the class teacher in this example may well be the school's specialist music teacher.

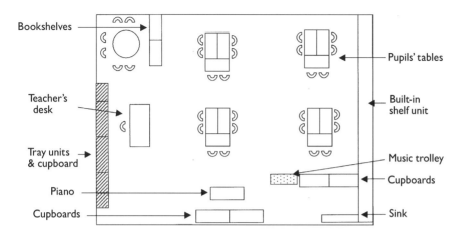

Bookshelves

Teacher's desk

Tray units & cupboard

Piano

Cupboards

Pupils' tables

Built-in shelf unit

Music trolley

Cupboards

Sink

Figure 6.4

The third type of classroom layout (Figure 6.5) would commonly be used in Early Years classrooms. It allows for a range of different curriculum areas to be organised to take place in the classroom at the same time. This classroom arrangement would support children working in groups or individually.

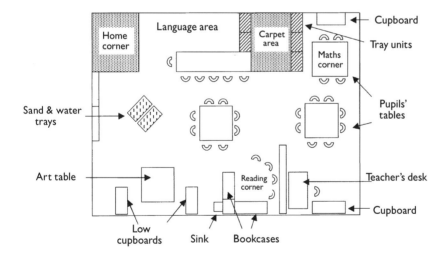

Cupboard

Language area

Home corner

Carpet area

Tray units

Maths corner

Sand & water trays

Pupils' tables

Art table

Reading corner

Teacher's desk

Cupboard

Low cupboards

Sink

Bookcases

Figure 6.5

The fourth kind of layout (Figure 6.6) has a range of a number of dedicated curriculum areas. Within this classroom environment you would expect children to work in groups either collaboratively or independently with each group working on a different curriculum area at any given time. During the course of the day groups would move from one curriculum base to the next so as to complete work in all the subject areas.

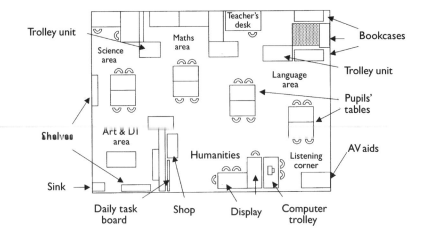

Figure 6.6

Teachers most commonly use the second and third layout types.

McNamara (1994) describes a fifth layout (Figure 6.7) in answer to the question:

How is the classroom to be organised so as to enable the smooth transition from one organisational form to another?

(McNamara (1994) in Pollard 1996, p. 196)

Desks are arranged around the sides of the classroom in a pattern similar to the one shown below.

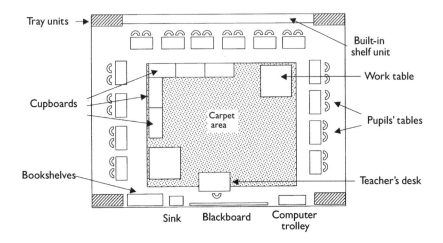

Figure 6.7

Children can sit either on the inside of the tables facing the wall when carrying out individual work or on the outside of the tables for whole-class work. The central area can be used for practical activities requiring more space, as a resource base or for discussion work. The advantages of this layout are:

- **Children can see each other (when seated outside the tables) and are more inclined to listen to each other's contributions than when seated in rows with their backs to colleagues or in groups where eye contact and audibility are difficult.**
- **A large space is available in the middle of the room for stories, large pieces of artwork etc.**
- **Children are able (when required) to work in pairs or threes, i.e. group sizes which are productive and unlikely to exclude people.**
- **The teacher can see, at a glance, what every child is doing and reach those with problems quickly.**
- **Desks can be quickly formed into tables for groups of four when required.**
- **When the children are seated on the inside facing the wall, they are less easily distracted from individual work than when sat in groups.**

(Adapted from McNamara in Pollard 1996, p. 196)

Action planning: how do you want to organise the class?

To organise the class effectively, you will need to take a series of decisions. These decisions have implications in the long, medium and short term. As a student teacher, it is unlikely that you will be able to influence all or indeed any of the long-term decisions; the school or class teacher may already have taken these. Nevertheless, you should be aware that these have been taken and will reflect the ethos and ideology of the school and classroom.

Long-term decisions

- **What particular ethos do you want to develop within the classroom?**
- **How much autonomy/responsibility do you want to give the children?**
- **What relationship do you want to have with them? What role(s) are you going to adopt?**
- **How can you organise the layout of the classroom to support their learning effectively?**
- **How can you utilise displays to support the children's learning and to celebrate their achievements?**
- **How can the available time be utilised across the curriculum to ensure breadth and balance?**
- **How much integration will there be between different areas of the curriculum? What structure should the day have to support this?**
- **How will the classroom environment support the raising of the children's self-esteem?**

Medium-term decisions

- What is the most effective range of classroom organisations for this particular learning programme?
- What skills/attitudes/understandings will need to be developed to support this?
- How is the available time most effectively used?
- How will your classroom management appropriately differentiate the learning to meet the needs of all the children?
- How will you monitor and assess the children's learning?
- What resources will you need to gather to support the learning programme?
- What classroom displays will you organise and how will these be constructed? To what extent and in what ways will the children be involved in this?
- What skills will you need to develop as a teacher to enable you to carry this out?
- How will you utilise any classroom support that is available (support teachers, classroom support assistants, parents, etc.)?

Short-term decisions

- What is the most effective organisation to promote the particular learning within a lesson?
- Will individual work, group work or whole-class activities most effectively promote learning in a given area of learning?
- If the children are working in groups:
  - on what basis will the children be allocated to groups and why?
  - will the children work individually or collaboratively on assigned tasks?
  - how much support will each group need and how much help can each group be given? What is the balance between teacher intensive tasks and tasks where children work independently?
  - in what way will the groups work on collaborative tasks?
- Will you utilise circle time?
- What resources will be used? How will these be arranged?
- How will you manage transitions between one part of a lesson and the next?
- What role(s) will you adopt?
- How will the classroom management support the equality of opportunity of all the children?

Practical task

Reflect on a recent teaching practice (or school visit). What long-, medium- and short-term decisions were you able to affect?

Conclusion

Many readers, particularly students new to teaching, may be overwhelmed by the complexity of classroom management. Like many areas of activity, some authors have reduced this complexity to a few basic rules. Focus on these and much of this complexity falls into place.

Laslett and Smith (1984) have identified four rules of classroom management which are:

1. Get them in.
2. Get them out.
3. Get on with it.
4. Get on with them.

Rule 1 – 'Get them in' – is made up of three aspects, *greeting*, *seating* and *starting* and is concerned with the start of the lesson. *Greeting* means being at the classroom before the children and making sure it is ready for the start of the lesson, thereby underlining your authority. *Seating* means making sure that the room is appropriately arranged for the activity and the children. *Starting* means making sure that children are immediately usefully occupied when they enter the classroom.

Rule 2 – 'Get them out' – is made up of two aspects, *concluding* and *dismissing*, and is concerned with the end of the lesson. This is a frequently neglected part of the lesson. All lessons should end with a conclusion where resources and materials are put away and the learning is suitably and effectively reviewed and reinforced. When the bell goes, you should set up a routine so that the children leave the room in an orderly way. Children are not just leaving the classroom – they are going to their next activity and need to be cued in to this.

Rule 3 – 'Get on with it' – is made of three aspects, *content*, *manner* and *organisation*, and is concerned with the main part of the lesson. In terms of *content*, variety is needed to maintain interest, curiosity and motivation. Different types of activity and different kinds of organisation (whole-class, group and individual work) will enliven lessons. Pace is important and where possible all children should achieve some target in each lesson which means breaking programmes of learning down into manageable chunks. *Manner* is concerned with the classroom atmosphere and how you promote a positive, supportive ethos. Key aspects are the plentiful use of praise, appropriate facial expressions and tone of voice, keeping eye contact with those you are addressing and having a quiet but clearly audible voice. *Organisation* is concerned with meeting individual needs and the recognition that all classes are mixed attainment. Groups are commonly used to organise for this and this is done in three ways – rota, quota and branching. Rota refers to children moving in rotation round the room from one activity to the next. Having appropriately constructed learning centres is essential to this approach. Quota means setting each child an appropriate amount of work to be completed within a lesson. And branching means having a common activity in which children engage at the outset and then follow up and extension work which is adjusted to meet the needs of children of differing levels of attainment.

Rule 4 – 'Get on with them' – is made up of two aspects, 'Who's who?' and 'What's going on?' These are essential to good, effective working relationships between teachers and children. 'Who's who?' concerns developing personal relationships with children by first learning their names and calling them by them whenever possible and secondly taking a personal interest in them as an individual. 'What's going on?' is about keeping in touch with what is happening within the class. Anticipation and prevention of difficulties is invariably the best practice. This involves scanning and monitoring what is happening in front of you on a very regular basis (like looking in the mirror when driving a car). Use both sight and hearing when you are doing this. Mark work in progress to see what learning is taking place. Avoid sitting at the teacher's desk; keep moving round the classroom. Above all try to return children to working with the minimum of confrontation.

Further reading

Alexander, R., Wilcocks, J. and Kinder, K. (1989) 'The classroom: messages, decisions and dilemmas' in *Changing Primary Practice*, London: Falmer. The chapter describes the effect of a local education authority initiative on the organisation of primary classrooms. Aspects covered include classroom layout, grouping and group work, planning and record keeping. It gives a clear insight into how teachers' ideological perspectives affect the decisions they take about their classrooms.

Bennett, N. and Dunne, E. (1992) *Managing Classroom Groups*. Hemel Hempstead: Simon and Schuster Education. This book discusses the importance of co-operative grouping in terms of children's learning. It describes how groups should be composed, the design of appropriate collaborative tasks and how group outcomes can be assessed. The book is based on extensive classroom research with teachers and children.

Jackson, P. (1994) 'Life in classrooms' in Pollard, A. and Bourne, J. (eds) *Teaching and Learning in the Primary School*. Buckingham: Open University Press. An alternative and insightful view of classroom organisation which contrasts with the more analytic approaches in the other further reading.

Proctor, A., Entwistle, M., Judge, B. and McKenzie-Murdoch, S. (1995) 'The contexts for learning' in *Learning to Teach in the Primary Classroom*. London: Routledge. This chapter provides clear and practical guidance on how the physical, psychological and social contexts influence learning in primary classrooms. Guidance is given as to how to make the organisation of the primary classroom effective.

Rogers, C. and Kutnick, P. (eds) (1994) *Groups In Schools*. London: Cassell Education. This is a detailed and comprehensive overview of group work in primary schools. Issues covered include the historical, theoretical, experimental and practical foundations of group work in primary classes. Based on a sound understanding of the principles of group work the book describes how to carry out group work in practice by giving examples of successful implementation.

By the end of the chapter you should:

- *recognise the importance of establishing a positive classroom climate with and between the children you teach;*
- *know that the relationship you have with pupils is an interpersonal one;*
- *understand how the ways in which you structure learning is as important as what you teach;*
- *understand that the 'hidden' curriculum is an important contribution to the overall experiences provided for pupils.*

This chapter addresses the following Professional Standards for QTS:

➔ **1.1, 1.2, 1.3, 3.3.1, 3.3.9**

(The Standards are reproduced in full at the back of this book.)

Learning: more than an academic exercise

Section 351 of the Education Act (1996) states that schools must:

- **promote the spiritual, moral, cultural, mental and physical development of pupils at the school and of society;**
- **prepare pupils for the opportunities, responsibilities and experiences of adult life.**

See Chapter 10 on p. 124 for further discussion of the aims of education.

This statement focuses not only on the academic aspect of school life, but also on personal and social development – both while at school and as a preparation for later life.

It is quite clear, then, that a major intention of the Education Act is to educate the child as a person (as well as a pupil), in terms of behaviour, roles and relationships in school and with a regard to behaviour, roles and relationships outside of school and beyond the years relevant to a particular phase. This intention is strongly reflected in recent intiatives to promote citizenship.

How individual schools provide for this – and the extent to which they are successful – varies, but it should be remembered that schools are social communities and institutions as well as educational establishments. Much attention to what goes on in schools is directed at the subjects taught – the **formal** curriculum; but, because schools are communities also, the school's behaviour patterns, roles and relationships are of equal importance in the development, both academic and personal, of pupils.

All that a child experiences in school is part of his/her personal and social and health education (PSE). The teacher has a central role to play in this:

> Parents have the major part of play, but the role of the teacher is vital because personal and social development and responsibility are intrinsic to the nature of education. It is something from which no teacher can opt out.
>
> (HMI 1989 p. 1)

This chapter in many ways brings together the key elements covered elsewhere in this book. You will understand already the need for teachers to have a sound grasp of subject knowledge, learning theory, assessment, differentiation and special educational needs. But the nature of primary education makes teaching in this phase very much an interpersonal activity, and one where the relationship established between you and the pupils can enhance or diminish the quality of learning that takes place. Therefore it is essential to match the 'whats' of your teaching with the 'hows'. The importance of this is made explicit in the introduction to the Professional Standards for QTS (DfES/TTA 2002 p. 2):

> Teaching is one of the most influential professions in society. In their day-to-day work, teachers can and do make huge differences to children's lives: directly, through the curriculum they teach, and indirectly, through their behaviour, attitudes, values, relationships with and interest in pupils.

Before you read the remainder of this chapter, think about *why* you have decided to become a teacher. The reasons often given by both students and qualified teachers include:

- **because I love working with children;**
- **because I want to do a worthwhile job;**
- **because I would get a lot of satisfaction from helping children develop;**
- **because I had difficulties at school and would know how such children feel.**

These all relate to and derive from the personal and social dimensions of the classroom and you, as the teacher, are not just an influence on these but are the director. It may help to think of yourself as the conductor and the class as an orchestra. The difficulty lies not in getting one person or section to play an instrument but in getting everyone to play in time, with the same feeling and expression and the same tune!

Just as a conductor needs to plan rehearsals, practices, discussions of the music etc., so you, the teacher, must plan for the interpersonal relationships which exist within the classroom. That is, you need to be clear about the type of relationship and classroom climate you wish to foster; how your behaviour and responses influence these; and how the children will know the sort of climate you want to establish and foster.

Practical task

What do you consider to be the key influences/factors in achieving a positive classroom climate?

A positive classroom climate:

- **has attractive displays based on children's work;**
- **is tidy;**
- **has a purposeful atmosphere when children are working;**
- **promotes children's self-esteem.**

In a classroom with a positive climate children:

- **are generally happy and enthusiastic about their work;**
- **feel valued;**
- **want to do well, for themselves as well as for the teacher.**

The teacher in a classroom with a positive climate:

- **does his/her best not to have favourites;**
- **respects the children as people;**
- **has a good relationship with the children.**

See Chapter 15 on p. 183 for what pupils expect.

The teacher/pupil relationship

When you are working in school, you probably want your pupils to like you – and why not? Depending on the length of a placement you are likely to spend many hours with the children and of course you do not want to be disliked. But the teacher/pupil relationship needs to be established carefully.

Extreme familiarity and/or informality does not, usually, make you more popular. Children know that the teacher is supposed to be 'in charge' and they will expect you to behave accordingly. So, whilst the relationship you have, and hopefully enjoy, is interpersonal, it must be professional also. There is a clear purpose to your being there with the children, you each have a role (teacher/pupil) and the power balance is not equal.

What you need to aim for is an approach which:

- **is friendly but not over-familiar;**
- **fosters a close relationship but is not cloying;**
- **has some professional distance so that you command respect but is not so distant that you seem aloof or indifferent;**
- **is challenging but not overly-critical or hostile;**
- **helps children feel secure but does not encourage their over-dependence on you;**
- **values the children as individuals but develops their own interpersonal skills and promotes co-operation;**
- **accepts the uniqueness of each child but requires some degree of conformity from all pupils.**

and so on.

A tall order, especially for a student teacher in training!

However, if you are able to establish a good relationship with pupils and establish the right sort of climate then the rewards are plentiful. You will find that the majority of children:

- settle more quickly;
- are more motivated;
- enjoy being at school, and working hard;
- have a higher standard of behaviour;
- become much more co-operative, willing to share and sensitive to the needs of others;
- have a heightened self-image and self-esteem.

Self-esteem

There are three important points which affect self-esteem:

- a comparison of one's self-image with an ideal self-image – the kind of person one would like to be;
- internalisation of society's judgements – self-evaluation is based on the evaluation of others and involves position, status and culturally learned standards;
- personal competence in relation to taking on various roles in life – every role embodies a set of expectations and is related to 'finding one's place in society', feeling that you are good at what you do and being able to express yourself through what you do. (Tyler 1992 p. 3).

There are two distinct areas in the day to day life of a primary school. The first of these is the stated or formal curriculum of subject matter, knowledge and skills. The second comprises attitudes, values and relationship and is usually called the **hidden** curriculum. Whether you plan it or not, the two operate side by side.

Consider: which will have the more lasting imprint on a child:

- the facts of a history (or any other) lesson;

or

- the humiliation of being an isolate?
- the fear of being teased?
- the confusion arising from being unexpressed?
- the ways that decisions are made and rules enforced?
- the partiality of a teacher towards other pupils?

Factors which influence self-esteem

It is important to remember that:

- **positive peer regard improves self-image;**
- **teaching and learning methods employed by teachers influence and affect achievement;**
- **a positive classroom climate enhances motivation and improves behaviour.**

If the classroom climate is right, then there is a much greater chance that children's self-esteem will be enhanced.

But there is no fairy dust available to help you establish the right climate. Besides giving serious thought to the sort of climate you desire in the classroom you need also to think through how you are going to achieve it.

Research shows that you as a student teacher are likely to have a clear, if idealistic, idea about the sort of teacher you want to be, the kind of relationships you want to develop with the children you teach, the physical appearance of the classroom and the class-room atmosphere you want to create. (Furlong and Maynard 1995 p. 74).

You may feel that the views of two students in their study reflect your aspirations.

> I want people to come into my classroom and automatically feel it is a really happy place to be. The kids know exactly what to do and are enjoying it and everyone is getting on with it.

> [It is important] that we care for each other, look after each other and are there for each other ... I would like to be part of that sense of belonging.
>
> (Furlong and Maynard 1995 p. 75)

However, only one student out of the eleven in the study made an explicit reference to the need for additional aims beyond giving pupils knowledge (Furlong and Maynard 1995 p. 149).

It was evident from the students' classroom practice that they did make some connections between the formal and hidden curricula. But if you approach classroom climate in an ad hoc or unfocused way, there is a good chance that you will overlook or not develop sufficiently one or more important contributory factors.

You will need to consider the following factors:

- *routines and procedures* **which form part of your classroom management**
  - **transition from one activity to another, movement from the classroom to a**

different part of the school, access to resources, tidying away at the end of sessions.

- *classroom habits* that can discriminate unintentionally against some children –

  selecting children to undertake 'jobs'; identifying children for a special mention in assembly, focusing on academic achievement only when giving rewards (merit marks, table points, certificates); your responses when children 'tell tales'; the extent to which you model what you probably preach with regard to classroom tidiness (especially your desk and resources).

- *approaches to the management of learning* which may enhance or diminish the climate you create –

  whether children contribute to the setting of classroom rules;
  whether positive personal skills and attributes are encouraged (co-operation, perseverance, collaboration, independence, a questioning approach, confidence);
  how you respond to children's answers, especially if they are wrong;
  the extent to which tasks and activities are interactive;
  whether you share with the children what your learning aims are for lessons;
  how you mark children's books (work which is incorrect, untidy, unfinished, of a different standard from usual etc);
  whether there is consistency in each of these;
  whether your behaviour offers a positive role model for the children.

- *rapport* –

  whether you pronounce and spell the children's names correctly;
  whether you engage children in personal talk about their interests, hobbies, views, feelings etc;
  the extent to which you do this with all of the class;
  how you respond to an 'unlikeable' child (clingy, attention seeking, know-it-all, dirty, smelly, cheeky, unattractive etc);
  whether the children have to 'read your mood' each day;
  whether children feel able to approach you with personal information or questions about the nature of the work you have set.

Practical task

Focus on your current or last school placement and write a short evaluation of how well you managed routines and procedures, classroom habits, approaches to the management of learning and rapport. Indicate your strength(s) and weaknesses (w). In preparation of your next placement (or your first class as a Newly Qualified Teacher), identify three targets which will help you in establishing a positive classroom climate with your next class.

In establishing a positive classroom climate you will need to weave together all of the elements covered in the other chapters of this book with each interpersonal element of your teaching so that a genuine congruence is built up; a congruence, or agreement, between what you say you want with what you do to bring it about.

In doing this you will be better placed to match the hidden curriculum of your classroom with the formal. The formal subjects taught cannot be separated out from the overall and complete interpersonal package experienced by the pupils, and it is the remainder which comprises the hidden curriculum:

- accepted conduct towards and between each and every member of the class;
- how you organise and manage the formal curriculum;
- the teaching methods used;
- the learning styles promoted;
- the combination of attitudes, values and procedures.

Day-to-day relationships and interactions, then, all make an important and significant contribution, not just to personal and social education but also to learning and achievement in curriculum areas. Tattum (1988) suggests that these relationships and interactions are ongoing, reciprocal, lifelong and cumulative. The whole curriculum experience that you present either enhances or diminishes the very qualities and skills which are essential to growth as a person.

The implication for you as the teacher is to examine the ways in which the formal curriculum is planned and delivered so that it actually does help children acquire appropriate and positive attitudes and values and a healthy self-esteem.

Worthwhile learning approaches

In 1989, HMI identified the following **worthwhile** learning approaches as being features of quality education and of relevance to pupils of all ages:

- **pupils are encouraged to take responsibility for their learning; pupils develop self-confidence and judgement; from the earliest age, pupils are encouraged to exercise informed choice within and between activities;**
- **there are opportunities for all pupils to achieve, irrespective of their particular strengths and abilities;**
- **pupils understand that everyone's contributions – including their own – deserve attention; pupils are able to work in and help foster a supportive context;**
- **pupils have the opportunity to work in groups of different size and purpose as well as on their own; they experience leadership as well as membership of a group; they can offer and respond to ideas; they can argue a case and defend sensibly a decision or course of action;**
- **pupils have the opportunity to explore PSE through role play – roles perceived as good or bad; roles which explore different ways of life; roles which challenge views held in society; roles which reveal a range of feelings and beliefs;**
- **pupils have the opportunity to use their imagination and to develop personal ideas and insights.**

(HMI 1989 pp. 5–6)

Although these were produced over a decade ago, they relate well to more recent publications: *National Curriculum 2000, Early Learning Goals, Personal, Social and Health Education and Citizenship.*

QCA guidance on Personal, Social and Health Education and Citizenship (2000) states that:

> Children and young people need the self-awareness, positive self-esteem and confidence to:

- **have worthwhile and fulfilling relationships;**
- **respect the differences between people;**
- **develop independence and responsibility.**

Further on, the guidance points out that a range of teaching strategies are needed if all pupils are to be provided with a breadth of effective learning opportunities — active learning, enquiry and discussion.

As discussed earlier, you will need to consider how you present and manage lessons so that your teaching strategies contribute to and promote a positive classroom climate.

It is worthwhile, at this point, to look at what teachers are asked to provide in terms of children's personal and social development.

At Key Stage 1, children:

- **have opportunities to show they can take some responsibility for themselves and their environment;**
- **learn social skills such as how to share, take turns, play, help others, resolve simple arguments.**

At Key Stage 2, children:

- **become more mature, independent and self-confident.**

At neither key stage can you the teacher assume that such developments occur automatically. Even if you tell the children that these key stage statements are what you want to promote, there is no guarantee that you will be successful if you do not give equal attention to how you are going to promote them.

Towards the end of Curriculum 2000 you will find an extract from the Statement of Values by the National Forum for Values in Education and the Community. With regard to the values which underpin relationships, the forum agreed the following:

We value others for themselves, not only for what they have or what they can do for us. We value relationships as fundamental to the development and fulfilment of ourselves and others, and to the good of the community.

On the basis of these values, we should:

- **respect others, including children;**
- **care for others and exercise goodwill in our dealings with them;**
- **show others they are valued;**
- **earn loyalty, trust and confidence;**
- **work co-operatively with others;**
- **respect the privacy and property of others;**
- **resolve disputes peacefully.**

(DfEE/QCA 1999 p. 148)

The 'we' referred to includes you the teacher because these values are considered necessary for all people. It is heartening to see this, a statement of values which is inclusive of all, teacher and pupils, because a climate which is based on these values, and which is promoted with what Pollard (1997, p. 101) terms 'genuineness', will be all the more positive and closer to the ideal.

Discussion point

Tyler (1992, p. 4) offers a list of questions for teachers wishing to test their commitment to a good, interpersonal classroom climate:

- **Do children work in silence or can they collaborate?**
- **Is there an atmosphere of co-operation or competition in the classroom?**
- **Is all the work defined and imposed by the classteacher or can children sometimes develop their own interests?**
- **Does all work require close supervision or does it also involve initiative and independence?**

Other questions you may like to ask are:

- **Do children take part in assemblies, helping to plan the content and delivery also?**
- **Are children actively involved in setting their own targets?**
- **Do children contribute to assessments of their performance, achievements and attainment?**

Practical task

When you are next working in school, ask your class teacher to tell you about his/her approach to fostering, establishing and maintaining a positive classroom climate. When you evaluate this discussion think about whether you have noticed a congruence between what s/he said and what s/he actually does.

The climate in action

Three features of your practice which can reinforce the classroom climate and cross subject boundaries are:

1. circle time
2. productive talk
3. interactive tasks.

Circle time

One way of fostering and maintaining a positive classroom climate is through circle time. Circle activities can help to develop self-esteem, an understanding and appreciation of community and listening and speaking skills (Braddy 1988).

The teacher and children sit in a circle so that everyone can see each other and take part equally. Simple ground rules should be established – such as everyone has a turn if they want one, that everyone is listened to, that there is only one speaker at a time, that all contributions are respected, there are no put downs, it's OK to pass.

Begin with a common phrase –

> *My good news is …*
> *My favourite food is … (toy, game, story, TV programme etc.)*
> *Hello, my name is … (when there are new children or visitors)*
> *I can hear …*

This allows feelings, experiences, ideas and information to be shared. Children can be asked for their own suggestions for a 'circle'.

Once the children are used to circle time and a sense of trust is shared within the circle, it is possible to deal with issues of importance within the class/school.

For example:

> *In the playground, I feel unsafe …*
> *When I have to write a story, I feel …*
> *I think we should … to improve our school …*
> *A secret I can share is …*

Some of these statements relate to **child protection**. It is important that you deal sensitively with the children and in response to their comments.

(You will find Jenny Moseley's book particularly helpful if you wish to read further on this – see Further Reading).

Productive questioning and talk

Teachers talk a lot, don't they? Routine talk, expositions, explanations and questions are all part of a teacher's job, so to speak. It has been suggested that teachers ask a question every 70 seconds on average, and that teachers themselves answer at least 40 per cent of them (Hargie 1978 cited Fontana 1995, p. 83).

You will have your own observations about the effectiveness of your placement-teachers in presenting expositions, explanations, questions and so on; and you will certainly have a view of your own effectiveness. If you can focus also on the type and purpose of the approach used and on your responses and the way in which you present them, you will be able to make explicit links between your oral/verbal skills and techniques and their impact on the classroom climate.

The type of talk you use will depend mainly on what information you expect in return, your purpose in framing your speech in the way that you did and how involved you want the respondent to be.

Teacher-talk can be productive or unproductive. This is covered in greater detail in Chapter 6 but it is relevant here to make a direct link.

See Chapter 6 on p. 74 for more information on teacher-talk.

Remember, teachers ask lots of questions. That means you do, also, in your role as the teacher. The questions you probe may be productive or unproductive.

Productive questions are likely to be:

- **open – respondents answer as they see fit;**
- **probing – further information or clarification is sought;**
- **reflective – the respondent has to consider and evaluate;**
- **hypothetical – the respondent considers situations and conveys opinions, values and perceptions.**

Unproductive questions are likely to be:

- **several questions in one;**
- **closed;**
- **ambiguous;**
- **rhetorical;**
- **leading.**

The link between your approach to questioning and classroom climate is, I hope, obvious but it does need to be explicit. When you plan for your teaching, you need to think through not only what questions you are going to ask but also which children you are going to ask, and your likely responses. How you do this will be a manifestation of the classroom habits discussed earlier which impinge on your teaching.

Therefore, consider the extent to which your approach to expositions, explanations and questions:

- **is inclusive of all children;**

- is clear and unambiguous;
- presents an encouraging tone;
- allows children time to think before they are expected to answer;
- is personable and incorporates humour when appropriate;
- motivates or sustains the children's interest/enthusiasm;
- accords dignity to children in how you phrase a question or accept an answer;
- allows them to 'have a go' at answering questions/contributing even though they may be wrong (no put-downs);
- displays consistency and fairness in how you respond to different children;
- models what you expect from the children when they talk to each other;
- recognises the interpersonal nature of the exchange.

This list is not exhaustive and you will work with teachers who vary in their ability to mould this element of their practice with a positive classroom climate.

Interactive learning

It is probably true to say that we all learn in different ways but there are general principles about how we achieve this – and we tend to read, do, watch and listen. You need to ensure that a range of learning approaches is incorporated into the curriculum. A better learning atmosphere is secured if children are actively engaged, understand what they have to do and the purpose of an activity, and believe it matters that they do their best.

In most primary classrooms children sit alongside at least one other and in many they sit as a group, typically in 4s, 6s or 8s. The children more often than not do not have the opportunity to function as a group. This, according to Dunne and Bennett (1990), means that opportunities are lost to enhance children's social relationships. You will find further information on grouping children in Chapter 6. The purpose of including it here is to emphasise its link with classroom climate.

 See Chapter 6 on p. 74 for more information on grouping.

GROUPING PATTERNS
1. Working individually on different tasks for individual products.
2. Working individually on identical tasks for individual products.
3. Working individually on jigsaw elements for joint outcome.
4. Working jointly on one task for joint outcome.

(ibid. pp. 10–14)

If children are provided with opportunities to participate in jigsaw and joint tasks, then they experience collaboration and co-operation, awareness of their own and others' needs, decision making, problem-solving and listening. Such experiences can help develop the classroom climate by promoting a 'spirit of co-operation' that goes beyond that found in many classrooms. However, group work is not a panacea for deficiencies in teaching, organisation or management and it requires proper planning and structure. So, you will need to think through:

- ground rules;
- fitness for purposes;

- practice for pupils;
- incorporating group work into routines and procedures and classroom habits also.

Again, further information on this can be found in Chapter 6.

Conclusion

The importance of classroom climate to children cannot be overstated. Children in the primary phase of education need to feel secure and valued as individuals so that they come to school willingly, are motivated to learn and develop appropriate social skills.

A congruence between what you say/expect as the teacher and what you do and how you do it will influence this greatly. You the teacher determine the classroom climate.

A final thought: how can children be expected to display:

- even-handedness;
- tolerance;
- sympathy;
- politeness.

if the teacher:

- treats children with manifest inequality?
- is intolerant of some children?
- lacks sympathy for some children?
- sweeps past a door held open for them without a word of thanks?

Further reading

Barnes, P. (ed) (1995) *Personal, Social and Emotional Development of Children.* Buckingham: Open University. An easy read about key aspects of children's development with particular reference made to children's self-esteem.

Best, R., Lang, P., Lodge, C. and Wilkins, C. (eds) (1995) *Pastoral Care and Personal and Social Education.* London: Cassell. A wide range of issues related to personal and social education is covered including the impact of a teacher's interpersonal style on pupil behaviour and the link between personal and social education and the whole curriculum.

Biott, C. and Easen, P. (1994) *Collaborative Learning in Staffrooms and Classrooms.* London: David Fulton. This book widens the definition of collaborative learning beyond formal group work in classrooms and promotes active forms of pupil learning.

Bottery, M. (1990) *The Morality of the School.* London: Cassell. A book which poses teachers moral challenges. Attention is given to the roles of teachers and pupils and various co-operative group activities.

Cullingford, C. (1990) *The Nature of Learning.* London: Cassell. This book outlines the holistic nature of learning. Inner meanings and emotion, relationships with others and a sense of self are addressed in a practical way.

Dowling, M. (2000) *Young Children's Personal, Social and Moral Development*. London: Paul Chapman. A book which draws together the theory and practice of personal and social development in young children. Emphasis is placed on the need for sensitive interventions from adults who understand children's needs.

Dunne, E. and Bennett, N. (1990)*Talking and Learning in Groups*. Macmillan. A good overview of the principles of group work, together with approaches and strategies for implementing it.

Dunne, R. and Wragg, T. (1994) *Effective Teaching*. London: Routledge. A book which is part of the Leverhulme Primary Project. Of particular interest are the references to ethos.

Edwards, J. and Fogelman, K. (eds) (1993) *Developing Citizenship in the Curriculum*. London: David Fulton. A collection of articles on how the cross-curricular theme of citizenship may be incorporated into the curriculum. Chapter 2 outlines how to create a climate for citizenship education and makes explicit reference to personal qualities and relationships, self-esteem and giving pupils responsibility.

Fontana, D. (1995) *Psychology for Teachers*, (3rd edn) Basingstoke: BPS/Macmillan. A comprehensive and practical guide to psychology. A number of chapters are of particular interest with regard to personal, social and moral development and teach attitudes and personality.

Furlong, J. and Maynard, T. (1995) *Mentoring Student Teachers*. London: Routledge. This book draws on research on students' school-based learning to analyse how student teachers learn to teach.

Galloway, D. and Edwards, A. (1991) *Primary School Teaching and Educational Psychology*. Harlow: Longman. The authors demonstrate how an understanding of teachers' day-to-day work in the classroom helps teachers tackle everyday problems related to children's learning and behaviour. The chapters on Interactions in Classrooms and Personal and Social Education are very useful.

Kerry, T. and Tollitt, J. (1989) *Teaching Infants*. Oxford: Blackwell. A practical exploration of both the essential skills and the key issues involved in teaching infants. There is much of value for the teacher of juniors also, especially the unit on understanding social relationship issues.

Mills, R.W. (1988) *Observing Children in the Primary Classroom*, (2nd edn) London: Unwin Hyman. A selection of case studies examining the impact of classroom situations on pupils aged 5-10 years. Gives a useful overview of good talk.

Mosely, J. (1993) *Turn Your School Round: a Circle-time Approach to the Development of Self-esteem*. Wisbech: Learning Development Aids. A highly practical book which contains many suggestions for circle-time sessions supported by photocopiable handouts. Important links are established with behaviour management.

Pollard, A. (1997) *Reflective Teaching in the Primary School*. London: Cassell. A comprehensive book dealing with all significant aspects of primary school teaching. It is full of practical ideas and support for reflection on classroom experiences. There is much of interest on the theme of classroom climate.

Pring, R. (1984) *Personal and Social Education in the Curriculum*. London: Hodder & Stoughton. This book maps out personal, social and moral education and identifies practical implications for the curriculum. It is of relevance still, incorporating philosophical questions with a systematic consideration of personal, social and moral education.

Robertson, J. (1989) *Effective Classroom Control*. London: Hodder & Stoughton. Plenty of practical advice on how to keep order in the classroom. The concepts of authority and power are identified and a co-operative relationship between the teacher and pupils is promoted.

Robson, S. and Smedley, S. (eds) (1996) *Education in Early Childhood*. London: David Fulton. A consideration of a wide range of early childhood issues that have relevance across the entire primary phase. Chapters of particular interest are those covering personality, professionalism and politics; roles and relationships; and meaningful interaction.

Rodd, J. (1996) *Understanding Young Children's Behaviour*. London: Allen and Unwin. A focus on teaching children to behave in socially acceptable ways whilst fostering self-esteem also.

Rowland, V. and Birkett, K. (1992) *Personal Effectiveness for Teachers*. Hemel Hempstead: Simon and Schuster Education. A book in which emphasis is placed on personal relationships and the interpersonal skills necessary for a successful career in teaching.

Steiner, M. (ed) (1996) *Developing the Global Teacher*. Stoke-on-Trent: Trentham Books. 'You can only teach about justice and democracy by just and democratic means.' This book helps answer questions related to dealing with prejudice and value diversity, self esteem and a commitment to justice and sustainable development. See Chapters 3 and 10 on teaching for justice and philosophical enquiry.

Wragg, E.C. & Brown, G. (1993) *Questioning*. London: Routledge. A book which is part of the Leverhulme Primary Project. Of particular interest is how teachers may best respond to questions.

Useful websites

Centre for Citizenship Studies in Education	www.le.ac.uk.education/centres/citizenship
Citizenship Foundation	www.citfou.org.uk
Emotional Literacy	www.anitdote.org.uk
General PSHE Materials (Lucky Duck Publishing)	www.luckyduck.co.uk
Healthy School Standard	www.wiredforhealth.gov.uk
Institute for Citizenship	www.citizen.org.uk

8 CLASSROOM INTERACTION AND MANAGEMENT

ROBIN BUNDY

By the end of the chapter you should have:

- understood that classrooms are complex environments;
- recognised that teachers and pupils interpret each other's words and actions with potential for misunderstanding;
- understood the principles involved in:

    explicitly defining the rules you wish to establish;
    establishing classroom routines;
    presenting yourself effectively;
    developing a positive reputation;
    gaining attention;
    being vigilant;
    managing resources, children and ideas;
    dealing with deviance.

This chapter addresses the following Professional Standards for QTS:

 1.3, 2.7, 3.3.1, 3.3.7, 3.3.8, 3.3.9

(The Standards are reproduced in full at the back of this book.)

Introduction

Interaction in classrooms

The concept of interaction is useful in getting to grips with what happens in classrooms where potentially life is chaotic and unpredictable. Seeing life in classrooms in terms of interaction suggests that there are several participants, usually a teacher and a number of pupils, all of whom have their own intentions, some of which fit together and some of which conflict. In developing and carrying out their intentions, the teacher and children make use of the meanings they have built up and although each person's meanings will have much in common with those of others, each will be idiosyncratic. The thoughts and actions that are generated are often not the same as those intended at the beginning. In order to establish and maintain discipline you, as a teacher, need somehow to manage the meanings and intentions that are brought to the classroom: you need to influence the thoughts and actions of your pupils so that there is harmony. The roles taken by you and the pupils in the classroom are not set and mechanistic, but have to be extemporised. The experience is less like playing an instrument in a symphony orchestra where the music is written and each instrumentalist follows his prescribed part, and more like playing jazz where all have an idea of the basic tune but each player has to listen to what is being played by others and construct his part to fit in. Thus classroom harmony is never attained once and for all; you must continually work at it. The experience can be like trying to run up a descending escalator: soon after you stop running, you end up at the bottom again. So with establishing and maintaining discipline, you can never let up or become complacent.

The material that follows presents a framework of concepts and principles which will help you to make sense of establishing and maintaining discipline and to take decisions as you interact.

Practical task

Take opportunities to observe classrooms in action. Try to discern patterns of interaction that are functional, e.g. routines such as children raising their hands to signal that they wish to contribute to a class or group discussion. Try also to discern patterns which are dysfunctional, e.g. children talking when the teacher is explaining something to the class. At times when you will not disrupt the flow of the interaction, ask participants to explain why they interacted as they did, and remember to question the class teacher as well.

Defining the situation

If you, the teacher, are going to take the leading role in the interaction in the classroom, there are two ways in which you will need to be able to *define the situation*. Firstly you need to be able to make sense of what is going on; you must be able to see clearly what is happening in the classroom, what the children are doing as well as what you are doing, and the effects of the interplay of all these actions. To do this you need to separate yourself from what is going on and take a cool calm look at it. See if you can spot any patterns in the actions, consider which patterns are functional and which are dysfunctional, look at the way one thing seems to lead to another and get a clear idea of the roles played by individual children. Secondly you need to be able to influence the central understandings being taken into account by the children in constructing their actions and ideas. You should be setting out to influence the definition of the situation that each child is using, and, of course, that is not easy. Nevertheless there are a number of aspects of defining the situation in this way which you can profitably consider.

Trying to be explicit

We can never be totally explicit about what we mean. There is always a qualitative change between what we mean and the words we choose to express it. However, we can make a conscious effort to express ourselves as clearly and explicitly as possible. This is often quite difficult though, because we act most of the time in a taken-for-granted way without thinking about what we are doing or what we expect. In such situations we often only become aware of the taken-for-granted reality when it is in some way or other jarred. This can be dangerous if you enter a classroom for the first time, take it for granted that the children know how you want them to behave, and give no thought yourself to how this actually is. You will find then that your *definition of the situation* only begins to come into your awareness as it is violated by the children's actions. Such actions will then appear deviant to you and you are likely to respond negatively to them, with the strong possibility that the children will feel resentful because you failed to point out in the first place what you were expecting.

Before you take your first lesson then, get a clear picture in your mind of the rules that you want to implement in your classroom. Take every opportunity you can to observe other teachers and work out the rules that are in play in their classrooms. Sometimes these rules will be explicit and may be on display in the classroom. More often they will be implicit and will only be evident in the behaviour patterns of the children, or on occasions when the rules are violated. Do not be afraid to ask teachers what their rules are and why they use them.

Reflect also on your own school days and work out the rules that were in play then. Consider what your views were on the rules when you were a pupil and whether those views would be useful in deciding the rules you should adopt for yourself. Daydream your way through some lessons which you have experienced as a child and which you would like to give now. Begin to develop your own set of rules so that in future you have a clear idea of what you expect and can make this explicit to the children in your care.

Of course when you are taking over another teacher's class on a school placement, it might not always be possible to implement your own set of rules if they conflict with those already in play. Nevertheless, even in such circumstances, having your own set of rules to bear in mind and compare with those in play will help you to get a clear idea of the amalgamated definition of the situation you will be seeking to set up.

Use of classroom routines

When you first take over a class, it can seem like an uphill struggle. You need to make the rules that apply to each event throughout the day explicit; this means that you not only have to define the situation at the beginning of each lesson, but also for each phase of the lesson and each change of activity within each phase. Eventually, though, you and the children will begin to be aware of repetitions of patterns which will soon turn into routines. When this happens the rules will begin to be taken for granted and will not need to be made explicit every time. Examples of such routines might be ways of entering and leaving classrooms, procedures for the distribution of materials, putting up hands to make a contribution to group or class discussion, and clearing away materials at the end of a lesson. The establishment of such routines is vital for the development of an ordered and peaceful classroom climate. They not only begin to make life predictable and therefore less stressful, but they also provide you with opportunities to step back and look at what is going on, as opposed to being centre stage in the limelight.

Practical task

Build up an explicit definition of or your ideal classroom situation in terms of the rules and routines you will seek to establish. Your previous consideration of functional and dysfunctional patterns of interaction will help here.

Presentation of self

Whether or not children take notice of you when you try to be explicit or establish classroom routines depends very much on how they see you. The more you are able to influence the meanings they attach to you, the more chance you have of getting them to take notice of you. You have, then, to pay careful attention to the way you present yourself to them; you need to make the right impression. There are two means at your disposal in order to achieve this. The first relates to the impressions over which you have a considerable degree of control, such as what you say to the children or the way that you dress. Much of what you have already covered in 'Trying to be explicit' relates to this. The second relates to the impressions over which you have much less control, often those that are related to the emotions, such as blushing or stammering. The first kind of impressions tend to be the more explicit, giving a relatively clear message, and the second tend to be the more implicit, and give veracity to the message. Thus what you say is important, but it is not just what you say, it is also the way that you say it.

It is also important that your *presentation of self* is consistent. When you first meet the children, they will be picking up messages about you by the impressions that you give them. This will establish expectations on their part about the sort of person you are and what you expect. If at a later date, you reveal yourself to be different, for instance by not being as tolerant as you first appeared to be, then the children may feel cheated, and they could quite reasonably get resentful. Thus it is particularly important to be clear about what you expect and present yourself in a manner which is consistent with that right from the start.

Practical task

Take opportunities to practise your presentation of self. Such opportunities may occur in professional situations, e.g. on a school placement. However, they may also occur in more personal situations, e.g. reading a story to a younger member of your family or even when you are alone in the bathroom!

Developing a reputation

If you are consistent and successful in your presentation of self, the children eventually take it for granted that you are the sort of person you appear to be. There is then an onus on you to continue to present yourself in that way, but the demands of doing so become less. First, you begin to take your presentation of self for granted and carry it out automatically without having to think about it. However, secondly, and possibly more importantly, you find that you have developed a reputation. That reputation then precedes you when you meet fresh classes of children in the school. You find that the children you have taught act on your behalf, marketing your image to the rest of the school. The result is that you never have to work as hard again to establish yourself in the way that you have chosen. As a trainee teacher, this might not provide you with very much comfort because you are never likely to be in a school long enough to get the chance to work with more than one class. However, you can see how once you have a permanent post, even though responsibilities might increase, this at least is one aspect of the role that gets easier.

Gaining attention

Perhaps the fundamental strategy in the establishment of discipline is that of gaining attention. If you cannot do that, you have little chance of making your definition of the situation prevail. Yet paradoxically, everything that has been written above about the definition of the situation contributes to the effectiveness of any strategy that you use for gaining attention. Decide what you see to be involved in the act of paying attention: it is likely to be something like sitting quietly, not moving and looking at you. Construct a speech which encapsulate these requirements: it might be something like, 'Stop! I want everybody to be quiet, sit still and look at me.' Then practise saying it a few times in a clear voice at a volume that is loud enough to be heard, and accompany it with dramatic intonation, gestures and body language so that when you are teaching and want attention, it just comes automatically. However, do not overdo the drama to the extent that it generates unwanted emotions, such as fear or over-excitement; the trick is to keep a balance, and that probably only comes with experience.

Practical task

Become aware of strategies that you might use to gain attention and practise them. Once again you may carry this out on school placements, but you can also do it in interactions with friends in those few off-duty moments at the pub!

Vigilance

In our society it is considered very rude not to look at a person when you are talking to him, or he is talking to you. In life in classrooms, such conventions are often ignored. Your first concern as a teacher is to keep an eye on what is going on around you all the time. As a result, even when you may be talking to an individual child, you find yourself moving your gaze from side to side rather like some sort of radar scanner as you keep the whole class in view. This not only allows you to monitor the actions of the children, but often also enables you to make necessary contact with children without even moving your position. Some children will need your reassurance and you can give that by meeting their gaze. Other children will be losing concentration on their work and a nod and wink can get them back on the job. Similarly, deviant behaviour may be addressed in the same way. The effectiveness of eye contact in dealing with deviance and lack of concentration, of course, depends on your having defined the situation in the first place. Then the children know what they should be doing and hence the eye contact becomes a cue to remind them to do what is expected.

Management

The ideas and principles dealt with under 'Defining the situation' are mainly concerned with looking at how you might with deal with discipline during teaching interactions. This is when you have to think on your feet, dealing with an unpredictable, potentially chaotic situation in as ordered a way as possible. The nature of interaction is such that you cannot expect events always to go as planned. However, that does not mean it is not useful to make plans. Your plans constitute your intentions and they need to be clear in your mind if you are going to have the determination necessary to bring them about in the face of what could be conflicting intentions on the part of the children. In making your plans, you are essentially thinking about the future in terms of how you will be managing a number of elements. We shall now look at what the main elements might be and some considerations you might make in managing them.

Management of resources

Problems of discipline often manifest themselves in those lessons which involve the use of complicated, abundant or unusual resources, such as is often the case in science, art, and technology lessons. Decisions must be taken about how these resources are to be distributed and cleared away. It is usually more efficient if you involve the children in these tasks, but as with planning the lesson itself, you need to define the situation clearly; you must define each task, define which children are to carry out each one, and define what the remainder are to do while the tasks are being carried out. Alternatively you may allow children access to the resources on an individual basis as they need them. If this is the case, you must make sure that the children and any support staff working in your classroom understand the rules and routines that regulate such access.

Practical task

Think rigorously about activities that you are going to implement in the classroom well in advance, and carry them out yourself before giving them to the children. Then make careful notes to include in your lesson plans so that you can define clearly what the children will need to do.

Management of groups, time and space

You will need to take decisions about when the children will be working as a whole class, in groups of various sizes and as individuals. You will have to define carefully how the groups will be composed, considering whether you will decide on this yourself or, if not, how the children will decide for themselves. You will also have to decide where the children will work. When the children are working as a class or as individuals, it is often taken for granted that they will work in their normal allotted places. Group work often involves a disruption of this normality, and therefore its location needs to be carefully considered and made very clear to the children.

See Chapter 6 on p. 74 for more information on managing the classroom.

Management of ideas

If the management of everything else seems complicated, it is nothing compared with the management of ideas. You are concerned now with the management of the children's experience and to do this in an educational manner you must initiate them into the subjects on the curriculum. To do this you must understand the subjects yourself. It is not enough for you to be able to deliver some content to the children. You must teach them how to construct for themselves the different forms of knowledge appropriate to each subject. You must therefore consider the concepts that each subject uses to make sense of the world, the skills or procedures it uses to build up knowledge about the world, the attitudes that generate a commitment to the subject, the criteria that are used to evaluate the knowledge that is produced and the different forms in which the knowledge is expressed. In order to get to grips with these elements for a particular lesson, it is often useful for you to carry out the activity you have chosen. This often not only enables you to present the children with an example of what they are going to produce themselves, but it gives you a clear conception of what they are going to have to do and think. You are then in a position to convey to the children the nature of the task and also to work out what needs to be assessed in the lesson and how.

Thus you have begun to think yourself into a future interaction in which you have serious intentions about what the children will do, the resources with which they will do it, when they will do it, where they will do it, the others with whom they will do it and how you will assess it.

Dealing with deviance

However carefully you try to implement the advice we have already considered, it is inevitable that you will find that on occasions children will resist the definition of the situation you are seeking to establish and maintain. When it does occur you have two problems. The first is bringing the child concerned back into line. The second is maintaining your definition of the situation among the other children once it is clear that it can be resisted. If you can do the former straight away, the latter is also safely dealt with. If you cannot, then it is rather like finding a leaking hole in a dyke. The longer you leave it before you plug it, the greater the danger that the whole dyke will burst. A fairly effective routine is to attempt to remind the miscreant of your definition of the situation. You might do this implicitly by catching the gaze of the miscreant or calling out his name. In doing this you are assuming that he knows what he should be doing and knows that he is not doing it currently but, having been implicitly reminded of all this, will now resume what he should be doing. If this does not work, then you need to state explicitly what he should be doing and maybe make it clear what he is doing that is wrong. Ask him if he understands and, if so, ask him to get on with his work. If that fails, and you have the time available, spend time with him and work alongside him for a while, praising him for any achievements he makes. Alternatively, if he is not disturbing the other children, tell him that you wish to see him at the next playtime. Even if it appears now that he is resisting your definition of the situation, you have indicated to him and the rest of the class that he is not getting away with it.

It is especially important to deal with deviance after the event, as opposed to in the event, if the child has become emotional in any way and does not appear to be open to reason at that time. When the child does come to see you at playtime, do not attempt to punish him. Your reason for seeing him is for both of you to develop a better understanding of his deviance and try to work out a way to avoid it in the future. First ask him why he behaved in the way that he did and do not let him avoid the question. Consider then what each of you can do to avoid it happening again. Remember this is all part of an interaction situation in which people are coming with different intentions, and do not dismiss the possibility that his resistance to your intentions may be in some way or other reasonable. Emphasise, however, the detrimental effect this deviance is having on his success and draw attention to what you see to be his strengths so that he feels you are concerned with his well-being. Finally, work out an agreement regarding how he is going to behave in the future and include a target which involves him cashing in on whatever you and he feel to be one of his strengths. The idea is to condemn the deviant behaviour, generate repentance for it and then look to a bright new future together.

Quality of relationships

Ultimately your success in maintaining discipline is going to depend on the quality of the relationships you establish with the children. If you generate a climate of fear in your classroom, it might work while you are standing over the children in terms of keeping them subdued, but you will never get the best out of them and whenever you turn your back they are likely to turn to their own devices. It is important that you show the children that, in attempting to establish your definition of the situation, you have their interests at heart. You need to show them that you understand them as individuals and respect them. When they co-operate with you it is vital that what they do leads to achievements on their part that can be seen by them and by others who are significant to them. They will then have an investment in your definition of the situation, because the interactions on the basis of it will be generating self-esteem on their part and good opinions of them by others, most notably you. They will not want to lose any of that.

Further reading

Blumer, H. (1969) *Symbolic Interactionism*. Englewood Cliffs: Prentice Hall. Blumer develops a coherent readily graspable model of serial interaction in the form of 'symbolic interactionism'. The three fundamental premises of the theory are presented and explained in the first chapter (c.f. The nature of interaction in classrooms).

Canter, L. (1989) 'Assertive discipline — more than names on the board and marbles in a jar', in *Phi Delta Kappa*. 71 (1) pp. 57–61. Canter presents thought-provoking advice on the development of discipline which, despite having a distinct behaviourist flavour, is similar to some of the advice in this chapter.

Goffman, E. (1968) 'Presentation of self to others' in Manis, J. and Meltzer, B. (eds) *Symbolic Interaction*. Boston: Allyn & Bacon. Goffman presents a dramaturgical model of social interaction, suggesting that our actions are like dramatic performances directed to presenting meanings about ourselves to an audience of significant others (c.f. Presentation of self).

King, R (1978) *All Things Bright and Beautiful*. Chichester: John Wiley. In Chapter 2 King applies the concept of 'definition of the situation' to the exploration of the meanings that an infant teacher has used to make sense of, and direct, the interaction in her classroom. In Chapter 3 he looks at the way in which some infant teachers implemented their definition of the situation to establish social control in the classroom (c.f. Defining the situation).

Rogers, C. (1983) *Freedom to Learn for the 80s*. Columbus, Ohio: Merrill. In the chapter entitled 'The interpersonal relationships in the facilitation of learning' Rogers presents an inspiring prescription of the qualities that a teacher should seek to establish in the relationships that are developed with pupils (c.f. The quality of relationships).

Stenhouse, L (1975) *An Introduction to Curriculum Research and Development*. London: Heinemann. In Chapter 7 Stenhouse develops a model of curriculum design directed towards the initiation of pupils into the structure of subjects (c.f. Management of ideas).

By the end of the chapter you should:

- *know the importance of management of emotions;*
- *understand the difference between discipline and control;*
- *recognise the difference between day-to-day behaviour maintenance and serious behavioural incidents;*
- *know how to react to challenging behaviour;*
- *understand the implications of exclusion.*

This chapter addresses the following Professional Standards for QTS:

 2.7, 3.3.9

(The Standards are reproduced in full at the back of this book.)

The previous two chapters gave guidance on how to create positive classroom climate and encourage positive interactions between pupils. Creating the right tone in the classroom is the most effective way of keeping poor behaviour to a minimum. The purpose of this chapter is to provide you with strategies for dealing with difficult behaviour. Even the most well-regulated classroom will experience some disruption at some times. Like most trainees you are probably more concerned about the maintenance of discipline in your classroom than almost any other aspect of teaching. You need to remember that most classrooms and schools are well-ordered, well-managed, communities of people who work well together. Serious disruptions are, on the whole, rare. It is true that in some schools, in some areas, challenging behaviour is more of a problem and there are reasons for this. In general, children will behave how they have been taught to behave and where poor behaviour is tolerated or ignored, children will continue to behave in that way. So it is important from the outset that you establish the sort of behaviour you expect and that the class know and understand that you are in charge, but that you are neither a dictator nor a tyrant. The relationship you have with each child in the class is, possibly, the most powerful tool at your fingertips. If you respect children and hold them in high regard, they will do the same to you. At least that's the theory, I hear you say! Truly, it does work, but there are children for whom life is very difficult, life may have treated them badly and, as a result, they behave badly. This does not mean that you have to tolerate poor behaviour in your classroom. Simply knowing why a child behaves differently from other children helps you to determine the best strategy for dealing with the child's difficulties. Many children come from quite difficult home backgrounds, even in well-heeled homes there can be emotional neglect. Some children are abused or leave home each morning without having had any breakfast, some children are the victims of constant bullying, either at home or in the school playground. Part of your job is to work out strategies for reducing poor behaviour and that may mean understanding why a child is behaving in a particular way. From the start set high standards and expect them to be met. Recognise that, for some children, meeting these high standards will be more difficult, but expect them anyway.

Be aware of emotions! Much has been said lately about emotional intelligence. This term is used to describe the levels of sensitivity and understanding of other people and situations. Different people have different degrees of emotional awareness. Goleman (1996) suggests that proper management of emotions can influence success more significantly than academic achievement. Whether this is true or not, our emotions play a significant role when dealing with difficult or disruptive situations. The more we are able to understand ourselves, the more we will be able to understand the effect on others and theirs on us. Children know when the teacher arrives in the morning in a 'bad mood' or in a 'good mood'. Mood swings are not helpful when trying to manage groups of children. Therefore, know your emotional state when you arrive at school in the morning and ensure that if you are upset, this is not communicated to the children; if you are angry this is not communicated to the children; or if you are disappointed that this is not communicated to the children. You need also to be aware what makes you angry and that you do not, inadvertently, overreact if a child irritates you. Children want a teacher who is largely calm and self-controlled. Similarly, you want children who are calm and self-controlled. If you can manage your own emotions and recognise feelings and sensitivities which are sometimes inappropriate, then you are in a better position to help children learn about and manage their own emotions.

Practical task

Reflect on the last time you were in a classroom and write down three things which irritated you about pupil behaviour. Ask yourself if your feelings affect your performance in the classroom.

Children's emotions can be volatile and you need to be sensitive to children and how they manage their own emotions. Temperament and personality do play a large part in how children behave; you need to recognise this. Some children do not know how to deal with anger and they may become violent. Encourage talk about emotions and feelings. Use circle time to allow you and your children to be open about feelings and discuss ways of dealing with anger, disappointment, hostility and discrimination.

Discipline and control

'Discipline and control' are frequently used as though they meant the same thing. (Rogers 1998). They are not the same. Discipline is about good order, complicity about agreed behaviour. A disciplined classroom is one which is well-managed and where agreed modes of conduct predominate. Classroom control, on the other hand, implies power and containment. It places the teacher in a position of authority over the children. The teacher, of course, is in a position of power and control to some extent but it is how this is employed which makes the difference to teacher/pupil relationships. The ideal classroom is one where the teacher is ensured of good behaviour, good inter-personal relationships and a good work ethic. This ideal classroom relies on the children subscribing and agreeing with the teacher. The teacher does not have to tell the children what to do because they know what to do and how to do it. The explicit and implicit rules have been agreed. An authoritarian classroom on the other hand, relies on the teacher being 'in control' and telling the children frequently what they must and must not do. In an environment where children feel 'controlled', they are more likely to engage in disruption if that control is weakened for any reason – for example, if the teacher leaves the classroom. Could you rely on the behaviour of the children if you were distracted? Think back to your own strategy in the classroom, do you believe that you are more preoccupied with discipline or preoccupied with control? At first you need to use a combination of both but reflect on your personal style and consider how you manage behaviour.

Here are some suggestions for managing day-to-day maintenance of good behaviour:

- **Know the school behaviour policy and what it states and ensure that the children also know the school behaviour policy.**
- **Have agreed rules of behaviour displayed somewhere in the classroom. These should not be a series of 'don'ts' but a series of acceptable behaviours, for example, 'In Class 4 we all agree: (i) To be careful with other people's belongings (ii) To treat each other with respect (iii) To help each other to learn (iv) To listen to each other's ideas (v) To keep our classroom tidy and safe'.**
- **Always head off trouble by being punctual and organised.**
- **Avoid scrambles at the start of the day or at the start of the lesson, make sure what you need is to hand and cut down the excuses for chaos.**
- **Rehearse the classroom agreement at different times during the day, so that children know it is to be taken seriously.**
- **Practise strategic ignoring, don't react to noisy pupils on every occasion or reinforce attention seeking.**
- **Praise pupils at every opportunity.**
- **Deal with pupils calmly and quietly. Indicating your firm disapproval is sometimes quite appropriate, but losing your temper is not. Never threaten what you cannot, or should not, do.**
- **Avoid unnecessarily prolonged, public confrontations. If this does happen give pupils the space and opportunity to back down and never, ever, humiliate a pupil in front of others.**
- **Don't give pupils the opportunity to 'play to the gallery'. If a pupil's behaviour is getting out of hand, remove him or her from the situation. A 'slanging match' between you and a pupil does nothing for your image.**
- **Use your voice wisely. Remember the effectiveness of shouting is inversely proportional to its frequency. Noisy teachers help create noisy classes!**
- **Insist on basic politeness, but don't be pompous. You are entitled to be treated as a human being.**
- **Treat pupils fairly and with consistency.**
- **Ensure the classroom is attractive and welcoming and always tidy and organised.**
- **Ensure the classroom takes account of all pupils from different cultures and backgrounds and uphold a strategy for equal opportunities.**
- **Ensure that each day has pace and structure and that children are not left hanging around or doing one activity for too long.**

Practical task

Write a behaviour agreement which you would like to use in your own class.
Make it appropriate to the age-range you are likely to teach.

Challenging behaviour

Every teacher at some point in their career will deal with unexpected and outrageous behaviour and you will not be any different. The important thing to remember is that how you deal with it is what matters, not that it happened. Let us assume that two children have a disagreement over a book which leads to a serious confrontation where one child strikes another. What do you do?

1. First, stay calm and approach the scene purposefully without giving rise to alarm in the classroom.
2. Give clear instructions to the aggressor to stop and to move away from the other pupil.
3. Avoid confrontation and endeavour to defuse the situation, keep your voice calm and steady and ask all other pupils who have been distracted to return to their work.
4. Separate the pupil from the rest of the class in order for the pupil to regain control and calm down.
5. If the matter gets seriously out of control, send another pupil for help, especially if physical restraint is necessary.

Incidents such as this need to be followed up with the pupils concerned. All those involved need to talk about how it happened and the events leading up to the incident. It is important that you are seen to listen and to be fair. It is important also that you re-establish your relationship with all the pupils involved and that if a punishment is required, it is the behaviour that is being punished, not the individual child. After any incident it is important that you quickly bring the classroom back to some normality. Be calm but firm and ensure that all pupils return to their activities. It is useful to give reminders of the agreed rules around the classroom, especially those about how we treat each other.

Rewards and punishment

In order to manage pupil behaviour, some schools employ various systems of rewards and punishments and these can be effective. There is debate about the appropriateness of rewarding good behaviour with stickers or small treats since it could be assumed that good behaviour is the norm. Nevertheless, poor behaviour has to be seen to be punished and has to be recognised as unacceptable. It is quite difficult, however, to use punishment effectively and can sometimes be counter-productive. It can generate hostility and resentment. Verbal reprimands can work successfully with some children, but for those for whom petty misbehaviours are part of their daily life, it is difficult to see sometimes if behaviour is improving, therefore conventional punishment may not be the answer. The aim, therefore, must be to minimise the opportunities for punishment to be an outcome. If, however, some punishment needs to be applied, and if it is threatened, you must apply it. The following might be used:

- *Extra work*: **This can have the unsatisfactory effect of reducing the status of the work, but it does deprive the miscreant of time.**
- *Detention*: **Content of detention may vary, for example, sitting in silence outside the headteacher's office or a task may be given during a playtime. It can be time-consuming if teachers have to supervise detention.**
- *Informing parents*: **A letter to parents informing them of serious incidents at school can have a powerful effect on altering the behaviour of pupils.**
- *Conduct marks*: **Some schools support the distribution of bad conduct marks for poor behaviour which are made public around the school at the end of each week and if a certain number is achieved, this may lead to detention.**
- *Loss of privileges*: **A pupil may be deprived of attending a school trip or a school function following poor behaviour.**
- *Exclusion from school*: **Expulsion is the most serious sanction and follows only the most serious of offences. However, schools are being discouraged from using exclusion as a punishment since this rarely helps the child and certainly doesn't help society.**

Punishments do not always work and success may depend on the nature of the child and the nature of how the punishment was applied. Praise and approval from the teacher is much better and likely to have an effect and helps promote a more positive classroom environment.

Exclusion or inclusion?

The point at which behaviour becomes so unacceptable that the headteacher and governors decide to exclude a pupil is more of an issue in seconday rather than primary schools.

The power of the teacher

Recent research by Morgan and Morris (1999) reveals how teachers under-estimate the impact they have on children's behaviour and learning. The children in the study were very clear that they behaved differently for different teachers and that some teachers commanded, and received, more respect than others. Most trainee teachers can reflect back to their own school-days and recall the classes in which they were more likely to misbehave. Take a few minutes to look back at your own school days and to a teacher whom you thought was ineffective in maintaining discipline. What was it about that teacher that made pupils, perhaps even you, want to 'play-up'? Was it timidity? Was it being poorly organised? Was it being badly prepared? Was it just lack of confidence? It is true that maintaining classroom discipline comes easier to some trainee teachers than to others, but everyone can learn strategies and techniques which work. Knowing how to use one's own style and personality to best effect in creating a positive classroom climate takes time. If natural authority does not come easy to you it will also take some self-discipline and some practice to work on it. For example, respect cannot be learned if the children are not treated with respect. Trainee teachers need to ask 'How do I come across to this class of children?' 'Do the class regard me as valuing their ideas and each one as an individual?' 'Am I always scrupulously fair, even to those children whom I do not like?' (and there will be some of those!).

When faced with a difficult class, the tendency for trainees and even experienced teachers is to blame the children and attribute the bad behaviour to all sorts of factors. While it is true certain conditions create opportunities for poor behaviour, a windy day for example, or the visit of the school nurse, different conditions simply mean that different behaviour strategies have to be employed. Recognising the extent of the power teachers have over children is part of that strategy. Ginott (1972, cited by Rogers 1998, p. 7)) observed that 'as a teacher I possess tremendous power to make a child's life miserable or joyous. I can be a tool of torture or an instrument of inspiration. I can humiliate, humour, hurt or heal.' If this is the case, there should never be an opportunity for a class to become 'out of control'. We argued earlier in favour of achieving a disciplined classroom rather than a controlled one. However, if circumstances mean that the class does need to be controlled, then remember that you have the power and the authority to do something about it. So what do you do if chaos breaks out and the children go berserk?

First, some don'ts:
- *Don't* start screaming at the top of your voice.
- *Don't* start chasing around after one or two culprits.
- *Don't* try and drag anybody to the front of the class (remember it is illegal to hit anyone).
- *Don't* tear your hair out.
- *Don't* run out of the room.

What to do
Rehearse in your mind a scenario so that should this ever happen to you, you have thought some strategies out:

- Keep calm and keep your dignity.
- Position yourself in the centre of the room and project your personality dramatically.
- Speak firmly and clearly and vary the volume and emphasis in your voice. Use pauses; make dominant gestures, such as hands on hips, or arms folded, or point; use an exaggerated stare at two or three people; walk slowly around the room; stop, wait, stare; repeat firmly, clearly, earlier instructions for everyone to stop what they are doing and sit still.
- Write the names of two or three ringleaders on the board or in a notebook.

This strategy may take two or three minutes but should work. Remember, you have to use the power of your personality and your charisma. However, if things are not calming down and may even be getting worse, send a child for help to the headteacher or deputy.

Such a scenario represents the worst nightmare for all trainees; fortunately it rarely happens, because you learn how to manage a large class of children over time and, after a while, managing 35 children becomes second nature – like driving a car, you forget how you are managing to do it. Experienced teachers know how to ensure that a riot does not break out. Bassey (1989) argues that children will not become disruptive if they are busy. He suggests there are two aspects to this:

(i) The children should know for every minute of the time that they are in the class-room *what* it is you want them to do, *where* and *when* you want them to do it and *what* it is they are to do *next*.
(ii) The children should *want* to do it.

(Bassey 1989 p. 55 emphasis original)

He repeats the traditional advice: 'The Devil makes works for idle hands, but keep 'em busy and you'll have no bother'. This is sound advice but often hard for an inexperienced trainee when a piece of work has been set which is expected to take 40 minutes and the children have done it in four!

This chapter has attempted to provide some guidance and help on maintaining an orderly and well-disciplined classroom. There will be days when maintaining discipline feels like a battle, but these will be few. As you grow in experience, your competence in maintaining a purposeful, working classroom will be such that you won't know you're doing it!

Further reading

Barnard, S. (1998) *Developing Children's Behaviour in the Classroom. A Practical Guide for Teachers and Students*. London: Falmer Press. This book develops some interesting and different systematic approaches to managing behaviour. In particular it focuses on children with special educational needs and gives guidance on how to negotiate with some difficult children.

Commissions for Racial Equality (2000) *Learning for All: Standards for Racial Equality in Schools*. London: CRE. This publication gives useful general advice and guidance on the legal position on acceptable and unacceptable behaviour.

Hopkins, D., West, M., Ainscow M., Beresford, J. and Fielding, M. (1997) *Creating the Conditions for Classroom Improvement*. London: David Fulton. This book has lots of ideas for INSET on behaviour and discipline. It develops ideas for improving relationships in the classroom and for improving the climate of classrooms.

Rogers, B. (1998) *You Know the Fair Rule*. London: Pitman Publishing. This book contains lots of good advice and strategies for making management easier and also good fun. This should be recommended reading for all trainee teachers.

By the end of the chapter you should have:

- *reflected on and refined your understanding of the notions of pupils' spiritual, moral, social and cultural (SMSC) development;*
- *developed ideas for promoting SMSC issues through the teaching of the subjects of the curriculum;*
- *considered how the climate of values and relationships in the classroom helps to shape pupils' attitudes and behaviour ;*
- *reviewed your understanding of the purposes of education with particular reference to children's personal development.*

This chapter addresses the following Professional Standards for QTS:

 2.2, 2.4, 3.3.1, 3.3.6

(The Standards are reproduced in full at the back of this book.)

The purpose of this chapter is to help you to explore how children's education can contribute to their development as persons. The first part introduces SMSC development as an educational aim, with a brief consideration of each of the four elements.

Next, some ideas will be suggested for raising SMSC issues through the teaching of the subjects of the curriculum.

Thirdly, the teacher's role in creating and maintaining a classroom environment conducive to SMSC growth will be tackled, and finally some questions will be posed to help you think through your own view of the purposes of education.

What is SMSC and why is it a teacher's responsibility?

The Education Act of 1944 required local education authorities to promote 'the spiritual, moral, mental and physical development of the community' and that requirement has never gone away. The 1988 Education Reform Act added 'cultural' to the list of adjectives while 'social' was added in the 1992 Education Act.

You will not be surprised as a trainee teacher to be asked to foster children's mental and physical development, since the idea of a 'healthy mind in a healthy body' is a very ancient aim of education. But you may be taken aback by an expectation that you have some responsibility for children's spiritual and moral development and more recently for their social and cultural values too.

The tradition of education in England and Wales has always emphasised the importance of the development of the whole person. Some visiting trainee teachers from other European countries recently noted the following aspects of English primary schools as being significantly different from their own experience: an emphasis on good manners and a high standard of behaviour; school uniform; school assemblies, collective worship and RE; clubs and other extra-curricular activities; and what they called 'the spirit of the school'. How have these differences come about?

Part of the answer is the close relationship between the state and Christian churches in providing education. In England and Wales most church schools are also state schools, whereas in other countries religious schools are independent of the state. The inter-twining of religion and politics has ensured that education in England and Wales has a strong values base. The phrase 'spiritual, moral, mental and physical' springs from a biblical verse about 'heart, soul, mind and strength', and its place in the Education Acts emphasises that people's beliefs, feelings, opinions and values cannot be divorced from their minds and bodies (Ewens 1998 p 107f).

This concern for the education of the whole person permeates the education system, particularly in the primary school sector. Whereas secondary teachers, when asked, may say that they teach mathematics or German or whatever subject, primary teachers tend to look smug and say that they teach children! This is partly a way of saying that most of them teach all the subjects, but it does also reflect a view that education is about personal formation as well as learning subjects.

The foursome of SMSC provides a useful means of categorising the broader purposes of education, and you need to think through their distinctive characteristics and con-tributions. However, you also need to keep in mind the 'mental and physical development' aim set out in the Education Acts, so that you keep asking the question, 'How can I promote SMSC through my teaching of the curriculum?'

What do you mean by SMSC?

This section looks briefly at each of the four elements, spiritual, moral, social and cultural and indicates how they can contribute to children's education.

Spiritual

It is important to distinguish 'spiritual' from 'religious'. While it is true that some people associate their spirituality with a religious faith and outlook, others find great signifi-cance in their spiritual experiences without holding formal religious beliefs.

Schools receive the following guidance about what inspectors will look for when judging schools' provision for children's spiritual development:

Judgements about the opportunities for spiritual development will be based on the extent to which the school provides its pupils with knowledge and insight into values and beliefs and enables them to reflect on their experiences in a way which develops their spiritual experience and self-knowledge.

(Ofsted 1996)

The key ideas here are the notions of:

- **insight (as well as knowledge);**
- **values and beliefs;**
- **reflection on experience;**
- **self-knowledge.**

Pursuing these as desirable ingredients of education is incompatible with reducing the curriculum solely to the transmission of factual information. Facts are important; however, they do not exist in a vacuum but in a value-laden context. Consider a study of Ancient Egypt in the National Curriculum for history (DfEE/QCA 1999). The decision to include Egypt in the history curriculum is driven by value judgements. Why Egypt? Why not Finland, Paraguay, Mongolia or Papua New Guinea? Why Egypt in the second millennium BCE rather than in the 18th century or the 8th?

Primary children can certainly gather many facts about Egypt. But good history teaching also engenders a 'feel' for Egyptian civilisation and some insight into various aspects of Egyptian society. It provides opportunities for direct experience, perhaps through seeing and touching appropriate artefacts, and allows space for pupils to reflect on similarities and differences between 'then and there' and 'here and now'. An appreciation of a shared humanity between ourselves and the people of ancient Egypt is an important device in nurturing spiritual insight.

The importance of spiritual development is illustrated in the remark that 'education is what remains when you have forgotten everything they taught you at school'. The academic study of school subjects cannot be divorced from the formation of pupils as people with feelings, ideas, intuitions, emotions, opinions and beliefs. You will need to make sure that the commendable aim of raising test scores is not achieved at the expense of the broader purpose of fostering lively, enquiring and reflective spirits in your pupils.

Moral

According to the inspectorate:

Moral teaching 'teaches the principles which distinguish right from wrong'

(Ofsted 1996)

You may encounter a dilemma here. Is it your role as the teacher to tell children what is right and what is wrong? If so, whose moral code do you follow, in an era when there are sincere differences of opinion? On the other hand, is it the teacher's job to help children to make their own moral decisions and devise a personal moral code? What do you do, then, with a child who concludes that it is right to bully other children, swear at teachers or microwave the class guinea pig?

The following statements summarise my own view of a practical and principled approach to moral education:

- **Despite differences of opinion on the detail of moral behaviour, there is a considerable degree of agreement in society about underlying principles which distinguish right from wrong.**
- **The 'Golden Rule', (Don't) treat others as you would (not) want them to treat you, is applicable to many situations and is universally accepted as a basic principle.**
- **Children develop morally first by experiencing a disciplined regime in which a moral code is imposed on them, secondly by having the opportunity to test and question this code in a safe, supportive environment, and thirdly by internalising moral principles so that they can apply them to new situations.**

You have only to observe a teacher for half an hour to notice how frequently s/he imposes a moral code on the class: be quiet, don't interrupt, wait your turn, remember to say please and thank you, and so on. One piece of research noted that around 50 per cent of the interactions between teacher and children in a Key Stage I class were of this kind. You will undoubtedly find yourself operating in a similar way in your own class-room, if only to secure good order. As a good teacher you will also make a point of explaining the reasons for your strictures and periodically discussing moral issues with your class.

You can, however, go somewhat further in helping children to understand how moral discourse and decision-making work. A number of authors have produced classroom materials designed to help with this. These often use fictional situations in which characters are faced with moral dilemmas to enable children to explore moral decision making as an example of problem solving. Children discuss, dramatise or draw cartoon-strips to work through the issues. As the teacher, you direct the learning process by drawing attention to the consequences of alternative choices.

You may also wish to emphasise the impact on the characters' feelings of the different solutions proposed. This calls for quite sophisticated teaching skills, since your prime motive is to promote enquiry and investigation rather than teach a known 'right answer'.

Social

According to Ofsted, social development:

> encourages pupils to relate positively to others, take responsibility, participate fully in the community and develop an understanding of citizenship.
>
> (Ofsted 1996)

Social development is concerned with the relationship of individuals to groups. There are two main ways, which complement each other, by which you can assist this process for your pupils. One is through the content of the curriculum. For example, you may study interactions within groups through literature or in history, or when undertaking a health education project. The other is by means of your organisation of the class, which can enable children to gain experience of belonging to and working in a variety of groups. In this case your intended learning outcomes for the lesson will include some which are related to the process of learning (for example, that children will succeed in working collaboratively and that each child will make an appropriate contribution) alongside others linked to curricular content. More generally, but no less importantly, the school provides opportunities for social development by providing supervised, unstructured playtimes and lunch-breaks.

Cultural

Cultural development is concerned with:

> teaching pupils to appreciate their own cultural traditions and the diversity and richness of other cultures
>
> (Ofsted Framework 1996)

The emphasis on 'own cultural traditions' is a useful counterbalance to the common view that cultural development is solely about 'other people's cultures'. But what is meant by 'culture'? Verma offers the following definition: 'the unique values, symbols, lifestyle, customs and other human-made components that distinguish one social group from another' (Verma 1994 p. 5), which makes it clear that culture is not confined to issues of ethnicity or religious faith. The Ofsted framework draws attention to the importance of developing positive attitudes towards culture, hence the word 'appreci-ate'. Just as with social development you can adopt approaches based on content and process. History, geography, RE, music, art and PE provide opportunities to learn about a host of cultural issues, but you should also find occasions for children to express their own cultural traditions, share them with the class and have them affirmed by peers and teachers. This can range from telling stories and singing songs to talking about practices and customs in families, faith communities and social groups.

SMSC and the curriculum

Consider three aspects of the curriculum:

The *formal* curriculum comprises the planned, intended programmes in the various subjects taught in the school, together with the other aspects of school life such as assemblies for collective worship, the school's rules and procedures and educational outings, provided as part of the taught programmes.

The *informal* curriculum consists of the planned, but non-compulsory activities offered by the school, such as clubs and societies, and optional excursions offered as 'extras' outside school hours: everything, in short, that is often described as 'extra-curricular'.

The *hidden* curriculum refers to unplanned, unintentional consequences such as the positive or negative effects of the teacher's personality upon his/her relationship with the class.

The formal curriculum provides many opportunities to promote SMSC . The following suggestions are designed as starting points to set you thinking.

Spiritual

In addition to the history example given earlier:

- **Mathematics: the concept of infinity. Children experienced a sense of wonder and mystery as they explored the idea that you can always add one more to the largest number you can think of.**
- **Science: some six-year-olds cut through some daffodil bulbs and were mystified because they could find no yellow colouring inside.**
- **English: ten-year-olds read Libby Purves' book *The Hurricane Tree* and discussed whether there was any point in planting some acorns since every member of the class would probably be dead before an oak tree was fully grown.**
- **ICT: eight-year-olds marvelled at the fact that human beings were able to invent a computer with a huge memory in a small space.**
- **RE: children wrestled with questions such as, What makes a friend? Who loves me? Why do people die? What makes me sorry? They also learning about answers to such questions offered in Christianity and other principal faiths.**
- **The Arts: children expressed their emotions and ideas through music, poetry, visual art and dance and gained inspiration through experiencing the compositions and performances of famous artists.**

Moral

- **Science: a class of nine-year-olds discussed how to persuade older children not to spoil their plant experiment in the school grounds.**
- **ICT: a group of seven-year-olds discussed how they could politely suggest that another child should not monopolise the computer.**
- **History: some eleven-year-olds argued passionately against the slave trade.**
- **PE: a five-year-old group talked about how to prevent anyone being hurt by careless use of apparatus.**
- **RE: ten-year-olds discussed whether Jesus' advice to 'turn the other cheek' was always right.**

Social

- **PE: children worked collaboratively to set out games equipment.**
- **Geography: juniors planned and conducted a traffic survey and shared their data.**
- **Design & Technology: seven-year-olds worked in groups of six to produce working models.**
- **Art: eleven-year-olds designed and made a large collage.**
- **Music: groups of children composed pieces then performed them to another class.**

Cultural

- **Geography: nine-year-olds spoke about the village, town or country in which they were born.**
- **Music: six-year-olds played rhythms on percussion instruments from Eastern Asia.**
- **English: ten-year-olds read poems written in England between 1850 and 1900, wrote some in a similar style and gave a presentation.**
- **History: seven-year-olds collected items from their grandparents for a display about the 1940s, made captions and a programme and held an exhibition for the rest of the school.**
- **PE: eleven-year-olds learned dances from India and Ireland.**

The essential point about these examples is that they are an ordinary part of everyday school life. As the teacher you will need to seek a balance in your planning to ensure that each element of SMSC is present, and that every subject of the curriculum plays some part in the development of SMSC values.

The informal curriculum

The informal curriculum is the set of non-compulsory activities offered outside formal teaching time. These voluntary activities range from sports, music, drama and arts clubs to optional excursions outside school time. The social and moral value of these activities is fairly self-evident. Children have the opportunity to opt into groups, often across age groups, in which their relationships with each other, and with their teachers, are developed in less formal circumstances.

Team sports offer chances to collaborate in playing games according to rules, experience winning and losing and learn that referees are fallible people whose decisions are nevertheless accepted. The arts give access to the spiritual insights and cultural expressions of a variety of artists, composers and writers.

Residential excursions provide settings for communal living and activity, and can entail visits to places belonging to a range of cultural groups. The quality of pupil-pupil and pupil-teacher relationships during so-called 'extra-curricular' activities is often of a different routine. You would not be the first teacher to discover that your extra-curricular link with a 'difficult' child transformed the way in which you could work with him/her in the classroom.

The hidden curriculum

Apart from the taught programme derived from the subjects of the curriculum, children are strongly influenced by the quality of the relationships which they experience in school and by the values promoted, intentionally or unintentionally, by their teachers. You need to be aware of the climate of values that you are creating, and to consider the effect of your own attitudes and beliefs upon the class.

It is easy for teachers to underestimate the impact that their personal style and behaviour has on children. Parents, however, are only too aware that the teacher is a focus of great authority in their child's life, especially during the primary school phase. Parents' authority is challenged on the grounds of the teacher's observations and actions; you have a frightening degree of influence over your pupils.

Consider the following qualities:

- **Do you convey your personal enthusiasm for some subjects, or antipathy towards others, albeit unintentionally, by your approach?**
- **Do you only put the very best work on display, or do you ensure that every child has some of his/her work valued in this way?**
- **Do you distribute appropriately graded questions around the class, or do you just ask those children likely to know the answer?**
- **Do you discriminate inappropriately among children in the way in which you organise daily routines, for example lining up after break?**
- **How do you greet children in the morning and say goodbye in the evening? One headteacher I know used to shake hands with every child at the end of the school day.**
- **Do you, however inadvertently, indicate some tasks as fit for girls and others for boys? If children express such judgements do you challenge and discuss them, or ignore them?**
- **Do children slow to complete tasks in English and maths have to continue with them during arts or humanities lessons or does each child experience a broad curriculum?**
- **How do children perceive your view of what is an appropriate relationship between pupils and teacher?**
- **How do you use humour? Do you ever use it to demean a child before his/her peers?**
- **Does your demeanour towards the class change if the lesson is being observed, for instance by an inspector?**

This list of questions, to which I am sure you can add others, demonstrates clearly that learning to teach is far more than demonstrating competence against a list of Standards. It challenges you to clarify your own values and to check your actions against your principles. Teaching is inevitably a moral, as well as an intellectual and skilled, activity. Children are quick to spot inconsistencies between the teacher's words and deeds. While it is good for them to learn that adults can differ in mood, tempera-ment, opinion and belief, you need to consider any significant differences between the school's proclaimed ethos and your personal views. Arguably, if you can portray to your class your own adherence to agreed policies, despite personal misgivings, you have taught them an invaluable lesson about society and contributed valuably to the SMSC programme.

Personal development as an aim of education

Fashions in education come and go. A current public concern with regard to primary education is the need to improve standards of attainment in literacy, numeracy and ICT. At other times the emphasis has been on enabling children to express themselves through a rich arts curriculum, to explore their place in the world through a diverse humanities curriculum and to analyse and order their experience through a detailed scientific and technological curriculum.

The curricular pendulum will no doubt continue to swing at regular intervals. But confining educational debate to a discussion of the curriculum is to avoid the central question: 'What is the purpose of education? Is it to transmit a culture, to mould a future workforce, to help individuals to realise their personal potentials, to impose order upon the population – or some mixture of these and other aims?'

The aspiration that children should be helped to achieve higher standards in curriculum areas is incontrovertible; a counter argument would be difficult to imagine. Strictly speaking, however, such intentions are educational objectives, rather than aims. They prescribe targets to be achieved in a short to medium time-span, but say nothing about why those particular targets are important.

Those who framed the major Education Acts in 1944 and 1988 ensured that the fundamental aims of education were addressed, albeit in a broad way. The requirement to address people's spiritual, moral, social, cultural, mental and physical development indicates that a concern for the development of the whole person is central to the aims of education. The 1988 Act adds flesh to this outline by stating that the school curriculum should prepare pupils for 'the opportunities, experiences and responsibilities of adult life' (DES 1988).

Conclusion

It is important that you, the teacher, should:

- **formulate your own understanding of educational aims;**
- **consider how fostering children's spiritual, moral, social and cultural development can contribute to those aims;**
- **develop a view of the role played by the curriculum subjects in reaching the aims;**
- **think about the part played by non-statutory, extra-curricular activities;**
- **reflect on the quality and tenor of your interpersonal relationships with pupils as a means to the desired ends.**

I'm sorry that you cannot just tick a box to show that you meet the standards addressed by this chapter. Generating a vision of what you want for your pupils, then striving to help them to achieve it is far too important for such a simplistic device; it's also far more satisfying.

Further reading

Best, R. (ed.) (2000) *Education for Spiritual, Moral, Social and Cultural Development*. London: Continuum. This edited collection of articles includes theoretical issues and practical guidance.

DfEE/QCA (1999) *Non-statutory Frameworks for Personal, Social and Health Education and Citizenship at Key Stages 1 and 2*. London: QCA. This sets out clearly the expectations of pupils in the primary years.

Francis, L. and Thatcher, A. (1990) *Christian Perspectives for Education*. Leominster: Gracewing. Written from an explicitly Christian perspective, this describes itself in its introduction as: 'A compendium of articles to stimulate reflection on the complex relationship between Christian faith and classroom practice.'

By the end of the chapter you should:

- *understand the legal and administrative framework related to equal opportunities in schools;*
- *be aware of some of the evidence for systematic inequalities in pupils' achievement;*
- *have considered some ways in which greater opportunities for all pupils might be promoted in the primary school;*
- *recognise some of the problems inherent in the concept of equal opportunities.*

This chapter addresses the following Professional Standards for QTS:

 1.1, 1.2, 1.8, 3.3.14

(The Standards are reproduced in full at the back of this book.)

This chapter introduces the topic of equal opportunities in relation to pupils in school. It outlines the legislative and policy background and the evidence for patterns of achievement. It briefly considers some requirements of school policies and the individual teacher's responsibilities in the classroom.

'Equal opportunities' and education: the legislative background

You will be aware that there is general UK legislation against discrimination on the grounds of race, sex and disability and that there are statutory bodies to pursue their enforcement. These major pieces of anti-discrimination legislation are essential background to any discussion of the concept of 'equal opportunities' though they constitute only a limited aspect of its application to your teaching in school.

Sex Discrimination Act 1975

This Act (extended and amended 1986) established the Equal Opportunities Commission (EOC) and outlaws discrimination on the grounds of sex. Anybody, including children (or those acting on their behalf), may make a complaint under the Act if they believe they being discriminated against on the basis of sex. Discrimination need not be direct and intentional for a complaint to be made. If the indirect outcome of a policy is unfair to males or females, then a complaint of discrimination may be upheld by the courts. In education if the outcome of a policy is that females (whether teachers or pupils) receive less favourable treatment than males (or vice-versa), then discrimination may be judged to have occurred. It would not be illegal, for example, to separate boys and girls for certain teaching purposes, but it would be deemed discriminatory if one sex had access to curricular opportunities or advantages which were denied the other.

Race Relations Act 1976

This Act created the Commission for Racial Equality and outlaws discrimination on the grounds of colour, race, nationality or ethnic and national origins. Anybody, including children (or those acting on their behalf), may formally complain under the Act if they believe they are being discriminated against or receiving 'less favourable treatment' on these grounds. Again, discrimination need not be direct and intentional. If the *indirect* outcome of a policy is that one group receives less favourable treatment than another, then a complaint of discrimination may be upheld by the courts. The law does, however, allow for particular measures to help designated groups who have defined needs, for example those whose first language is not English.

The Race Relations Amendment Act 2000 made even more explicit the responsibility that all designated 'public authorities', including schools, have to eliminate unlawful racial discrimination and promote equality of opportunity and good relations between different racial groups.

The Disability Discrimination Act 1995

In its original form the Disability Discrimination Act (DDA) 1995 had limited application to schools (see Circular 20/99). Having been subsequently amended by the Special Educational Needs and Disability Act 2001, it now applies firmly to education. Since September 2002 it has been unlawful for providers of education and related services to discriminate against disabled people. Schools and LEAs have a duty to make 'reasonable adjustment' to ensure that pupils who are disabled are not put at a substantial disadvantage compared to their peers. Parents who believe that discrimination has taken place can take a claim to the SEN and Disability Tribunal (SENDIST). You should note that whilst there is obviously some overlap between disability and SEN, these are not synonymous. Pupils with some physical conditions (severe asthma or diabetes, for example) may have rights under the DDA but not necessarily be registered for SEN purposes.

The Disability Rights Commission Act 1999 created the Disability Rights Commission (DRC) in 2000 with statutory duties to work to eliminate discrimination, promote equal opportunities, encourage good practice and advise government. The DRC has produced a Code of Practice for Schools (DRC 2002) which, though not statutory, is an authoritative interpretation of the application of disability discrimination legislation.

Educational opportunities and 'social exclusion'

Though these are the main planks of anti-discrimination policy, there are other wide concerns about various forms of inequality in society. You will recognise the concern with gender and race but will also be familiar with broader notions of social and economic disadvantage. The current Labour government has established a Social

Exclusion Unit to pursue its concern for greater 'inclusion' of all those who appear to be significantly disadvantaged or on the margins of contemporary society. In a speech at Stockwell Park School, Lambeth, in 1997, Prime Minister Tony Blair explained:

> Social exclusion is about income but it's about much more. It's about prospects and networks and life chances. It's a very modern problem, and one that is more harmful to the individual, more damaging to self esteem, more corrosive for society as a whole, more likely to be passed down from generation to generation than material poverty.' (cited in Blunkett 1999)

The education system features prominently in policy debates about different forms of inequality and social exclusion in British society. It does so for two broad sets of reasons:

- **Schools, colleges and universities are commonly recognised as the principal public mechanism for the distribution of opportunities in the modern world. In the modern 'credential society' (Collins 1979) educational institutions both prepare and certificate their clientele as *qualified* for subsequent academic or occupational destinations. Directly or indirectly they may act as filters or gatekeepers for access to many of the more desirable opportunities.**
- **Educational institutions, and particularly schools, are widely believed to have a major role in the formation of social attitudes. These may include personal educational or vocational aspirations and views held towards different groups in society.**

Neither set of arguments is entirely beyond criticism and you will recognise that there are clearly other factors involved in each, but these are the assumptions of much public policy in education. The Department for Education and Skills (DfES) official website claims that one of the department's twin aims is to 'build a fair and inclusive society' in which 'everyone has an equal chance to achieve their full potential'.

Equal opportunities and education policy

Beyond the requirements to comply with anti-discrimination legislation, there appears to be widespread formal support for the principle that schools should provide 'equal opportunities' for their pupils. At a national level a DfEE Circular on *Social Inclusion* made clear its importance:

> 'Commitment to equal opportunities: parents and pupils should know that the school has an equal opportunities policy and is committed to equality of opportunity for all pupils. Schools should monitor the impact of their policies and procedures on different groups (by race, gender and disability). The effectiveness of such policies should be assessed at governors' meetings.'
>
> (DfEE Circular 10/99 para 2.1)

In its curriculum guidance the Qualifications and Curriculum Authority (QCA) also refers to the importance of securing equal opportunities for pupils. The Office for Standards in Education (Ofsted) *Handbook for Inspecting Primary and Nursery Schools* requires inspectors to take equal opportunities into account in making their judgements and to consider the extent to which the school 'is socially inclusive by ensuring equality of access and opportunity for all pupils' (Ofsted 1999b: section 4). Local authority policy statements commonly make some reference to the promotion of equal opportunities and many have specific guidance for education. Most schools have equal opportunities policies and when working in schools you may encounter these and find an individual teacher is sometimes given this brief as a whole school responsibility.

Though at all levels of the education system there appears to be a concern to foster equal opportunities, there is rather little by way of agreed definition. Nevertheless, in employing such a term we incur some obligation to think clearly about what we might mean and work towards some sort of shared understanding.

Practical task

Equal terms?

Given the apparent official support for the concept, it is difficult to imagine, say, in a job interview, responding to a question about this topic: 'Actually, I don't believe in equal opportunities...' But what exactly do you understand by the term? Before you go any further, briefly jot down how you might define 'equal opportunities'. What is the difference between 'equality' and 'equality of opportunity'? Exactly which opportunities are to be 'equal' in education? When can we say that opportunities are 'equal' or 'unequal'? It is important that you try to work out your own lines of thought in arriving at some sort of provisional answers to these questions.

The above activity will very likely demonstrate at least *some* problems in closely defining what we mean by 'equal opportunities'. Closer examination will show that far from being the straightforward term it might initially appear, equal opportunities turns out to be a shifting, slippery, sometimes elusive and essentially 'contestable concept' (Riley 1994: 12). Despite the official endorsements outlined earlier, there remain serious arguments as to just what formal commitments to equal opportunities in education actually entail. Clarifying meaning will resolve some questions but you will find it also reveals some disagreement over underlying values and social objectives (Foster et al 1996).

Equality of educational opportunity

Defining 'equality' is a task which has engaged teachers and educationalists for long enough, though this is not the place to rehearse all the arguments (see, for example, Peters 1966; Cooper 1980). In some respects a degree of *inequality* seems unavoidable, even fundamental to any form of school system. Children do not all achieve the exactly same level of formal educational success and it is inconceivable that this could be otherwise. Pupils do not have exactly the same educational potential, those interests and capacities – whether we think they are inherent or acquired – which might be relevant to their learning.

Whilst some level of educational inequality is an inescapable fact of life, we can still argue that 'equality' is an important aim in education. Estelle Morris, subsequently Secretary of State for Education, wrote in *The Times*: 'At the core of Labour's education policy is equality of opportunity – the opportunity for every child, in every school to succeed.' (Morris, 1996)

State schools in a democratic society must broaden the opportunities which all pupils have to reach their individual potential. The objective is not equality in the absolute sense of everybody achieving the same, but the removal of what are often referred to as 'barriers' to educational success. Unsurprisingly, this often shifts the political argument to just exactly which factors should be regarded as 'barriers' to be dismantled.

Inequalities in educational 'life chances'

Barriers to equality of opportunity emerge from an examination of patterns of inequalities in educational *outcomes*. Given we recognise some obvious differences between children, attempts to chart educational inequalities examine populations and groups rather than individuals; claims of inequality must be demonstrated in differences in the educational performance of pupils which are significant, systematic and sustained.

The principal claim is that various social groups appear to have very different 'life chances':

> life chance: probability of a person of a specified status achieving a specified goal or suffering a specified disadvantage.
>
> (Reading 1977 p. 120)

This encompasses such things as employment, health care and not being detained at Her Majesty's pleasure; it includes material goods and less easily definable benefits like status, job satisfaction and personal autonomy. It is argued that these are not simply the result of individual ability or effort, but also relate to the opportunities which – by accident or design – are available to different social groups. Most crucially for our purposes, 'life chances' include the greater or lesser probability of achieving educational success. Whilst in law all children have the same formal entitlement to a 'broad and balanced' National Curriculum, there may be certain background factors which appear to constrain individuals' chances of educational achievement.

Practical task

Unequal chances?

What factors in a pupil's background might influence his or her educational 'life chances' or capacity to benefit from the opportunities of the compulsory years of schooling? List the relevant factors – these can be positive or negative – and try to organise them into some pattern and rank them in significance.
Which do you think are the most significant?

Evidence of educational achievement

See Chapters 12 and 13 for more information on special educational needs.

Research into educational opportunity and achievement has focused on three categories – in accelerating order of inexactitude: sex/gender; race/ethnicity; social background. Special educational needs, with its variety and gradient of divisions, is a rather different type of analytical category, though very much an equal opportunities issue. The three categories have been extensively researched in terms of opportunity and achievement. Below are some broad conclusions on the basis of recent evidence (see references and further reading for more details).

Sex/gender

Sometimes a distinction is drawn between biological sex and sociocultural gender (e.g. Hughes 1991: 12), but this is commonly ignored.

The longstanding concern has been with the way the school system appeared to be more geared to the needs of boys than girls (e.g. Stanworth 1983; Weiner (ed) 1985; Tutchell 1990). There are certainly still concerns about sexism in schools, but in terms of academic achievement there is evidence that girls are now outperforming boys on almost every attainment measure up to age 16 (Mitsos and Browne 1998). At the primary stage girls have long outperformed boys. The 1999 statistics for the National Curriculum Assessment results at ages 7 and 11 indicate the pattern:

Key stage 1 test results 1999:

PERCENTAGE OF PUPILS ACHIEVING LEVEL 2 OR ABOVE BY GENDER

Reading	girls 71%	boys 60%
Writing	girls 61%	boys 46%
Mathematics	girls 65%	boys 62%

(*Source*: extracted from DfEE SFR 29/1999 table 5a)

Key stage 2 test results 1999:

PERCENTAGE OF PUPILS ACHIEVING LEVEL 4 OR ABOVE BY GENDER

English:	girls 75%	boys 64%
Mathematics	girls 68%	boys 68%
Science:	girls 78%	boys 78%

(*Source*: extracted from DfEE SFR 29/1999 table 9)

This sort of data, plus the evidence that boys are more likely to be excluded or to exclude themselves from school, have led to some recent claims that schools need to do more with 'disaffected boys' (Morris 1996; Wragg 1997a). These arguments have provoked some controversy (Wragg 1997b; Weiner et al 1997; Epstein et al 1999) but are strongly reflected in current policy debate.

Race/ethnicity

You will find the word 'race' is often placed in inverted commas (e.g. Gaine and George

1999); this is to draw attention to the fact that it is a highly debatable term and not a straightforward biological category (Klein 1993, p. 4). 'Ethnic group' is a broader and more serviceable term; it can include racial, religious, national and cultural factors. These factors are often confusingly mixed, even in official classifications; there is no limit to the number of categories which can be employed and much depends on the purpose. Travellers (commonly referred to as 'gypsies', though this word is best avoided) are often included as an identifiable category of ethnic minority. It is important to recognise that everybody has an ethnic identity; to talk of visible minorities alone as 'ethnics' is absurd as well as potentially offensive.

Recent reviews of the educational achievement of ethnic minorities attainment (e.g. Ofsted 1996; Gilborn and Gipps 1996) have suggested that as a whole this is improving, though the performance of some groups continues to be depressed relative to the population as a whole. Some broad conclusions are:

- **Many pupils from ethnic minority backgrounds are doing very well on formal measures of attainment. Chinese, some Indian groups and what were once termed 'East African Asians' are amongst the highest achieving groups of pupils.**
- **Pupils whose families originate in Pakistan and Bangladesh still have difficulties in the early years of primary school. Much of this seems related to acquiring English. Subsequently, however, their performance may match or surpass that of English first language pupils *in the same social circumstances*; Bangladeshi background pupils, in particular, still underachieve at the higher grades of GCSE.**
- **Afro-Caribbean pupils make sound progress in the early years but performance shows a clear decline during the secondary phase. They have a disproportionate number of exclusions from school (CRE 1997) and underachieve at GCSE.**
- **Traveller pupils do least well. Although some make a reasonably promising start in primary school, by the time they reach secondary level their attainment is generally weak.**
- **Girls from minority ethnic groups do better than boys.**

Social background

Traditionally social and educational researchers have talked about 'social class'. We can agree that notions of social class are imprecise, yet we will probably use class categories as part of our explanation of social events and people's behaviour, including our own! Several classification systems have been adopted, and though all are open to objection, researchers necessarily have to offer some sort of model and categories. The Registrar General's five-point scale has been one of the most common. This is based on occupations: classes I and II are professional/managerial; class III non-manual/skilled manual; class IV semi-skilled manual; class V unskilled. Some of the official measures of the social composition of a school's intake are even cruder; often they are simply calculated on the percentage of pupils eligible for free school meals.

There has been longstanding debate in the USA and UK about the effects of social background on educational attainment and the evidence for what schools can do is contested (Davies 1999). In crude terms, children of professional parents (classes I and II) are around four times as likely to gain five passes of C grade or above at GCSE as children of unskilled workers (class V). One conclusion is overwhelming: regardless of both ethnic origin and sex, pupils from more economically advantaged backgrounds outperform those who are poor (Gilborn and Gipps 1996). Patterns of inequality do change, but the great intractable issue remains what schools can do about the most disadvantaged or 'socially excluded'.

Confirming or confronting disadvantage?

It is important to recognise that the evidence is shifting and that the negative and positive effects of social background, ethnicity and gender are inter-related in complex ways. Whatever may be statistically true of 'group averages', there will always be more variation within than between groups (Gilborn and Gipps 1996: 1). There is one simple lesson: you must never make assumptions about the potential achievement of pupils based on stereotypical views of group identity.

The accusation sometimes made, not least by a former Secretary of State for Education, David Blunkett, and former Chief Inspector of Schools (Woodhead 1998), is that some schools which have a disadvantaged intake often confirm rather than challenge low expectations of achievement. This point may be rather harsh on teachers 'at the sharp end' of social and educational inequality, but the danger of overemphasising pupils' backgrounds and deficiencies is that you lose sight of what might be achieved if you concentrate on the quality of opportunities which you are providing *now* in your lesson. This particular twist to the opportunity debate is not one you can afford to ignore; it is an extension of arguments about the 'self-fulfilling prophecy'. It also brings the argument right back to the level of the classroom and the way you approach the curriculum and the hour-by-hour business of teaching.

School policies for fostering social inclusion and equal opportunities

Promoting access to the curriculum

Your duty as a teacher is not just to offer or even teach a curriculum: it is to do your best to ensure that the pupils in your care have a realistic chance of 'accessing' that curriculum. Behind this piece of jargon is an important idea: equality of opportunity has to be more than simply the formal right to be present whilst something is happening.

You can promote greater equality in pupils' capacity to access the curriculum through the specific content of your lessons and the way they are taught. This is part of what should be your general commitment to providing appropriate work for individuals. Gender, ethnicity and social background are key elements in this and the selection of appropriate materials and activities can reinforce both understanding and identity. It is particularly important to acknowledge cultural differences, religion, traditions and language as positive features whilst recognising that they may affect learning in specific areas. At the same time as building upon existing sociocultural knowledge you should always be seeking to broaden a child's understanding of the world and give them new experiences. You should provide work to which pupils can relate, but provide bridges to cross from the familiar to the unfamiliar.

Practical task

Strategies for the classroom

In planning work you should consider:
Choice of topic – Whose interests does this reflect? Does it appeal to boys and girls?
Does it exclude anybody? Are there any cultural or religious sensitivities to be
observed?

Displays and visual materials – Do they reflect different cultures? Do they show
appropriate male and female role models? Do they avoid stereotypical images of
different groups?

Language – Is your language and that of books and other resources accessible to all?
Will the vocabulary and concepts be culturally unfamiliar to some pupils? Is English a
'second language' for any of your pupils? How can you help those who may have
difficulty?

Promoting attitudes and values

A further aspect of education for greater equality is the commitment to promoting particular knowledge, skills, attitudes and behaviour which help all pupils take their place in a complex society. Schools are not just concerned that children should achieve in academic terms, they are also concerned with the promotion of values for all pupils.

Teachers have a significant role in preparing pupils for life in a multicultural society. The Swann Report (1985) made it clear that 'multicultural education' was not just for minority groups. All pupils should be encouraged to show respect for that which is of value to others and to try to understand things which may at first appear culturally unfamiliar. Britain's multicultural society should be reflected in the curriculum. Schools can also approach diversity and equality as more explicit issues in assemblies and wherever personal and social education is carried on. This is as true for pupils in so-called 'all white' schools as those in multi-ethnic areas (Epstein and Sealey 1990).

There is also a concern that schools should explicitly combat racist attitudes and practices. Anti-racist education arose out of a sense of the limitations of multicultural education in the face of racism. It has long been a controversial area, but the underlying causes for the emergence of anti-racism have not gone away. In giving evidence to the Lawrence Inquiry (into the death of the black teenager Stephen Lawrence and the subsequent police investigation) on behalf of the Commission for Racial Equality Sir Herman Ouseley, then Chairman of the CRE, said:

> 'The starting point for prevention of racist crime is in the education of our children … at the present time is that there is no anti-racist teaching within the National Curriculum. We are not doing anything coherently as a nation to counter racial prejudice through formal classroom activity … there will be pockets and examples of good work … but there is no coherent programme that addresses this system- atically across the teaching environment.'

> (CRE 1999)

The MacPherson Report (1999) made three recommendations relating to education: there should be amendments to the National Curriculum to combat racism; local education authorities and school governors should implement anti-racist strategies in schools; and Ofsted inspectors should comment on these strategies in inspection reports. What is very clear is that the argument which Chris Gaine has characterised as 'No Problem Here' (Gaine 1988, 1995) has still to be faced in many schools; racism cannot just be an issue for schools with significant visible minorities, it is an issue for all.

The same sorts of underlying principles also apply to gender. The curriculum and the way it is taught must both recognise the preferences and needs of boys and girls and prepare both for life in modern society. One of the challenges you will find in the primary classroom is to attempt the education (rather than simple coercion) of boys to allow a more equitable distribution of your attention. This is a very definite equality of opportunity issue. It has to be more than just anti-sexism for boys, however necessary that may sometimes be; there are some very positive values to be promoted.

Practical task

Heart and minds?

In what ways can a school foster tolerance, understanding and opposition to discrimination and prejudice amongst its pupils concerning:

- *socially disadvantaged groups?*
- *ethnic diversity?*
- *gender?*

Promoting [e]quality in your classroom

The objective of equal opportunities policies is to reduce any disproportionate educational disadvantages experienced by members of particular groups. It may sound trite, but there is little point in simply promoting equality of opportunity within the school without promoting quality of opportunity. The most fundamental aspect of both quality and equality in your classroom is that all pupils must have the opportunity to learn, to make progress in academic and personal terms. However 'equal' the experience you provide for pupils may be, unless they make solid educational progress your achievement as a teacher is rather hollow.

There is no escaping that the issues which come under the heading of 'equal opportunities' are some of the most controversial in education: they are obviously political and often deeply personal. How teachers, individually and collectively, may enhance or diminish the opportunities available to pupils is always an awkward question: it is nonetheless a question which reflective teachers ask repeatedly of themselves.

Practical task

Your policy for [e]quality

What can you as an individual teacher do to promote greater and more [e]quality *opportunities in your classroom?*

Further reading

There are many books on these issues. Below are just some available sources.

Arnot, M., Gray, J., James, M. and Rudduck, J. (1998) *Recent Research on Gender and Educational Performance*, London: Ofsted/The Stationery Office.
This summarises what researchers have discovered about the different educational achievements of boys and girls.

Cole, M., Hill, D. and Shan, S. (eds) (1997) *Promoting Equality in Primary Schools*, London: Cassell. This includes both theoretical background on equality issues and practical guidance geared to primary teachers.

Epstein, D., Elwood, J., Hey, V. and Maw, J. (eds) (1999) *Failing Boys? Issues in Gender and Achievement*, Buckingham: Open University Press. A range of authors place issues about boys' achievement in a wider context; they pose some serious questions about the underlying assumptions of recent debates.

Epstein, D. and Sealey, A. (1990) *Where it Really Matters... Developing Anti-Racist Education in Predominantly White Primary Schools*, Birmingham Development Education Centre. This makes clear the importance of anti-racism for all pupils and includes practical ideas.

Gaine, C. and George, R. (1999) *Gender, 'Race' and Class in Schooling: A New Introduction*, London: Falmer. This is a good introduction to research across the three areas; it discusses some of the complexity of concepts such as race and class.

Gillborn, D. and Mirza (2000) *Educational Inequaltiy. Mapping Race, Class and Gender: A Synthesis of Research Evidence*. London: Ofsted. Available online via: http://www. ofsted.gov.uk

Klein, G. (1993) *Education Towards Race Equality*, London: Cassell.
This book traces the social and political background of education for race equality. It also includes guidelines for reviewing practice across the curriculum. Though some of the specific points relating to the earlier National Curriculum have become outdated, the underlying principles have not.

Runnymede Trust (1993) *Equality Assurance in Schools: Quality, Identity, Society*, London: Runnymede Trust /Trentham Books. This Runnymede Trust publication on includes references and resources and discusses a range of practical issues in a readable style. It includes useful lists of objectives for pupils in multiracial education.

Multicultural Teaching: this journal (published by Trentham books) is a good source of informed but relatively brief and accessible articles.

ELECTRONIC SOURCES
Equal Opportunities Commission: http://www.eoc.org.uk
EOC site includes links, lists of publications and some on-line material.

Commission for Racial Equality: http://www.cre.gov.uk/index.html
CRE site includes links, lists of publications and some online material including the *Code of Practice*.

Disability Rights Commission: http://www.drc-gb.org
DRC site includes links, lists of publications and some on-line material including the *Code of Practice for Schools*.

The Guardian website: http://www.educationunlimited.co.uk/specialreports/
This includes access to a series of special reports in 1999 and 2000 by Nick Davies and
ensuing correspondence; several of these discuss evidence of inequalities in educational
provision, poverty and achievement.

DfES website: www.dfes.gov.uk includes information, circulars and guidance, links to
legislation and statistics on many issues related to equal opportunities and social
exclusion. Because information is changing you are best advised to access the home
page and use the directory and search functions.

By the end of the chapter you should:

- *be aware of some of the major issues relating to special educational needs;*
- *be aware of a range of needs that children are likely to present in the mainstream classroom;*
- *be able to identify children who have special educational needs;*
- *be able to clarify some of those needs;*
- *be able to begin to offer structured and targeted support at the classroom level;*
- *understand how the 'Revised Code of Practice on the Identification and Assessment of SEN' might work in practice;*
- *be able to construct and implement an Individual Education Plan.*

This chapter addresses the following Professional Standards for QTS:

 2.6, 3.2.4, 3.3.4

(The Standards are reproduced in full at the back of this book.)

Most trainee teachers are at least a little apprehensive about SEN and yet once you are involved in this area you may find it to be the first time you begin to understand your children.

The chapter will help you to recognise and make effective provision for children with special educational needs. You should keep in mind, however, that the chapter is related to mainstream classrooms and that you need to read further to prepare for work in specialist units or special schools. For the most part, teachers who work in those settings will have completed courses of further professional development following Initial Teacher Training. If you intend to work in such settings, you will normally require at least two years' experience in a mainstream setting.

Read the desired learning outcomes at the beginning of this section carefully. You will see that they fall into two parts. Firstly, we need to be able to *recognise* special educational needs and identify particular difficulties. Once we are familiar with a child's needs, we can call on a range of strategies to *provide effective help.*

In practice, schools are currently required to address the requirements of the Code of Practice for the Identification and Assessment of Special Educational Needs (DfES, 2001), usually simply referred to as the Code of Practice. This, and the SEN Tool Kit (DfES 2001), will provide you with excellent advice about how to manage your work in special educational needs.

A very important aspect of special educational needs is to recognise and accept that individual need is a continuum. You will already have recognised that all children have individual needs and you will probably feel you have some real experience of differentiation, in which case you should already be able to:

- **identify the differentiated needs of children;**
- **understand the purpose of matching work to children's differentiated needs;**
- **recognise the importance of planning, assessment and evaluation in effective differentiation;**
- **recognise and develop teaching strategies and skills to achieve successful management of a variety of methods of differentiated learning for children.**

Bearne (1996, Chapter 13) contains some very helpful advice if you wish to revisit this area. A more practical way to explore how teachers differentiate is to observe then try some of the ideas for yourself. Teachers use a variety of strategies that have stood the test of time and many have developed their own particular style. They differentiate by setting a range of tasks and by varied use of support and resources. They also differentiate in more subtle ways. Talk with them about it!

When providing for special educational needs, we need to think carefully about the variables that contribute to needs and to understand their effects on the individual. Only then can we provide *real help*.

The 'problem' with special educational needs

Dave was a fourth-year undergraduate student, thoughtful, alert and highly successful in his school placements. Subsequent to his final experience in schools he had chosen to take a special option in special educational needs, working closely with a group of children in school. He had worked alongside a number of children with difficulties in his earlier placements. He definitely wasn't the student I expected to be knocking on my door for advice.

D (apprehensively) 'Any chance of five minutes?'
B 'How can I help?'
D 'I simply can't suss out Jack.' (a case study child)
B 'Go on...'
D (with furrowed brow) 'I can't work out what his problem is ... he can't settle and he disturbs the rest of his group all the time. He has difficulty reading. He seems tired and looks worn out. It's difficult getting him to write anything at all. I can't seem ... to make any contact. And I really don't think the class teacher and I see eye to eye on Jack. What do you think I ought to do?'
B 'I'm not sure unless you give me some more clues. From what you've said the problem appears to be yours as much as Jack's.' (I could usually be fairly honest with Dave.)

Of course, there are any number of issues here. Dave was a 'clued up' student who was struggling with a situation just 12 weeks before gaining Qualified Teacher Status. He was confused by just some of the difficulties that Jack was experiencing. He wanted to do something. He was feeling frustrated, vulnerable and – if truth be told – a little angry with himself.

'I think you have some decisions to make', I said. These were going to be Dave's decisions, not mine.

We can return to Dave later. His problem illustrates a common enough dilemma, not exclusive to teachers-to-be. We all meet these difficulties constantly in every interaction in school. However, it seems that once we have assigned the label 'special educational needs' to the difficulty, we swiftly move into personal guilt mode if we perceive ourselves as being unable to solve it. I couldn't solve Dave's dilemma. Perhaps it was partly solved when he came for help.

Dave was just one of thousands of students who work with tutors on undergraduate and postgraduate teacher training courses and who have 'needs'. Sure enough, Jack had needs, but then so did Dave. Once Dave had recognised this, we were on our way to providing some *real help*.

'Real help', in this case for both Jack and Dave, is a term that was usefully coined by Freeman and Gray (1989) and which has for some time formed the basis of meaningful, practical and worthwhile support. We need to keep this in mind constantly by asking: 'Is what I'm doing for Jack really helping? What's the *real* priority and how can I turn this into meaningful action?' As with Dave, we need to perceive the 'problem' not as Jack's alone, but as a shared problem *always capable of some degree of solution*.

Real help through case studies

Many final year students may have carried out individual case studies, often of children with special educational needs. This will have helped them to explore methods and approaches used to identify and help pupils with special educational needs. As you read on, try to visualise some children you met on placement who needed extra support. There are a lot of them! One of the things case studies consistently reinforce is the complexity and highly problematic nature of this area of provision. Once we have recognised that, it allows us to move on and attempt to make sense of a whole variety of practical situations and to extricate some commonalities, some ways of working that will support us in making sense of our work.

One aspect of this complexity that we feel should be tackled is the way in which our attitudes and values affect the help we provide for others, in particular the children in our class. One of the tasks you will have been asked to carry out is to consider, towards the end of any placement, how you have responded professionally and personally to the exercise. Just as many students report special educational needs as problematic and complex, so many report some degree of improvement in practice. Most discover strengths in the child that they might otherwise have missed, and many use the strengths to break the circle of failure. Many report a considerable degree of personal change in their attitudes towards children, the school that supports them and the system in general. Some report an affinity with the area that they had previously left unexplored. A few have suggested that the experience of working so closely with their child has taken them through a period of vulnerability, which has made them ask searching questions about themselves. A very small number decide that they found the experience unrewarding in many ways and distance themselves a little from the dilemmas. Yet almost all want to do more.

Back to Dave's dilemma

Dave's difficulties are common enough. Students report a number of common concerns:

- the lack of a knowledge base in special educational needs;
- lack of a skill base;
- confusion with terms;
- their status in relation to the class teacher;
- difference in perceptions of the child's difficulties;
- lack of experience in providing intensive support;
- not knowing where to start;
- not being able to manage support for the one child while teaching the whole class;
- not understanding the basics of provision for a child with a particular difficulty (for example, my child is dyslexic ... so what do I do?);
- and in many instances simply not being able to cope with the child's behaviour.

Perhaps you are already identifying with some of these. Once you have identified a child's need, the question that follows will probably be a deceptively simple one. What do I do now? Let's try to explore.

Some main issues

Special educational needs involves making suitable provision for a whole range of impairment, disability and difficulty together with the handicapping effects that society often brings to bear on these. It is a highly complex area of provision perceived as 'problematic' by all involved. It relies upon provision, not just by teachers, but by a range of professionals whose interests are often at odds and to whom access is not always easy. Responsibilities for provision are often confused and there are substantial resource issues. Historically, people with disability have been marginalised, stigmatised, persecuted, segregated, excluded, ridiculed and seen as objects of fear and abuse. There are significant personal and human rights issues and significant duties and responsibilities to be addressed. Equal opportunities are high on the special educational needs agenda.

Only comparatively recently has a more sensitive approach been brought to bear on provision for special needs in general and special *educational* needs in particular.

The definition

A useful starting point would be to consider the definition of special educational needs

(SEN) offered by the Warnock Committee (DES 1978), prior to the Education Act (1981). This was a time of considerable change in provision for young people with disability. The definition is also found in the Code of Practice. It is reproduced below:

> A child has a learning difficulty if he or she:
>
> (a) has significantly greater difficulty in learning than the majority of children of the same age
>
> (b) has a disability which either prevents or hinders the child from making use of the educational facilities of a kind provided for children of the same age in schools within the same area of the local education authority
>
> (c) is under five and falls within the definition at (a) or (b) or would do if special educational provision was not made for the child.

You will see immediately from this definition that SEN was perceived predominantly as a learning difficulty or disability. There are several reasons for this. This was the first time that the term SEN had been introduced. It was presented by Warnock as an attempt to cluster the range of need and focus on its outcomes for learning, particularly in the classroom. Previous legislation from the early twentieth century had resulted in attempts to provide descriptive labels for needs, which resulted in marginalisation and for the most part segregation of the disabled. For a few moments we can try to create a 'feel' for how history and legislation has changed the way we view special educational needs today.

In the 1944 Education Act, for example, the following categories of need were identified:

- **severely subnormal (SSN);**
- **educationally subnormal;**
- **blind;**
- **partially sighted;**
- **deaf;**
- **partially deaf;**
- **epileptic;**
- **delicate;**
- **physically handicapped;**
- **diabetic;**
- **speech defective;**
- **maladjusted.**

Such labels *created* need. For example, the term 'maladjusted' was used to describe a range of social, behavioural and emotional difficulty. In a very short space of time the term was in general use and over **30,000** children in schools had been identified as maladjusted within the space of a couple of years.

Let's consider this term as symptomatic of the provision of the times. Not only is the actual focus of this term hazy, but it also has strong negative overtones. Maladjustment is a comparative term and suggests deviation from an (acceptable) norm. It suggests a discrete 'condition', rather than a continuum of need. It may be that we all lack 'adjustment' at times and that it is 'normal' for this to happen.

It doesn't take much to move from describing 'maladjustment' as a descriptor of the behaviour to describing the child. 'Maladjustment' quickly became 'a maladjusted child' and then a cluster term to describe a sector of the school population – the 'maladjusted'.

Making sense of Madhur

We do the same thing with special educational needs, but perhaps less so. A child with a recognised special need quickly becomes 'a special needs child'. So 'Madhur has special needs' quickly becomes 'Madhur is a special needs child'. Her whole persona has now been subsumed within the difficulty. She is soon seen solely as a 'problematic child' rather than a 'child experiencing difficulty'. Assessments and reports concentrate on weaknesses rather than strengths. Yet strengths are potential growth points in taking Madhur forward. As a problematic child, she is easily seen as 'defective' in some way, even though this negativistic term was dropped some years ago.

What happens now is interesting. The difficulty has been perceived as Madhur's problem. When she doesn't respond to teaching, she may be seen as lazy, uncooperative, withdrawn or disruptive and so on. Her image of self is seriously affected. Self-esteem is depressed and motivation to achieve (possibly scant in the first instance) is reduced. The system that should have provided a way forward is now doing the opposite.

What happens to Madhur is symptomatic of several major issues in SEN provision and of one in particular.

Classroom practice: setting the climate

Providing for SEN in the classroom requires that we, along with others, recognise that many of the causal variables related to SEN lie not within Madhur but within the system that provides for her. This is often referred to amongst practitioners in SEN as the *child deficit/system deficit dilemma*. The 'system', by perceiving Madhur as 'problematic', is setting up conditions that may hinder rather than support. Once we perceive her as *having a disability* or *experiencing a learning difficulty* rather than *being a problem*, the onus shifts to the parent, the teacher, the school, the local authority, the 'system', to provide support in the form of 'real help'. Madhur should be included in this approach. Taking a client-centred approach enables us to work with Madhur to:

- **help her understand her own learning (metacognition);**
- **separate the disability from the persona;**
- **recognise needs and strengths;**
- **work together from a shared understanding of the difficulties which Madhur experiences.**

This is not a light touch or 'soft' approach. Madhur will have to take on responsibility and work hard to succeed. However, she will need the personal support and professional skill of those involved in taking her forward.

So, what are the issues which arise from our thoughts on Madhur and what might this mean for our practice?

Legislation in special educational needs

In Britain, the main thrust of legislation in the early part of the twentieth century was to identify and segregate people with disability. Much of the legacy of this can be seen in the institutionalisation and labelling of particular sectors of the population for social, psychological or medical reasons. During the 1970s and 1980s, movements from the USA and Scandinavia to include people with disability in the community filtered into the UK and resulted in the integration and inclusion movements. Subsequently, in the late 1980s and during the last decade many people with disability have been re-introduced into community and a significant number of institutions have closed.

In parallel with this, the inclusive education movement of the mid-1980s led, for a time, to efforts to close many special schools, although response to this varied in different LEAs.

It was within this context that the committee chaired by Mary Warnock was given the brief to investigate provision for SEN in the mid-1970s. It reported in 1978. Legislation followed in 1981. What were the intentions of this committee and subsequent Education Act?

The 1981 Education Act

Key features of this Act were to:

- **provide an overall descriptor (*special educational needs*) to reduce (negative) labelling effects;**
- **involve a range of professionals (*multi-professional approach*) in provision, thus capitalising on the range of expertise offered by these professionals;**
- **integrate provision (*in three levels*) in schools;**
- **define provision for children under and over two years old;**
- **provide a staged framework for the internal and external assessment of children with special educational needs and to provide a statement of these needs;**
- **require local educational authorities to provide suitable support and resources to meet needs identified on the Statement of Special Educational Needs.**

Provision during the 1980s therefore changed significantly from that earlier provided for schools. Significant issues did arise, however, particularly from the resource issues surrounding the provision of statements and subsequent support. Parents of children identified by the school as having a special educational need often experienced significant difficulties in accessing support and finding their way through the labyrinthine system of 'multi-professional' provision.

The Code of Practice

In the early 1990s there was a call for a more formalised system that would allow for closer definition of the responsibilities of LEAs and schools. The 1993 Education Act made various demands of schools, but its main effect was to place a duty on the Secretary of State to issue a Code of Practice for the Identification and Assessment of Special Educational Needs. The first Code of Practice was implemented from September 1994.

Following a consultation process with LEAs, schools, SEN voluntary bodies, the health and social services and others, the Code of Practice (2001) was revised. The revised Code retains much of the guidance from the original but takes account of the experiences of schools and LEAs since 1994. It also includes new rights and duties introduced by the SEN and Disability Act 2001 and Regulations. It is the model for practice currently used by schools.

In simple terms the main requirements for schools are that they should:

- **work in partnership with parents, operating key principles (para 2.3);**
- **appoint a 'responsible person' (a governor or the head teacher) for special educational needs (1.8);**
- **appoint a special needs co-ordinator (SENCO) with specific responsibilities (1.2, 4.4, 4.5, 5.10, 6.9, 6.10);**
- **provide, operate and publish a written special needs policy for the school containing specific sections (1.9);**
- **attend to the statutory duties of the governing body (1.8);**
- **set in place a 'graduated response' to provision as follows:**

   i)   early years provision (5.5), involving *Early Years Action* (4.7), *Early Years Action Plus* (4.11) (involving consultation with external specialists) and *Statutory Assessment* (4.13 and Section 7 onwards) (involving provision of the Statement of Special Educational Needs);
   ii) primary school provision (5.1), involving *School Action* (5.12), *School Action Plus* (5.16), and *Statutory Assessment* (5.17 and Section 7 onwards);
   iii) secondary school provision (6.1), involving a similar approach to that in the primary school (6.5, 6.12, 6.16), and *Statutory Assessment* (6.17 and Section 7 onwards);

- **incorporate Individual Education Plans (IEPs) (4.9, 5.14, 5.15);**
- **make provision for children under five with special educational needs (all Section 4);**
- **make provision for children under two with special educational needs (4.19, 4.20).**

(Numbers in brackets refer to the relevant Sections of the Code of Practice.)

In essence, there are three stages of provision. Initially the school responds (*School Action*), subsequently it may incorporate support from external services (*School Action Plus*), and ultimately it may refer the child for *Statutory Assessment*.

Before you read further, it will help you to skim the revised Code of Practice (DfES 2001) and read the chapter relevant to your particular key stages. Together with the Good Practice Guide (DfES 2001), this provides an excellent summary of how to manage SEN. Looking at it will be time well spent. Try not to rush it. Check that you can remember the key points. As a class teacher you will need to operate the Code effectively. If you have a more specific interest in the SENCO's role, it will become your key working document.

Practical applications in the classroom

Now you have read something of the background to special educational needs provision. It will help you to develop both understanding and practice if you are able to reflect on your experiences as a trainee teacher so far. The tendency is to see SEN as something different, a complex often quite frightening area which is controlled by 'people who are very knowledgeable'. Even the language of SEN can be daunting. However, in real terms it is all part of the continuum of differentiated need and you will have already had substantial experience of this. You may know more than you realise! The language is merely a system of shorthand codes used by those who devote significant time to this area. You will meet this as you do more and more work in school.

Although it may be something of an oversimplified exercise, let us try to cluster together some of the behaviours that children in your class might present. This is oversimplified because, in practice, the margins between the difficulties shown in Figure 12.1 are often blurred and the causal relationships complex. However, it may be useful to use the model from the Good Practice Guide as a starting point.

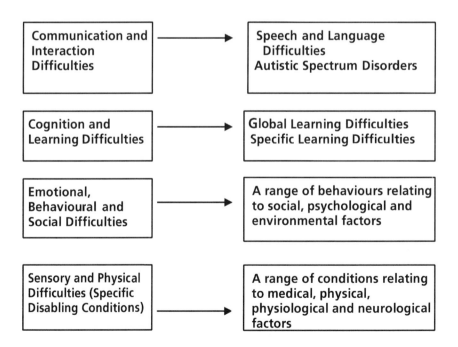

Figure 12.1 Special educational needs: presenting behaviours

Communication and Interaction Difficulties cover a complex range of need that may arise for a variety of reasons. These may present themselves as, contribute to or arise from any combination of the other three areas. Hence the complexity!

Cognitive and Learning Difficulties may be perceived as **global**, incorporating a general slowness of learning, difficulties in conceptualisation and mastery of cognitive and motor skills. They may also be perceived as **specific**. Specific learning difficulties may relate, for example, to difficulties in the acquisition or practice of language and communication skills. Further examples might be dyslexia or dyspraxia, which consist of clusters of specific difficulties relating to perception, discrimination, laterality, sequencing, short-term memory and, in the case of dyspraxia, significant co-ordination difficulty.

Emotional, Behavioural and Social Difficulties is a complex area consisting of various clusters and continua of need. Behaviour may be significantly withdrawn or isolative. A further example might involve disruption to self and others. The effect of behaviour on emotions and vice versa is complex. In either case, there may be significant effects on learning and learning difficulties may be caused.

Sensory and Physical Difficulties (Specific Disabling Conditions) are legion and in any case require some specialist knowledge to understand. Simple examples might be those that relate to specific impairment – for example, hearing or visual impairment. Asthma is a medical condition that we can identify in a significant number of children. Syndromes (for example Down's) are examples of more complex conditions.

As a classroom teacher, you will need to take specific advice and follow guidance on the range of specific disabling conditions as they occur, and you are more likely to encounter some than others. Opposite is a list of specific disabling conditions, together with their estimated incidence in a school population of 8,200,000. It was compiled by Comic Relief from a variety of sources. Note the terms but don't panic if some are new. It is very unlikely that you will meet them all in your teaching career!

Note: dyslexia, dyspraxia and speech and language difficulties are also recognised as specific learning difficulties. They are included here as part of the original list.

How do I identify these needs?

Identifying need is not always difficult but it may be! The rule of thumb here is to:

• **observe the child;**
If you are the child's teacher, you will be doing this every day! You don't necessarily have to read lengthy records at this point.

• **describe what the child knows, can do and understands;**
Always start with positives. These will provide you with a context for building on strengths and interests by teaching for the difficulties using the strengths as a context. For example, if the child enjoys working on the computer, this will provide you with an

Asthma	820,000
Dyslexia	820,000
Dyspraxia	820,000
Speech and Language Difficulties	250,000
Deaf and Hearing Impaired	65,000
Epilepsy	30,000
Blind and Partially Sighted	21,000
Autism	20,000
Cerebral Palsy	20,000
Diabetes	18,000
Juvenile Arthritis	14,000
Down's Syndrome	11,000
Fragile X Syndrome	10,000
Haemophilia	8,000
Sickle Cell & Thalassaemia	8,000
Muscular Dystrophy	8,000
Spina Bifida	5,000
Cystic Fibrosis	5,000

obvious way forward in providing a positive motivational force for the child (for some, but not all, activities).

• **describe what the child cannot do and doesn't understand;**
Initially, state what the difficulties are rather than why they occur. This will enable you to be clear about the learning activities you will need to put in place. You can approach the diagnostic process next!

• **try to access any missing evidence;**
Are there some records that you have not been able to access? What happened to the child in previous classes and/or schools? Now read the records.

• **infer why the difficulty may be occurring;**
Now you have a fuller picture, it is safe to make some informed guesses as to why the difficulties are occurring. Share these with colleagues, particularly the SENCO, and those who might have previously taught the child. Discuss your concerns with parents.

• **formulate your Individual Education Plan and share it with parents and the SENCO.**

Practical task

Individual education planning for special educational needs

By now you should be more familiar with:

- *the nature of the difficulty;*
- *some possible targets for learning.*

You can use this knowledge to help you clarify:

- *some activities and resources;*
- *a timescale for the learning.*

In your time in school, you will have probably identified children with special educational needs. Next time you are in a classroom setting, use the ideas above to provide an assessment and a plan of action for a particular child. Observe the child for about 30 minutes and take notes. (This is potentially difficult in an under-fives environment but will be well worth your while!)

First note down what you already know about the child's learning. Then describe and log what happens and what the child does over an observed session. Simply describe the child's functioning in this environment. Try not to infer anything. Note any work outcomes. Then add in any comments about the child's work in previous sessions. After school, take this away and try to identify any particular strengths and difficulties you have noticed in your school file. List your findings.

Focus on the four headings (the bullet points above) and write a short plan for your child. Try to incorporate this into your support. After a little while, evaluate its effectiveness. Keep monitoring and recording the child's development from time to time.

If you follow this approach, you should, like Dave at the beginning of this chapter, begin to achieve some success. Once you have done this a few times, you will find the construction of an Individual Education Plan much easier.

Individual education planning

The Individual Education Plan (IEP) illustrates, at a very simple level, the process of recording, monitoring and targeting action over a set period. The school will have provided further working notes outside this IEP, and provision will be monitored through the class teacher's (and possibly the support's) working records. Note the decision to discuss the long-term issue of Mary's overall difficulty with her development of literacy skills with the support agencies. At this point, the *School Action Plus* stage would come into force. However, notice that the class teacher and support are providing support in specific aspects of literacy development from the outset of the plan. The later support from the literacy team may come in the form of advice, provision of specific resources, or actual teaching.

An IEP should always provide *real help* for the child and should be closely monitored by the SENCO and class teacher, and reviewed with the parents to an agreed schedule. You may use your own style for constructing and recording the plan. Often a school will have its own in-house format.

When you construct an IEP, keep the following in mind:

- **the activities;**
- **the resources;**
- **the targets;**
- **the general workability for the teacher;**
- **the involvement of parents;**
- **the timescale;**
- **the value to the child.**

Remember that the plan should be explicit in its targets and the activities should be workable and sustainable. Before you finish reading this chapter, stop for a few moments to consider why you think the plan in Figure 12.2 could provide Mary with some real help.

Providing real help has been the focus of this chapter. You may now feel a little more confident in providing it.

Moving forward

The way forward in managing special educational needs in the classroom is possibly to remember that this is not a hundred-metre dash. It's fine to try and fail occasionally. We encourage our children to make decisions for themselves and to take calculated risks within a secure environment. The same applies to us. Having said that, we need to accept that it's a hurdle race and that knocks on the shins are part of the game. Perhaps this chapter will help to lower the hurdles a little.

Further reading

Roffey, S. (1999) *Special Needs in the Early Years: Collaboration, Communication and Co-ordination*. London: David Fulton. A thorough and readable review of the processes in which teachers, other professionals and parents must collaborate to secure effective support for young children with SEN.

Stobbs, P., Mackey, T., Norwich, B., Peacey, N. and Stephenson, P. (1995) *Schools SEN Policies Pack*. London: National Children's Bureau. Some excellent examples of individual education planning.

Widlake, P. (ed.) (1996) *The Good Practice Guide to Special Educational Needs*. Birmingham: Questions Publishing. A comprehensive guide to both general principles and strategies for all areas of the curriculum.

ELECTRONIC RESOURCES

www.dfes.gov.uk/sen/

This is the DfES special educational needs website. It includes links to the Code of Practice, Good Practice Guidance and further information for parents, teachers, SENCOs and LEAs.

Special Educational Needs Record

1 Personal information

Name of child:	Mary H
Date of birth:	02.07.95
Parent/carer:	Ms N
Class/form:	Y2

2 Other information

Health:	Dr X
EWO:	Mrs B
Social services	
School support team:	Mrs S

Area of concern	Date identified	Date resolved
Failure to eat and drink in school	October 1999	Late October 1999
No speech to adults or children on school premises	October 1999	November 1999
Not talking. Unable to assess language skills	October 1999	See 10.01.2000 Review Comment overleaf
Social isolation from other children	January 2000	See 10.01.2000 Review Comment overleaf
Sequencing skills	July 2000	See 10.01.2000 Review Comment overleaf
Development of early literacy	January 2000	Review May 2000

This can be added to at any stage. When a concern is identified, it should be noted and added to this record. The dates resolved should also be noted when action is successful.

Special Educational Needs Record

Name of student:	Mary
Date of birth:	02.07.95
Class/form:	Y2
Teacher responsible:	Mrs T
Date this plan started:	October 1999
Parental contact:	Mrs B (October 25 1999 – see file)

Targets Mary will be able to:	Action and provision	Outcome Date of review: 10.01.2000
Make a small contribution to small group discussion by November 1999.	Supported small-group sessions three times a week. Work linked to on-going topic work and language activities. Open-ended questions to promote extended responses.	Beginning to respond so progress has been made. Response is variable – more receptive than expressive, but answers the support teacher on some occasions. Beginning to relate to one child more than the others.
Read 25 words by sight, linking it with Oxford Reading Tree stage 2 reading scheme by December 1999.	Individual work with assistant/parent (ten minutes of four sessions per week) using modified teaching approach.	Mary partially achieved this by demonstrating an ability to read all words on some occasions, although she experienced difficulty with memory and recall, constantly needing reinforcement and support.
Sequence in order a series of four pictures and then tell the story in her own words by December 1999.	Picture story cards, sequencing two puzzles, comic strips, etc. Initially, twice per week out of class with assistant. Follow up in class.	Mary could order the sequence early (by early November). However, it is still difficult to draw a response from her in telling the story. Will point to appropriate picture while assistant recounts story. Review again March 2000.
Construct and write an ordered short sentence independently by December 1999.	Use of Breakthrough approach. Construct/read to adults/record sentence. Complete in class during writing activity time.	Some success working from own word bank constructed in Breakthrough. Vocabulary limited to 30 words. Review again May 2000.
External agency/school support team.	Contact County Literacy Support Team under School Action Plus. Discuss and take advice.	Literacy Support Team contacted. See Profile for detailed notes of assessment and advised provision. Review again May 2000.

Figure 12.2 Example of an IEP

By the end of the chapter you should:

- *have considered the pastoral needs of all children;*
- *be aware of the connection between effective teaching and interaction and a secure learning environment;*
- *be aware of the need to provide additional support for some pupils and to consider practical ways in which this can be provided;*
- *be aware of the importance of responding to individual social, emotional and academic needs;*
- *be aware of the need for effective liaison between all those involved with the child;*
- *have a positive and confident approach to diversity in the classroom, resulting in high expectations and the creation of an effective and inclusive learning environment for all children;*
- *have an understanding of the legal framework of care for children.*

This chapter addresses the following Professional Standards for QTS:

 1.4, 1.6, 3.1.2, 3.2.4, 3.3.6, 3.3.9

(The Standards are reproduced in full at the back of this book.)

This chapter considers the needs of all children as they enter and progress through school and reflects issues at government, whole-school and classroom level. The concept of pastoral care will be interpreted holistically, and policy into practice examined in connection with ethos, interaction and communication between all members of the school community. Emphasis will be placed on the importance of a rigorous approach to pedagogy and connections made between effective, motivating teaching and the reduction of frustration, anxiety and potential bullying. Detailed consideration will be given to the role of the class teacher in creating a safe and supportive environment in which pupils can thrive socially, emotionally and academically. Where appropriate, reference will be made to legal implications for the teacher in ensuring child protection. The chapter will include a range of practical ways to promote effective observation and intervention.

Needs of all children

All of us have basic needs regardless of our age. We need to feel that we belong, are safe and secure and our differences and contributions are valued by those around us. When these needs are met we are able to thrive and develop, both physically and emotionally. We feel able to explore, discover and take risks, in the knowledge that our efforts will be taken seriously and valued. In school, when children are away from the families that love them, this need to feel comfortable is essential if learning is to take place. It is also realistic to acknowledge that for a minority of children early childhood may have been a troubled experience. Sadly for some of these children it has been traumatic. For them it is vital that school provides a safe haven. Maslow (1968) presented these needs in the form of a pyramid which demonstrated that high self esteem is gained when these basic needs are met. Learning is maximised when self esteem is high and children feel confident. This philosophy influences many school policies and underpins most teachers' interaction with children.

Social and emotional support

Over recent years there has been an increasing awareness of the role of emotions in people's lives. Daniel Goleman's (1996) book on emotional intelligence has been a best-seller! We can all recall being unable to complete a task or learn a new concept, not because we do not have the capacity to achieve the learning but because we were not sufficiently engaged with the process. This engagement can be prevented for a number of reasons, and again we refer to Maslow and his 'hierarchy of needs'.

Jenny Mosley in her book *Turn Your School Around* (1993) fully explores questions around children's needs under the headings provided by Maslow. She suggests we need to ask if the children are hungry, cold, or lack a comfortable home or school. Do children feel safe, physically and emotionally in their environment? Do children have a sense of belonging, to a family, class, school, community? Finally have they had opportunities to experience success, to be valued and encouraged in order raise their self esteem? Maslow argues that until this happens people will not reach 'self actualisation' and become the unique individual of which we are all capable.

In school the 'caring' curriculum is often referred to as the 'pastoral' curriculum. Schools that feel strongly that these issues have a direct impact on learning will ensure that there is a whole school approach to caring for every person within it. This will manifest itself in many ways. You might reflect upon some of the schools in which you have been taught or placed for a teaching practice. To what extent do you think the school ethos has been one of mutual respect, care and support for the all of the children, regardless of individual differences, strengths and weaknesses? Consider what it is about the school which might convince the children that they are respected, valued, cared for and catered for in terms of their learning needs.

The class teacher: attitude, communication and empathy

One of the most powerful indicators of a school that respects individuals is the attitude of adults. For children in school the most significant adult is their class teacher. A negative, moody, inconsistent and uninterested teacher can diminish the curiosity and attention of the children. An atmosphere of fear is created where risk taking is minimised, individuality is depressed and creativity is stagnant. However, an alert, welcoming, open-minded teacher ensures each child is able to approach each new learning opportunity with an expectancy of success and confidence in all outcomes being valued. There is no failure in such a classroom; only feedback providing information which can be utilised in adjusting strategies and activities to ensure future success.

The manner in which the teacher communicates provides evidence of how the children are perceived. Interaction which is consistent, measured and respectful of children gives a sense of calm, organisation and purpose. Taking time to talk and get to know all the individuals, their family connections and current interests is important. This positive interaction between teacher and child needs to be modelled by all members of the school, including catering and secretarial staff and midday supervisors. This indicates that the environment is safe, comfortable and that there is a community to which all belong.

Having created this emotionally stable learning environment, we must be aware that for many children this is the most secure and constant aspect of their lives. For children whose basic needs are not met at home, it is often difficult to engage with school and the processes of learning. The emotions which are the outcome of fear and anger often spill into the school environment as it is a safe place to express the real self. These emotions can flood the thinking processes and distract children from what is happening in the classroom. It seems for some their whole being is angry, frightened, withdrawn and hostile. These children are disturbed as a result of their life experiences and it is a challenge for us as teachers to work with them and keep them within the school. All too often this disruptive behaviour leads to exclusion.

The ability to see the world from the perspective of another enables us to create a climate which reflects mutual respect. 'When teachers are empathically understanding, their students tend to like each other better. In an understanding classroom climate, every student tends to feel liked by all the others, has a more positive attitude towards self, and a positive attitude towards school. This ripple aspect of the teacher's attitude is provocative and significant.' (Schmuck in Rogers 1983, p. 128) Sadly, all too often adult learners can recall being intimidated and confused in the classroom, resulting in a detachment from some aspects of learning and even from school itself, which may have an impact for life.

Whole-school responses to meet the needs of all children

Induction into school

The first encounter with school is a vital time for the young child and his or her family. Successful induction is essential to effective pastoral care. School can be a very strange experience for a young child. For example, the child may be unfamiliar with:

- **separation from parents;**
- **size of the rooms;**
- **noise level;**
- **unfamiliar resources;**
- **numbers of unknown children;**

- toilet facilities;
- vastness of the playground.

The language of school is a critical factor in successful induction for many children. The language structures and style of interaction may confuse and alienate some children, leading to lowered expectations from teachers. Tizard and Hughes (1984, p. 210) have produced powerful evidence to show that the verbal behaviour of young children can be very different at home and at school. Some children are puzzled by the teachers' use of language, in particular 'teacherly questions' to assess understanding. These children all too quickly become the passive recipients of language, the answerers of organisational and procedural questions and not the askers of questions rooted in curiosity.

In order to ensure a positive start to schooling, nursery and primary schools establish induction programmes which value parents and children and prepare thoughtfully and sensitively for the transition ahead. This policy ensures children, parents and carers feel welcome and secure.

Maintaining a positive whole-school ethos

The positive attitude of the teacher is crucial for all children and for those who find learning difficult it is even more significant. For these children, the inability to achieve in areas of the curriculum can lead to withdrawal or hostility as they come to terms with their perceived limitations. They become aware of their difference from other children in their class, they can become fearful of failure, ashamed of not to being able to meet the expectations of others and angry that for them school may not be a happy place to be. It is the teacher's responsibility to ensure that all children feel successful and are not vulnerable to the domination of others resulting in bullying. A positive valuing attitude, coupled with careful assessment and planning can ensure that learning does in fact take place, albeit in small, managed, steps.

Practical task

To promote self-esteem and children's involvement in their own learning, create an opportunity for you to talk to children about their perceptions of their strengths. This can be done in small group work, in circle time or on an individual basis.

Special needs of some children

We need to recognise that some children may require additional support in order to meet a range of individual needs. Pastoral care should not simply relate to children's affective/emotional needs. If we are to provide a supportive learning environment we need to consider how we apply an empathetic approach to practicalities of meeting children's academic needs. Children with special educational needs will benefit from this fusion of a sensitive and supportive approach and a rigorous attention to detail when planning, implementing activities and interacting with individuals and the whole class. It is vital that this approach allows children to gain autonomy and respect. There is an inherent danger that an ineffective approach may create a climate of dependency or insecurity.

Even within a positive classroom climate some children will find it difficult to meet the social and academic demands. For the child and the teacher this can feel challenging, frustrating and confusing. Both can often sense that progress is not being made. In the past this may have resulted in the child being excluded from the curriculum or even the mainstream school. Two major Education Acts radically changed thinking and enhanced the possibility of a positive response to diverse needs. The 1988 Education Reform Act ensured that all children have the legal right to a broad and balanced curriculum including the National Curriculum.

> Aim 1: The school curriculum should aim to provide opportunities for all pupils to learn and achieve.
>
> (DfEE/QCA 1999, p. 11)

The revised National Curriculum (DfEE/QCA pp. 30–37) provides schools with a set of principles relating to inclusion in order to ensure that all pupils have access to effective learning opportunities. The three main principles for inclusion relate to setting suitable learning challenges, providing an effective reponse to diverse learning needs, and overcoming barriers to learning and assessment for individuals and groups.

As you will have noted from the previous chapter, the 1981 Education Act changed the focus from exclusion to inclusion and identified a continuum of needs. Legal recognition was given to the fact that some children would require extra provision to meet their 'Special Educational Needs'. These needs should not be considered simply in terms of what 'difficulty' a child might have, but in terms of the level and type of support required to enable maximum successful access to the curriculum and the classroom for the child and those with whom s/he works. Special needs may only influence certain aspects of a child's life in the classroom and may be transitory. They may not always be obvious and will be heavily influenced by the context in which the child operates, the nature of the learning environment and the approach of the teacher.

Additional support

The provision of additional support will play a major role in diminishing anxiety and frustration for some children. The source of a great deal of disruptive behaviour may often be traced to fear of failure: many children would rather opt out, refuse to participate or become aggressive, rather than to admit that they are unable to understand the demands of a task. Appropriate action usually promotes a positive learning environment for the whole class. Effective support for children with special educational needs is likely to lead to effective provision for all children.

Observation: the first step towards the provision of positive support

To provide effective additional support, ensure that children are identified and appropriate intervention takes places. Observation of children in the process of learning and interacting in the classroom gives you the opportunity to assess aspects of learning and behaviour for all children and to identify those who may need extra help and support. Working within the normal routines of planning, evaluation and assessment will help you to identify the nature of a difficulty and ask yourself questions about the form of effective intervention.

The first step is close, focused observation which reflects an open minded approach. Base your conclusion on evidence, not assumption.

Observation is a significant aspect of the process of identifying and responding to individual needs. Unstructured approaches may result in oversimplification of the process and an inaccurate and unhelpful picture of the child's needs. It is dangerously easy to adopt a deficit-based approach, in which the focus of the observation is restricted to all the aspects of classroom life which the child finds difficult. This produces limited information and a negative starting point for intervention, 'find out what the child can't do and give him lots more of it'. It is obviously important to identify areas of difficulty, but these should be counterbalanced by the assessment of the child's strengths and interests.

Special educational needs are not static, but context-specific. The interaction between the child, the teacher and the learning environment should be the focus of the observation. The child may struggle in one aspect of the curriculum, tending to be more disruptive in certain situations. It is important to adopt this holistic approach in order to obtain realistic and useful information.

Suggested areas for observation

- **What are the strengths of the child?**
- **What does the child perceive to be his/her strengths?**
- **How do other children respond to the child?**
- **What social aspects of classroom life present difficulties for the child and for those with whom s/he works?**
- **What aspects of the curriculum present the child with difficulties?**
- **What aspects of teaching and classroom management may result in difficulties for the child? Timing, whole class work, group work, communication?**
- **What physical aspects of the classroom present difficulties?**

It may be useful to focus on the response of the child when s/he struggles with the learning environment, identifying the overt response and the underlying trigger for the problem.

- **How does the child respond when s/he experiences problems?**
  - **By making demands on the teacher, according to a rule?**
  - **By attention-seeking behaviour to gain attention from the teacher?**
  - **By making demands on the teacher, not according to a rule?**
  - **By seeking assistance from other children?**
  - **By distracting other children?**
  - **By work refusal?**
  - **By adopting work avoidance strategies?**

The strategies children employ to avoid work are varied. They may choose to be openly confrontational. They may seek to distract all the children in a group, in order to ensure that no one succeeds and therefore no one child is seen to fail. The uncertainty which this engenders creates a lack of security which can be sensed by the children. In the extreme some children may respond to this by seeking to take control themselves and then to intimidate successful learners. This amounts to bullying which may begin in this specific classroom based situation but spill out into other aspects of school life.

It is also likely that you will encounter children who avoid work by adopting a helpful and supportive role in the classroom: these children are always willing to volunteer to help. The teacher may view this very positively, but the children may use this strategy, consciously or unconsciously, to avoid tasks which they consider to be difficult or worrying. Children are frequently more comfortable opting out, than putting themselves at risk of failure. Work avoidance represents a major source of stress in the classroom for all participants. Addressing this effectively and positively is an essential step towards meeting the pastoral needs of all children.

Observe the child in a range of contexts

Effective observation must be manageable, useful and provide a picture of the child in a range of situations, reflecting all areas of development, social, intellectual, physical and creative. You may wish to observe the child in whole class settings, e.g. literacy and numeracy hour, or in group or individual work.

Involve the child

Children may feel excluded from the process of assessment and identification of needs. In fact they have a great deal to contribute, they have first-hand experience of the situation and their own interpretation of events in the classroom. It is essential that you encourage children to enter into discussion with you, to set targets, to recognise strengths, to express anxieties and where appropriate, to realise the impact of their behaviour on their peers.

Involve the parents

It is essential to ensure parental involvement, encouraging them to identify the child's strengths and difficulties, both at home and school. This rapport with the parents establishes a positive working relationship in the interests of the child and maintains dialogue while needs are identified and interventions are planned. A collaborative approach is much more likely to promote learning, success and a happy child.

Practical task

Carry out a structured observation using the above suggested areas as a focus. Have you observed and recorded an equal number of strengths and weaknesses? What is your evidence for these observations?

What form might the support take?

Children may require support in the following areas if they are to gain access to the curriculum and to wider aspects of classroom life:

1. Responding to spoken language.

2. Responding to written language.

3. Gaining and retaining knowledge and skills.

4. Meeting the organisational demands of the classroom.

5. Meeting the social demands of the classroom.

Responding to spoken language

The most obvious response to the need to differentiate may be considered to relate to the modification of activities, the type of resources and to the adaptation of written work. However, often the most relevant starting point is the need for teachers to be aware of the complexity of the demands of their communication for some children and to adapt their spoken language accordingly. Children who experience difficulty in processing spoken language may be bewildered by the length of sentences, the complexity of the syntax used and the number of commands given in a rapid sequence. They may well be confused by the demands of technical vocabulary in the classroom, a demand that is growing as new initiatives are implemented in education, e.g. the National Literacy Strategy and the National Numeracy Strategy. Children experiencing hearing loss may find communication in the classroom demanding and tiring, leading to possible isolation and underachievement. It is important that you are aware of the significance of spoken language in promoting (or restricting) success for many children.

Clear communication is also a significant factor in the establishment of a positive classroom ethos. It is easy to confuse children by the volume or complexity of your language and then to apply value judgements to the children who are unable to respond to instructions, questions or advice. A child who has not understood may behave in a way which frustrates self, peers and, of course, you. The child may ask repeatedly for confirmation, may disrupt peers or may opt out of the task and the difficult situation. It is very easy to assume the child is attention seeking, lazy, uncooperative or stubborn, when in fact the underlying cause of the problem is unclear communication. The following suggestions do not provide an exhaustive list, but they may be a useful starting point for effective interaction in the classroom.

- **Be aware of the length of your utterances: are there times when it would be appropriate to reduce this? It is equally important to present children with good models of spoken language.**
- **Be aware of the complexity of your syntax, e.g. the use of the passive tense can be very confusing.**
- **Be aware of the demands of the vocabulary and the need for explanation.**
- **Be aware of the difference that making eye contact with some children can make in facilitating understanding.**
- **Be aware of the pace of your spoken language, especially in questioning. It is all too easy to 'fire' questions at children without allowing sufficient time to interpret the question or to respond effectively. This can lead to anxiety and frustration and responses which do not represent the child's understanding.**
- **Be willing to evaluate the effectiveness of your use of language.**

Responding to written language

Differentiation has been discussed in detail in an earlier chapter of this book. However, the following brief points may prove useful in establishing a positive learning environment.

 See Chapter 3 on p. 33 for more information on differentiation.

- Many children who struggle with written language need strategies to help the written word become more accessible. Colour coding of words, parts of speech or common spelling patterns, can help to reinforce the visual patterns which are an important aspect of reading.
- When preparing written materials, remember that some children may be daunted by the amount of writing. Attention to layout, avoiding dense passages of text, can prompt a much more positive response and more effective participation.
- Do children have the skills to identify key words to help make the text more accessible?
- Think creatively about recording; whilst it is clearly necessary to develop skills in writing, are there times when it is appropriate for children to present information in other ways, graphs, diagrams, pictures?
- Think about the self-esteem of the learner. Is it necessary for differentiated resources to look markedly different?

The factors outlined above are only a small part of successful differentiation. However, attention to these aspects of written communication may reduce the fear of failure, reduce tension and promote a more positive approach to learning.

Practical task

When planning your lessons consider the instructions which you plan to give to children verbally or in written form. Focus on two examples of these and analyse your use of language in terms of the complexity of syntax, vocabulary and the volume of information. Will this prevent some children from engaging in the activity?

Gaining and retaining knowledge and skills

Although this aspect of learning is addressed in an earlier chapter it has also been emphasised throughout this chapter that uncertainty about the likelihood of success in learning can result in tension and possible aggression. This obviously has an adverse effect on all those in the classroom. Some children are very aware of the fact that they have difficulty in gaining and retaining knowledge. This is exemplified by observation of a child with special educational needs who was working with a group of children in a mainstream class, she picked up her pencil at the start of a task, looked at it and remarked accusingly 'this pencil makes it come out wrong every time'. This anxiety prompts the child to anticipate failure and can result in a downward spiral, in which the child does not expect to achieve success, senses possible failure, fails and brings a sense

 See Chapters 7 and 9 for more information on gaining and reatining knowledge and skills.

of resignation to failure to any new task. If we are not careful, we as teachers can contribute to this process by low expectations. The following observations may help to combat difficulties in this area.

- **Provide the child with effective strategies to learn, based on the child's learning. You may wish to find out more about this by reading work by Alistair Smith on accelerated learning (1998).**
- **Recognise the need for consolidation activities in a range of contexts.**
- **Take the stress out of the situation by encouraging the child to identify strengths and recognise his/her interests in other areas.**
- **Set realistic and attainable goals, involving the child in the process.**
- **Positively interpret the errors which children make, using this as a way of gaining insight into their thinking and the opportunity to identify the strategies which the child uses. Child based strategies may be used consistently by the learner and may lead to success or error. The identification of inappropriate strategies may foster success and reduce frustration. It is essential to observe the child in the process of learning and to talk to the child, in order to identify the strategies which are being used.**

Meeting the social demands of the classroom

This can be the most challenging aspect of the inclusive classroom for you, for the child, his/her peers and other adults in the classroom. Social interaction is complex, dynamic and situation specific. It is not our intention to provide simplistic solutions for every occasion and every context. However, an awareness of some of the underlying tensions and a consideration of possible strategies may an informed starting point.

Acknowledge the complexity of classroom life

Interaction in the classroom is influenced by a range of factors, many of which are beyond your immediate control:

- **the requirements of the curriculum;**
- **the organisational demands of the whole school;**
- **whole school ethos and expectations;**
- **the previous experience of the children.**

Watkins and Wagner observe that classrooms are busy, public places and that classroom events are multidimensional (Watkins and Wagner 1988, p. 66). It is important to acknowledge the influence of these factors if you are to analyse events in the classroom and to respond effectively and consistently.

Carry out an audit to analyse the current situation

The ethos in the classroom has a powerful effect on all those who work in it. As teachers we wish to create a positive and supportive learning environment promoting confidence and enjoyment. Despite our best efforts it is all too easy to feel that this is under attack from all sides! A useful starting point may be carrying out an audit to ascertain the causes of frustration, irritation and disruption. Responses to the Elton Report on Discipline in Schools (DES 1989) revealed that the majority of teachers regarded the cumulative effect of a series of minor disturbances to be the major cause of disruption in the classroom. Ninety-seven per cent of secondary teachers reported that their lessons were disrupted by pupils calling out, distracting others, or chattering at least once a week. Eighty-seven per cent of teachers cited children's work avoidance strategies as a significant cause of disruption in the classroom. Carrying out an audit into the demands which children make on your time and your response to these demands may produce valuable information. This may reveal issues related to organisation, use of time, communication and expectation which could be addressed in order to enhance the learning environment.

Liaise effectively with other adults in the classroom

The presence of other adults in the classroom seems to offer an instant solution to many difficulties. However, benefits do not automatically result from an increase in numbers of support staff. Evidence from the Alexander Report (1991) revealed that in some classrooms which were observed, children actually spent less time on task in situations where there were three adults to support learning. (I adult 59% on task, 2 adults 67 % on task, 3 adults 61% on task). This is should *not* be taken as an indication that reduced staffing is desirable, it should indicate that there is a need for the following factors to be taken into account if children are to receive maximum benefit from the presence of several adults:

- **effective planning, which reflects all those involved in supporting learning;**
- **clear communication;**
- **clear assessment and the opportunity for all those involved to participate in the process of assessment;**
- **a shared understanding of the implications of organisational factors, timing, management, classroom routines, the availability of resources.**

Attention to these factors will result in a positive working relationship in which all those supporting learning feel valued and are able to function effectively. This, in turn, reduces the opportunity for children to engage in a range of work avoidance strategies by 'playing off factions'. Shared expectations and understandings will result in a supportive learning environment.

Social interaction between children

This is fostered within the positive classroom climate that has been promoted in this chapter. Teachers can model respectful dialogue and ensure that inappropriate talk is discouraged through recognising the effect upon others. There may be a tendency for some children to dominate others, resulting in bullying which is insidious and needs to be eliminated. It is easy to adopt a heavy-handed approach to bullying which can exacerbate the problem. You need to be able to observe and analyse the triggers of bullying behaviour and be able to listen to the victim, the bully and their parents. It is important to remember that no happy or confident child engages in bullying tactics,

 See p. 178 in Chapter 14 for a definition of bullying.

nor falls foul of a bully. Clearly, bullying must not be tolerated; therefore teachers need to recognise the complexity of the situation in order to make an informed and effective response. Schools adopt a whole school approach designed to minimise bullying. It is important for individual teachers to identify possible contributory factors relating to elements of their own teaching; including assessment, preparation, content, activities and evaluation. Many of these factors have been raised in this chapter. Meeting children's pastoral needs is dependent on effective teaching.

Exploring serious issues which may concern children

You will now be familiar with the Code of Practice (DfES, 2001) which stresses the importance of children expressing their opinion on their provision. The Children Act of 1989, implemented in 1991, gave legal recognition to the importance of the 'ascertainable wishes and feelings of the child' (Section 1(3) The Children Act 1989). This Act brought together all aspects of child health, welfare and protection and set out the legal framework for a multi agency approach to these issues. Parents and children were given new rights. Teachers in daily contact with children need to be aware of the legal position. This Act identifies four categories of abuse:

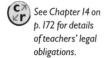 *See Chapter 14 on p. 172 for details of teachers' legal obligations.*

- **neglect resulting in failure to thrive;**
- **physical abuse including non-accidental injury;**
- **sexual abuse;**
- **emotional abuse, severe or persistent emotional ill treatment or rejection, resulting in adverse effects on behaviour and emotional development.**

As a result of this Act every school has a policy setting out the school's approach to Child Protection issues. When you go into a school it is essential that you become familiar with this policy and identify the 'designated' member of the teaching staff to whom you would refer any serious concerns.

It is important to remember that the majority of children are well cared for and protected. It is equally important to maintain vigilance through careful observation. You need to establish a rapport with children in by creating a supportive ethos enabling them to express their wishes and feelings. Also, individual children should feel able to disclose more sensitive information about their lives which may include abuse. This may be taking place in school also in the form of bullying. Here are some practical suggestions for allowing this process to occur:

- **use of circle time to build up a climate of trust in which sensitive issues could be explored;**
- **use of circle time to build up self esteem encouraging children to recognize their own strengths and the those of their peers;**
- **use of circle time to celebrate success in the classroom;**
- **use of circle time to discuss issues such as work avoidance and identify possible causes and solutions;**
- **use of circle time to discuss individual likes, dislikes and interests;**

- use of circle time to acknowledge the adverse affect of the behaviour of some children on the class as a whole.

Summary

Numerous issues relating to pastoral care have been raised within this chapter. Emphasis has been given to the importance of a whole school approach, ensuring children's legal rights are protected. The concept of partnership between all those involved in the life and work of the school has been stressed throughout. It has been our intention to acknowledge the importance of a policy reflecting clear principles and a shared philosophy which must be translated into action to influence all aspects of school life. Finally, a central theme of the chapter has been the role of the teacher in promoting a safe and welcoming learning environment. Good teaching is an essential aspect of the process of meeting pastoral needs.

Further reading

Alexander, R. J. (1991) *Primary Education in Leeds: Report from the Primary Needs Independent Evaluation*. University of Leeds School of Education.

Farrell, M. (1998) *The Special Needs Handbook*. London: David Fulton. A useful and comprehensive overview which would provide a valuable source of reference for all matters relating to special educational needs. It also provides useful addresses and sources of further support.

Fisher, J. (1996) *Starting from the Child*. Buckingham: Open University Press. This book provides a readable introduction to several of the aspects which are raised within this chapter. The starting point of this book is the recognition of the strengths of young children and an analysis of the ways in which class teachers can recognise these strengths, respond to them and take the learning forward. The book is well structured and set firmly in the context of the classroom.

Griffiths, M. and Davies, C. (1995) *In Fairness to Children*. London: David Fulton. The authors provide more detailed coverage of issues relating to pastoral care which ensure that children operate in a safe, secure and supportive environment. The importance of home, school and community links is recognised.

Mosley, J. (1993) *Turn Your School Around*. Wisbech: LDA. There are several references to circle time in this book. Mosley provides a model for whole-school development and for classroom practice. There is a range of materials to develop understanding and promote self-esteem.

By the end of the chapter you should:

- have considered some of the legal implications of becoming a teacher in England and Wales;
- understand the main features of the legal framework within which the teaching profession is regulated;
- be aware of a teacher's contractual obligations and rights as an employee;
- be aware of a teacher's statutory responsibilities in relation to pupils within and without the classroom;
- be familiar with the regulations which govern a teacher's actions in disciplining children, including the specific directives on the physical restraint of pupils;
- understand the role and purposes of school governing bodies.

This chapter addresses the following Standards for the award of QTS:

 1.8

(The Standards are reproduced in full at the back of this book.)

This chapter considers the individual teacher's statutory responsibilities and legal liabilities when working within state schools in England and Wales. These include: teachers' general contractual commitments; their common law duty to ensure that pupils are healthy and safe and their responsibility for promoting children's welfare; their obligations with regard to race relations and gender discrimination; and the rules which govern discipline and the physical restraint of pupils. You should note that whilst all schools have to abide by general UK legislation (e.g. employment and antidiscrimination laws) many of the details outlined apply to 'maintained schools' (i.e. state funded) in England and, sometimes with minor variations, in Wales. Scotland's and Northern Ireland's education systems are administered separately; independent (private) schools set their own pay and conditions. For fear of overexciting you, this chapter will not deal with pay scales.

A working knowledge

The standards for attaining QTS make it clear that you 'are not expected to have a detailed knowledge of the whole legal framework' but that you do need to be aware of your rights and responsibilities as a teacher. It is important that that you have an understanding of the major legislation and administrative regulations which apply to teachers in schools. Though some of this may seem rather remote at the beginning of your training, it is important that from the outset of working in school you understand some of the requirements made of teachers.

Once you accept appointment, signing your contract implies acceptance of roles and responsibilities which are framed by law. Many of the obligations and entitlements which will apply to you are rooted in general legislation which applies to all employees in the United Kingdom; others are specific to teachers. Not being familiar with laws and regulations will not excuse you from observing them: whilst you cannot hope to master *all* the intricacies of the rules and regulations which apply to schools, it is clearly important to know in broad terms just what you will be taking on in terms of responsibilities and obligations when you become a Newly Qualified Teacher. Similarly, though you do not need to know all the details of way schools are governed, it is important to understand the role of the governing body and its relationship to you as a teacher.

Teachers – a regulated profession

As you are doubtless only too aware, in order to become a fully qualified teacher you have to achieve Qualified Teacher Status and satisfactorily complete your Induction Year. But even when this has been achieved, it is important to recognise that your right to be a teacher is a conditional one: *your* right to practise as a teacher can be withdrawn. These are not matters upon which we shall dwell in this book, but you should never lose sight of the fact that teaching is quite properly a regulated profession.

The Standards for achieving QTS in England (1.1 – 1.8) make it clear that you have to 'understand and uphold the code of General Teaching Council for England'. Since September 2000 a General Teaching Council has been established in England (GTCE), and in Wales (GTCW); Scotland has had one since 1965. When you take a post as a teacher in a state school you are required to be a registered member of the relevant GTC. Though the teaching councils have an important new role in professional registration and discipline, you will nevertheless be joining a profession that is largely regulated by government: the key powers over entry, pay and conditions remain with the Secretary of State. There are laws and regulations setting out who may be a teacher in a school maintained by the state and what such teachers *must*, *may* and *may not* do. Also – as will become of increasing interest to you – there are laws and regulations that determine just how much you will be paid for your labours.

Being on the Sex Offenders' Register and certain other serious criminal convictions mean being debarred from teaching. Teachers are exempted from the 'spent convictions' provisions of the Rehabilitation of Offenders Act 1974. A check through the Criminal Records Bureau requiring 'enhanced disclosure' may be requested when you take up a new appointment with a different employer, have a break in service of three months or more, or if the school or LEA has 'grounds for concern' about your 'suitability to work with children' (DfES 2002 para 38). The CRB searches information held on the Police National Computer, the Department of Health's Protection of Children Act List, and DfES's infamous 'List 99' which identifies teachers deemed unsuitable to work in schools either for particular reasons of misconduct or on certain medical grounds. Though we trust *you* will never need these, you do have some rights of appeal and errors are not unknown.

The GTC (England) has issued a Code of Professional Values and Practice for Teachers (GTCE 2002); the GTC (Wales) has published its Professional Code for Teachers (GTCW 2002). At the moment these are not the legal basis for professional discipline, but are nevertheless a guide to what is expected of teachers. As with any employee, in addition to serious criminal or professional misdemeanours, proven professional incompetence or incapacity to fulfil your contractual obligations can result in your dismissal. All governing bodies are required to have 'capability procedures'. Through the Disciplinary Functions Regulations, the General Teaching Councils have been given the powers to investigate professional conduct and professional competence and can terminate a teacher's registration in ways similar to other registered professions. As a job applicant, employee or GTC registrant you are of course protected by employment legislation, the Race Relations Act 1976, the Sex Discrimination Act 1975, the Disability Discrimination Act 1995 and subsequent additions and amendments to them.

Teachers' conditions of employment

Teachers' contracts

If you become a teacher in a state maintained school in England and Wales your professional duties and the financial structure which governs the rewards you can expect for your work rest upon the School Teachers' Pay and Conditions Act (1991). This Act allows for the operating details to be set out in the *School Teachers' Pay and Conditions Document* (STPCD). This document (traditionally known as the *Blue Book*) changes annually, following the government's response to the report of the School Teachers' Review Body (STRB). An explanatory circular, *School Teachers' Pay and Conditions of Employment: Guidance,* accompanies the formal document to explain its application. Your contract of employment will apply to the version then current; it implies acceptance of subsequent versions as pay scales are adjusted and new contractual requirements are introduced.

In the STPCD and Guidance there are numerous references to 'relevant bodies' rather than 'employers'. This terminology is necessary because of some of the quirks of teachers' employment arrangements. If you work in a nursery or very small school without a 'delegated budget', or as an 'unattached teacher' for a central service, then the LEA is the 'relevant body' as well as your employer. However, in almost all maintained schools the governors will be the 'relevant body' for appointing you and determining your exact salary, but whether they or the LEA are your contractual employer depends upon the formal legal status of the school.

There are four categories of maintained schools in England, which may have some influence upon your contractual conditions:

- **Community schools (formerly known as 'county schools'): the LEA is the employer.**
- **Voluntary Controlled (usually Church of England, though there are some Methodist VC schools and some without religious affiliation): the LEA is the employer, but the governing body determines worship; it may make some conditions of appointment related to the school's religious ethos.**
- **Voluntary Aided (particularly Roman Catholic schools, but also some Anglican, Jewish and Muslim schools): the governing body is the employer, it determines**

religious instruction and may make some associated conditions of employment including religious commitment.
- **Foundation (a relatively small number, largely former Grant Maintained schools): the governing body is the contractual employer.**

Contracts of employment may be permanent, fixed term, or temporary. The contract of employment is a formal document but the contract to which you work also includes your job description and school policy documents. As a teacher you should expect a clear job description which can subsequently be changed through negotiation. Recent regulations and guidance mean that as a newly qualified teacher you should have an appropriately tailored job description and heads are to ensure this does 'not make unreasonable demands' (DfES 2002b para 109).

What do the 'conditions of service' demand of teachers?

Teachers' formal 'conditions of employment' are set out at the back of the *School Teachers' Pay and Conditions Document* (DfES 2002). There are some very particular conditions which apply only to headteachers, conditions which apply to all teachers other than heads, and a few additional conditions which apply to deputy and assistant headteachers or to advanced skills teachers.

The introductory part of the 'Conditions of Employment' section makes clear that a teacher 'shall carry out the professional duties of a teacher as circumstances may require' (para 64.1) 'under the reasonable direction of the head teacher of that school' (para 64.11) and 'such particular duties as may reasonably be assigned to him (sic)' (para 65.1). Though the document goes on to itemise duties 'deemed to be included', the language is very broad and inclusive: teachers have wide-ranging responsibilities.

The core responsibilities under 'teaching' include (para 66.1):

- **planning and preparing courses and lessons;**
- **teaching, according to their educational needs, the pupils assigned to him, including the setting and marking of work to be carried out by the pupil in school and elsewhere;**
- **assessing, recording and reporting on the development, progress and attainment of pupils.**

The document outlines a long list of further responsibilities associated with teaching. It makes clear your obligation to:

- **participate in public examination and assessment procedures;**
- **keep records;**
- **write reports;**
- **communicate with parents and attend meetings;**
- **attend staff meetings;**
- **contribute to your own and others' appraisal;**
- **review your methods of teaching;**
- **undertake further professional development;**
- **cover for absent colleagues (with some restrictions).**

Finally, you have to carry out the 'administrative and organisational tasks related to such duties as are described above' (para 66.12.1).

You should consult this section of the document and the accompanying *Guidance* (DfES 2002b) to see just how a teacher's duties are defined.

If you do so, you should be under no illusions on one point: the duties of a teacher extend some way beyond simply teaching pupils in the classroom. The teacher's 'working time' requires you to be available up to 195 days in the school year and you can be require to teach on 190 of these (para 67.2). Five days are normally reserved as training days. In addition to the normal school day, you have to 'be available to perform such duties at such times and such places as may be specified by the head teacher ... for 1265 hours in any school year' (para 67.3) though these have to be 'allocated reasonably' within the 195 days. In other words, headteachers have the authority to make your attendance at certain activities such as staff meetings and parents' evenings a contractual obligation within the 1265 hours, or what is commonly referred to as 'directed time'. Most of the voluntary extra-curricular activities to which you might contribute out of school hours are not usually reckoned within 'directed time'.

These 1265 hours include teaching itself, but not routine preparation, marking and general burning of midnight oil. The final paragraph of the document (67.7) deserves to be quoted in full:

> Such a teacher shall, in addition to the requirements set out in paragraphs 67.2 and 67.3, work such additional hours as may be needed to enable him to discharge effectively his professional duties, including, in particular, the marking of pupils' work, the writing of reports on pupils and the preparation of lessons, teaching material and teaching programmes. The amount of time required for this purpose beyond the 1265 hours referred to in paragraph 67.3 and the times outside the 1265 specified hours at which duties shall be performed shall not be defined by the employer but shall depend upon the work needed to discharge the teacher's duties.

Doubtless with one eye on the lawyers, the document had nevertheless earlier included one interesting and related clause: 'Nothing in this Document shall be taken to conflict with Council Directive 93/104/EC of 23 November 1993 concerning certain aspects of the organisation of working time' (para 54.3). This is the European Working Time Directive which came into operation in 1998 and limits the working week to 48 hours, but averaged over 17 weeks.

You are also entitled to a break in the middle of the day. Lunch-time supervision is not part of your normal contract. Attendance at 'assemblies' for administrative purposes is part of your contract in all schools, but outside of religiously affiliated schools attendance at school worship can be declared a matter of conscience.

Further details of non-statutory agreements between the National Employers Organisation for School Teachers (NEOST), which represents the LEAs, and the six teacher unions are set out in what is traditionally referred to as the *Burgundy Book,* more formally the *Conditions of Service for Schoolteachers in England and Wales* (NEOST/LGA/ ATL/NAHT/NASUWT/NUT/PAT/SHA, 2000). This is periodically revised as the details are renegotiated.

The 'remodelling of teaching'

Teachers' workloads and their exact responsibilities have been under review. Following a study by PricewaterhouseCoopers (2001) recommendations were made by the School Teachers' Review Body (STRB 2002). Outline proposals for dealing with 'excessive teacher workload' have been published by the DfES (November 2002). Legislation should follow in 2003 to clarify the responsibilities of teachers and to give them more time 'to focus on teaching' with increased support for administrative tasks. This is likely to have significant implications for the way schools operate.

The role and purpose of school governing bodies

As a teacher you will vote for a teacher governor (two in a large school) to sit on the governing body. There are also elected parent governors, non-teaching staff governors, local authority governors and co-opted governors. Religiously affiliated schools (as some are Muslim or Jewish it is necessary to move away from referring to them all as 'church schools') have foundation governors. In voluntary aided and foundation schools (see above) foundation governors are in the majority. In aided and foundation schools the governing body is also the employer.

School governing bodies have a central role in the overall direction of schools. Acting collectively, governors are responsible for determining the school's aims, for the appointment and discipline of the headteacher and staff, and for setting policies on a range of issues from pupil admissions to sex education. In all maintained schools they are responsible for the budget.

See Chapter 11 on p. 133 for more information on discrimination.

Legislation and regulations which apply to schools and teachers

Education law is both extensive and complex and this cannot be anything like a full list. Below are some of the key areas of which you should be aware.

Acts concerning rights and discrimination

Teachers, schools and education authorities are bound by many of the provision of national legislation on rights and discrimination: the Sex Discrimination Act 1975; the Race Relations Act 1976 and Race Relations (Amendment) Act 2000; and the Disability Discrimination Act 1995. These acts apply to your own rights as an employee and to the work you do. Some brief indications of their application to pupils are given in Chapter 11.

Since October 2000 the European Convention on Human Rights has been enshrined in United Kingdom law. The Human Rights Act (HRA) 1998 states: 'It is unlawful for a public authority to act in a way which is incompatible with a Convention right' (ch 42 para 6). Though the detailed application of the Act remains to be tested in the courts, the governing body of a state school is usually viewed as 'a public authority', as much as the DfES or LEA.

School policies on discipline

The legal framework for school discipline policies is set out in Annex B of DfEE Circular 10/99. This makes the governing body responsible for setting the discipline policy whilst the headteacher is charged with its day-to-day implementation. Parents must be clearly informed about the policy. The annex spells out what the policy should do:

> It should make clear the boundaries of what is acceptable, the hierarchy of sanctions, arrangements for their consistent and fair application, and a linked system of rewards for good behaviour. It should promote respect for others, intolerance of bullying and harassment, the importance of self-discipline and the difference between 'right' and 'wrong'. (Circular 10/99 para 1)

See Chapter 13 on p. 159 for some further points on bullying.

Schools must have a policy on bullying. This is defined in Circular 10/95 as: 'deliberately hurtful behaviour, repeated over a period of time, where it is difficult for those being bullied to defend themselves'. The circular identifies three main types of bullying (para 35):

- **physical (e.g. hitting, kicking, theft);**
- **verbal (e.g. name calling, racist remarks);**
- **indirect (e.g. spreading rumours, excluding someone from social groups).**

Bullying is to be treated seriously and as a teacher you cannot simply ignore it as commonplace.

Physical restrain and sanctions

You will not be surprised to find that this is a controversial and fraught area in law as well as in routine practice. It is important to be clear on certain basic principles. The Education (no 2) Act 1986 prohibited physical ('corporal') punishment in state schools; this was reaffirmed in the Education Act 1996. It is thus classed as a form of common assault and such a charge is a serious one. More difficult for teachers is that instant and informal actions taken to control a child could also be construed as assault.

The Education Act 1997 added a section to the 1996 Act to clarify when teachers may use physical force to restrain a pupil. It allows you to use 'reasonable force' to prevent a pupil from:

- **committing a criminal offence (or what would be if they were old enough);**
- **injuring themselves or others;**
- **damaging property;**
- **acting in a way that is counter to maintaining good order and discipline at the school.**

The provisions of the Act do not just apply in school, but whenever you have 'lawful control or charge of the pupil' (DfEE Circular 10/98 para 10).

not negligent. You should always assess the risks of an activity for pupils in view of such factors as their age, known health problems, skills and the level of supervision available. Accidents, including serious ones, can always happen but the duty of care demands that you take steps to prevent what might reasonably be foreseen. For many activities which carry some obvious risk, such as swimming, outdoor activities or the use of sharp tools, schools and local authorities should have explicit guidelines. You should adhere to these both for the safety of pupils and your own protection. If you are in *any* doubt as to the safety of an activity you should err on the side of caution and seek appropriate advice. You might also note that one of the Ofsted inspection points is: 'ensures the health, safety, care and protection of all pupils'.

A note on liability

Schools must have employer public liability insurance. This means that for most purposes you are covered against third party claims arising from your actions on school-related business. Provided you have not deliberately behaved illegally or dishonestly, you would normally be covered by this. If you are negligent in some way, however, you can expect that your employer might take some disciplinary action. You can also expect to feature in the media – this is not the fifteen minutes of fame you want!

There is, however, one aspect of insured liability which you are responsible for arranging. If you take pupils in your *own* car or otherwise use your vehicle on school business you must ensure – and *insure* – that you are covered by your policy to do so. You must not assume that your motor insurance necessarily covers this.

Concluding advice

As a teacher and a responsible professional you need to be personally aware of your rights and responsibilities. You need to be very clear about your legal and contractual obligations: in law, ignorance is not a good defence. As a professional employee you also need to understand your rights and entitlements: be assured, as a teacher you are unlikely to be paid much more than you deserve for doing much less than you should!

It is crucial you understand the basic principles but also that you appreciate these are complex matters. In the course of training or on joining school you will be approached by teacher unions inviting you to join. The most honestly expressed and sensible advice given by a union representative to a group of would-be teachers was: 'I want to persuade you to join my union, but the most important thing is that you join one.' This is sound advice: you never know just what difficulties you may be faced with. Nevertheless, you should not lose sight of the fact that most teachers pass their working life without legal drama or major contractual conflicts with their headteacher, governors or LEA. It is easy to forget that in most schools and for most of the time, most teachers are peacefully – and even more or less contentedly – going about their business of teaching pupils.

Further reading

A number of books are available which deal with education law and a teacher's rights and responsibilities. For a recent book by a barrister see:

Hyams, O. (2000) *Employment in Schools: A Legal Guide*. Bristol: Jordans.

Books quickly become out of date and many schools pay for a subscription service to *The Head's Legal Guide*, or *The Teacher's Legal Guide*, Kingston upon Thames: Croner. These are loose-leaf guides with regular updates; *The Teacher's Legal Guide* also includes an annual book, *Teachers' Rights, Duties & Responsibilities*.

The best source of current information and links is the DfES website and TeacherNet: http://www.teachernet.gov.uk/. This gives access to much useful information: there is an A to Z of School Leadership and Management and links to legislation, guidance and press releases on many topics. It is particularly worth consulting:

Circular 10/95, *Protecting Children from Abuse: The Role of the Education Service*;
Circular 10/98, *Section 550A of the Education Act 1996: The Use of force to Control or Restrain Pupils*;
Circular 10/99 *Social Inclusion: Pupil Support*. See Annex B for the requirements of discipline policies in schools;
DfEE (1998) *Health and Safety of Pupils on Educational Visits*. London: DfEE.
QCA/HSE (1999) *The New General Teaching Requirement for Health and Safety*. London: HSE.

On pay and conditions see the documents on the DfES website; a copy must also be made available in schools for teachers to consult. The Burgundy Book is not available online: NEOST/LGA/ATL/NAHT/NASUWT/NUT/PAT/SHA (2000) *Conditions of Service for Schoolteachers in England and Wales*. London: Employers' Organisation for Local Government.

Key documents relating to the proposed changes in teachers' responsibilities are also available online via TeacherNet on the DfES website:

PricewaterhouseCoopers (2001) *Teacher Workload Study: Final Report*. London: DfES.
STRB (2002) *Special Review of Approaches to Reducing Teacher Workload* (cm 5497). London: The Stationery Office.
DfES (2002) *Department for Education and Skills Response to STRB Workload Report*. London: DfES.

For information on the GTC (England) see: http://www.gtce.org.uk/
For the GTC (Wales) see: http://www.gtcw.org.uk/

The various professional associations all produce guidance for members. Union representatives in schools will have much of this published material. Some of this is available on their websites. See WWW sites for NUT, NAS/UWT, ATL, PAT; look also at advice from the headteacher associations: NAHT and SHA.

By the end of the chapter you should:

- **be aware of the importance of effective working relationships with children and all colleagues in the educational community;**
- **have an overview of the many different responsibilities teachers have outside the classroom;**
- **know that teachers have to take responsibility for their own professional development and career profile;**
- **have an understanding of the term 'professional' and what is meant by professionalism.**

This chapter addresses the following Professional Standards for QTS:

 1.4, 1.5, 1.6, 1.7, 3.3.1, 3.3.11, 3.1.3.

(The Standards are reproduced in full at the back of this book.)

Why become a teacher?

To be a real professional you need to be:

> **P**rofessionally autonomous
> **R**esponsible
> **O**rganised
> **F**air
> **E**ducated
> **S**killed
> **S**elf-regulatory
> **I**ndependent
> **O**pen
> **N**eutral
> **A**ccountable
> **L**earned

Above are listed some of the essential characteristics of a professional. How many of them apply to you? There are, of course, many other features of being a professional but the key ingredients are your attitude to your work and your ability to achieve the characteristics above and be effective. Moreover you need to be able to evaluate your own performance.

Elsewhere in this book there has been frequent references to the fact that teachers do much more than simply teach children in a classroom. Almost every school and class-room activity signals the need for you as a class teacher to have additional skills in dealing with parents, colleagues and support staff as well as children. It is the rich diversity of knowledge, skills, attitudes and understandings which makes teaching a unique profession and one which demands much more of the person than almost any other job.

This chapter is intended to clarify what teaching as a profession means and how we recognise and judge professionalism. Most importantly, it will give guidance on how to achieve and sustain the professional values and practice encapsulated in *Qualifying to Teach: Professional Standards for Qualified Teacher Status and Requirements for Initial Teacher Training* (DfES/TTA 2002). In many ways, Section I is the most significant part of the document because for many trainee teachers it encompasses the main reason teaching was selected as their preferred career. Teaching provides opportunities for highly professional behaviour in many areas and frequently attracts people who are conscientious, hardworking and committed to caring for and improving the lives of those with whom they work. These days teaching is demanding and only those determined to strive to the highest standards feel comfortable in the job. Achieving high standards is determined in part by the quality of your relationships with children, colleagues, parents and support staff and also the relationship you have with yourself and your career. Relationships have to be positive, optimistic and trusting. Most of all they must transcend divisions of race, culture, class, religion and ability and disability.

Talking to trainee teachers and newly qualified teachers there is little doubt that many want to be teachers no matter what the pay, no matter what the rewards. They feel they have a contribution to make in extending and developing the careers and lives of young people. You may be one of those who chose teaching because you wanted to create an environment where improvement is allowed to happen. Most trainee teachers want to make a difference to young people's lives and provide better opportunities. They want to have a strong, trusting relationship with pupils, parents and colleagues. Largely they subscribe to a principle that states that children and teachers should want to come to school, enjoy it when they are there and leave it each day better informed and more enriched than the previous day. Inevitably there will be factors that mean that some people have a more difficult job than others. But even in difficult schools, some heroic work is being done by excellent teachers, who have spirit, integrity and enjoy the demands of the job, remaining optimistic and enthusiastic. It is important, therefore, that you know why you want to be a teacher and the sort of teacher you want to be, as it will affect your approach to the job.

Many teachers enter the profession knowing that it is going to be hard, knowing that it is not well paid, knowing that it is not glamorous, but knowing that the rewards can be great. In a developed world where the workplace has been taken over largely by profit margins, image and ruthless competition, teaching still attracts many people who care about humanity.

In Chapter 7 four reasons were suggested why people pursue teaching. Here are some more:

- **a desire to work with children;**
- **a desire to create a better school experience;**
- **a desire to work as a member of a team;**
- **a desire to be creative and imaginative;**
- **a desire to be stimulated intellectually;**
- **a desire to have a job that is varied, challenging and worthwhile;**
- **a desire to influence the community and society.**

Practical task

Practical task

Write down the three main reasons you decided to choose teaching as a career. Now identify three concerns you have about joining the profession and explain why they bother you.

Is teaching a profession?

It would be useful at this stage to consider what the term 'profession' means and how it is applied to teaching. The Longman Dictionary of Contemporary English (1975) defines the term 'profession' in the following way: 'a form of employment especially one that is respected in society, as honourable and is possible only for an educated person, and after training in some special branch of knowledge'. Other definitions include the notion of being client-centred and the need for special expertise to support the interest of the client. In medicine it is clear the client is the patient, in law it is clear that the client is the victim or the accused, in commerce the client is the customer. Who is the client in education? Is it the child, is it the parent or is it the state? The answer to this question could be quite important in how you view your job as a professional. My view is that the best interests of children must come first and then the interests of other stakeholders.

Teachers are educated certainly and undergo very rigorous training in a special branch of knowledge. When the long anticipated point arrives and you assume the responsibilities of a qualified teacher you will define yourself as a member of the teaching profession. Later you will almost certainly complain about the public standing of the profession, its status and its rewards and you will wonder why schools and teachers attract criticism from the media. You will also begin to describe work-related behaviours as 'professional' or 'unprofessional' in a variety of contexts.

Children are very clear about their perceptions of professionalism in teachers. They observe very closely and have high expectations of their performance. To children it is important to be on time, to be well prepared, to be a competent class manager, to be honest and fair. They want their teacher to be a good role model, to be someone they can look up to. This does not mean to say mistakes cannot be made, it means that they are acknowledged. Being professional does not mean you have to be perfect, but it does mean you have to know how to handle yourself and present a professional image.

It is worth giving a couple of minutes to the traditional understanding of what was meant to be a professional or be part of a profession. In 1970 the Monopolies and Mergers Commission identified seven characteristics of professions. These seven characteristics concur with the original notion of professions, which were considered to be medicine, law and the church. The characteristics are as follows:

To be a true professional you must:

- **possess specialised skill to enable you to offer a specialised service;**
- **undergo intellectual and practical training in a well-defined area of study;**
- **maintain detachment and integrity in exercising personal judgement on behalf of a client;**

- establish direct personal relations with clients based on confidence, faith and trust;
- collectively have a particular sense of responsibility for maintaining the competence and integrity of the profession as a whole;
- belong to an organised body which, with or without state intervention, is concerned to provide machinery for testing competence and regulating standards of competence and conduct.

The teaching profession has some, but not all, of these characteristics. It is not autonomous, for example, but all professions and not just teaching are now subject to influence by government agencies.

Since September 2002 all teachers have been expected to be a member of the General Teaching Council. While the establishment of a Teaching Council may help to promote the status of teaching, the GTC cannot provide the professional autonomy some teachers desire. It is argued that teachers and schools are paid for out of public funds and, like all publicly funded services, must therefore be held accountable and rigorously scrutinised. Put this way it does not seem unreasonable that pressure should be exerted to ensure high quality provision and high quality performance from all teachers.

Eric Hoyle (1980) identified two kinds of teachers. He described one group as the 'extended professional' and another as the 'restricted professional'. The contrast between the two reflects an attitude to work and quality of performance. Restricted professionals work hard but have a limited view of their role. They see their job as doing what is necessary to get the tasks done but remain rigid in their interpretation of the employment contract. In contrast the 'extended professional' takes the full range of duties and tasks very seriously and does more than is expected. The extended professional seizes initiatives, works extended hours without complaint, and is committed, conscientious and diligent.

The restricted professional:

- has a high level of classroom competence;
- has a degree of skill in understanding and handling children;
- derives much satisfaction from personal relationships with pupils;
- evaluates performance in terms of their own perceptions of changes;
- attends short courses of a practical nature.

The extended professional has all of these qualities, but additionally:

- views work in the wider context of school, community and society;
- participates in a wide range of professional activities – for example, subject panels, governors, conferences, and so on;
- tries to link theory and practice;
- has a commitment to some form of curriculum development and mode of evaluation.

(Hoyle 1980)

A professional staff-room should be:

- **brightly decorated and well furnished;**
- **clean, tidy and well ordered;**
- **equipped with appropriate catering facilities;**
- **equipped with an area for staff study and/or preparation;**
- **equipped with a computer to provide access to the Internet and e-mail;**
- **equipped with an area for books, journals and other literature relevant to the profession;**
- **an area for serious discussion and meetings;**
- **an area where all support staff are welcomed.**

It should have:

- **well organised and differentiated notice-boards which indicate:**

  - **messages from the headteacher and others with leadership roles;**
  - **messages from the support staff and catering staff to teachers about matters that affect them;**
  - **messages and information from outside agencies including the LEA, education welfare officer (EWO), educational psychologists (EPs), child support, etc;**
  - **messages and information about trainee teacher placements and mentor training;**
  - **information about courses and conferences and other professional development opportunities including national initiatives;**
  - **information from governors;**
  - **information about parents and parents' evenings, etc.**

A professional staff room should:

- **promote a positive image of teaching;**
- **encourage engagement in professional advancement;**
- **encourage debate and discussion about educational issues;**
- **welcome into it all members of staff including assistants, trainees and technicians;**
- **provide an impression of which all staff would be pleased and proud;**
- **present an image of professionalism that would impress visitors to the school;**
- **promote the achievements of children;**
- **recognise disability and ethnic and cultural diversity.**

Professional relationships

Relationships with children

Building good relationships with all children is essential to effective teaching. It is the one area in which good NQTs start out with the best of possible intentions but most frequently misjudge. The secret is to keep the relationship professional. You do not want fans; you want achievers. If they achieve they are likely to be your fans too.

Remember, remember, and remember what it is like to be a pupil and speak to each one with respect! Ask yourself from time to time: 'What would it be like if I were spoken to in such a way? Would I be happy to be addressed in such a manner?' At times you will encounter difficult children and you will be under pressure. Keep your cool. The respect you get from children will depend on the respect you give them.

You will encounter children in contexts other than in the classroom. You will have to settle disputes in the playground, manage a whole school assembly and help manage the movement of children around the school. There will be children to manage other than those in your class. The image you portray to all children in the school is critical. You need to consider how children might talk about you when you are not there!

A number of studies have now been completed on children's judgements of their trainee teachers and teachers. The overwhelming demand is that the teachers are strict, fair, kind and humorous. The recently published Hay/McBer Report (2000) offers the following from pupils in describing a good teacher:

is kind
is generous
listens to you
encourages you
has faith in you
keeps confidences
likes teaching children
likes teaching their subject
takes time to explain things
helps you when you're stuck
tells you how you are doing
allows you to have your say
doesn't give up on you
cares for your opinion
makes you feel clever
treats people equally
stands up for you
makes allowances
tells the truth
is forgiving

Other responses from children about the characteristics they rate in teachers are as follows:

- **The relationship you have with them as individuals is as important as subject knowledge.**
- **Pupils appreciate teachers who are well organised, are predictable and have routines and whose expectations of behaviour are high, and well understood.**
- **Children say they want their teachers to be fair, kind and funny. Children are very clear they do not want their teachers to be over friendly, they want them to demand high standards of behaviour and performance from them and also from**

teachers. They want them to be fair. Nothing infuriates either individual children or whole classes as much as injustice and an intemperate reaction to incidents from the teachers. More than anything they dislike intensely the notion that it is possible to punish the whole class for the misdemeanours of one or two.

- Pupils claim they want to see their teachers as people in authority, with authority, but sympathetic to the needs of all children. The high fliers in the class appreciate evidence of understanding of the low flyers in the class. High fliers in the class who are unsympathetic to other children and their particular needs look to the teacher to instruct and improve the attitude of those children.

- Children appreciate their accomplishments being recognised and commented on. All children want to be treated with respect and regard and all teachers want to be treated with respect and regard.

Relationships with colleagues

In chapter 7 the importance of classroom climate was emphasised and earlier in this chapter we considered staff-room climate. Equally important is the notion of school climate and a positive school climate, which conveys to all who enter the school as one of trust, co-operation, collaboration and achievement. In a school where teachers work together, share the same goals and aspirations for themselves and for the children, and where the mission is understood there is likely to be a positive climate.

In the past teachers guarded jealously what went on in their classrooms and were frequently unwilling to share their practice or what the children were learning with anyone else and indeed resented the interference, even from the headteacher. Nowadays good teachers want to collaborate and share good practice and engage in the discussion which good teachers have about the quality of pupil progress and the quality of pupils' learning. Most schools these days have their staff grouped into teams, and teachers may belong to more than one team – for example, a year team in a large school or curriculum team. Teamwork is essential if sound planning is to be shared by all colleagues and a whole-school strategy developed around good practice and professional development.

See Chapter 7 on p. 93 for more information on classroom climate.

As a new entrant to the profession, it is important to understand and be sensitive to the feelings of experienced members of staff. Some will welcome you as:

- a breath of fresh air!
- the new expert!
- the one with all the new ideas!
- the fount of all knowledge around Curriculum 2000 and assessment!

Others will regard you as:

- a threat!
- an upstart!
- a novice!
- a probationer who needs to 'forget all that stuff from college and learn the real job'!

- one to be ignored!
- one who needs to be told what to do very often.

Most, however, will, treat you:

- with respect;
- with good humour and understanding;
- as a new colleague in need of support and guidance;
- as a human resource with additional skills and knowledge which will enhance the school;
- as a newly qualified teacher with entitlement for time each week from a mentor for support, for professional development, for regular feedback on performance.

It is easy to feel indignant and angry if you are made to feel small and undervalued by more experienced colleagues. If it does happen, keep cool, keep the matter in perspective and always be willing to reflect on your own inexperience. Humility can work wonders with the arrogant. Even when you feel done down, react carefully and remember that colleagues who react against trainees and newly qualified teachers tend to feel threatened and insecure.

If you are a good communicator you are likely to be an effective teacher, an effective colleague and an effective team leader.

As a trainee or newly qualified teacher, you will have a mentor who will be responsible for guiding and assessing your progress in school. The relationship you have with your mentor is critical. Again mutual respect is important if you are both to succeed. Your mentor will want you to succeed So remember that as part of your professional behaviour, you should be able to:

- take criticism without taking offence;
- respond to criticism without giving offence;
- avoid blaming others when things go wrong;
- seek help and support when you need it – you are entitled to it;
- learn from mistakes.

If you are a trainee you will be expected to complete a Career Entry Profile at the end of your training, which will identify your strengths, weaknesses and areas for further professional development.

If you are a newly qualified teacher, arrangements should be made for you to

- teach only 90 per cent of contact time;
- have opportunities for contact with experienced, good teachers;
- be mentored, observed and counselled regarding progress;
- receive appropriate professional development and training;
- receive help with special educational needs provision;
- be allowed to network with other NQTs.

Most mentors take their professional responsibility seriously and are anxious to ensure that you are well supported. In a minority of schools, mentors find they have not been allocated sufficient time to give you regular feedback. If this happens, you must employ your negotiating skills to let the headteacher know that you need more support.

Relationships with other support staff in school

Sound working relationships with the staff who support teachers and their work is essential. But there is another group of staff in the school who are very important too. Classroom assistants, secretaries, caretakers, catering staff and welfare assistants and then a whole range of trainees of one sort another who may be in the school; for example trainee nursery nurses, trainee teachers, and trainee child development students. There are many other people in schools beside teachers and it matters how you treat them.

First, keep in mind that, no matter to whom you are speaking, for whatever reason, everyone has a right to expect a high level of respect and regard and to get as much of your attention as is possible. The strength of a school can be affected enormously by the quality of the relationships between all the people in it. Many schools these days provide training and support for groups such as catering staff, secretaries, classroom assistants, nursery nurse support staff, to ensure that they too feel that they are as important to the welfare of the school as are the teachers. Without them the school cannot function. That is something the children need to understand.

Classroom assistants will be of particular importance to you if you have them in your classroom. If you have a classroom assistant, it is part of your role to manage them effectively so that they support your teaching and pupils' learning. They tend to be poorly paid but enjoy what they do, so it is important that you demonstrate how much you value their contributions. Ensure that they are included in the planning so that they are prepared for the week ahead. Each morning indicate to them what you would like them to do and be very clear about the instructions. It is important to be clear about:

- **how you employ them;**
- **what you ask them to do with particular children;**
- **how you feed back to them on their performance on what you have asked them to do;**
- **how they become involved in the planning and development of the classroom activities you wish them to support;**
- **how you use your authority and expertise.**

Practical task

Suggest three advantages of having a positive working relationship with all the support staff in your school.

Write a sentence about how you think the relationship between you and the headteacher should develop in your first year as an NQT, indicating what sort of professional development activity you would like to receive and making your career intentions clear to the head and to your mentor.

What should you do if your mentor is not finding time to give you feedback and support?

Let's look at how you talk to support staff, classroom assistants and all other support staff:

- **Do you treat them with the regard and respect you treat all other staff in the school?**
- **Do you consult them about the behaviour of children and respect and regard the comments they give back to you?**
- **Do you include them in regular meetings about the job they do and how it affects work in the classroom? Suggest a way this might happen**

Classroom assistants are probably the most high profile group in schools and you may or may not have a formal classroom assistant. This group are often striving towards a qualification and striving towards becoming a highly competent classroom support person, even if they are not intending to become teachers in the distant future. Find out what their career intentions are so that you can support their staff development and ensure that they have the appropriate kinds of experiences with pupils. Nothing is more frustrating than lack of clarity about what it is you have been asked to do, so make sure that your classroom assistant understands what it is you want them to do and what outcomes you expect. Used appropriately classroom assistants and other support staff will help you teach more effectively. They can relieve you of the many important, but non-teaching, tasks, which you would normally have to do. In particular, they can help keep your classroom and resources organised.

Classroom assistants tend to be highly motivated, well-intentioned, able and intelligent people. Thus they are an enormously valuable asset in the classroom and they can, if directed well by the class teacher, make a 100 per cent difference in children's learning simply because they are able to support the work of a good class teacher. You must try to assess the abilities of your classroom assistant and then determine how best they can assist the learning of the children in the classroom and compensate for the work that you are unable to do. Most important, however, is to recognise and utilise the skill and the knowledge they have. You have responsibility to guide and direct them clearly.

Working with support staff

Good support staff play a significant role in enhancing the quality of school life. The numbers of support staff in schools have grown significantly over the past 15 years and look set to increase even further in the future, with far more classroom assistants being employed to support class teachers. Other support staff in the school, including secretaries, bursars, catering staff, etc. all can make your job easier if they have a good relationship with you. Ensure that all support staff are treated with courtesy and respect and always thank them for their assistance. It is important, too, that if they ask for your help in dealing with challenging children, you give them that help.

Playground supervisors frequently encounter supervision difficulties with children. You are trained to deal with children who need to be disciplined and they are not, so even if it is your lunch period, do intervene and help support staff either if you can see they need it or if they ask for it.

Relationships with parents and significant others

Cementing good working relationships with other teachers in the school, your head-teacher and other line managers, and with all other support staff is important and once you have learned how to do that effectively you will understand just what a bonus that is. Parents of the children you teach are the other group to whom you must relate well. In the past a number of schools made misjudgements about working relationships with parents, but in the recent past this has improved. There was a time when schools discouraged parents from either meeting teachers frequently or allowing parents in to see classrooms and work that children are doing in school. That is not the case now and parents are encouraged to visit the school as often as they wish and talk to classroom teachers as often as they need to as well as talking to the headteacher.

If you think back to the early part of this chapter when we were asking whether or not teachers were professionals, the issue arose as to whether teachers were able to respond to their client group. It is an interesting question about teaching, 'to whom are teachers accountable?' Is it to children? Is it to government? Or is it to parents? The answer is that teachers are accountable to a number of different groups but parents, of course, are a particular and significant group. Parents deserve and need to know how well their children are doing in school and they need to be informed about any learning difficulties their child may have. They are entitled, also, to learn if their children have strengths and exceptional talents. Keeping records of the profile of children's attainments, as described earlier in this book, is an essential part of the teacher's job but in talking and working with parents it is important that the class teacher is able to discuss with them from an informed position the strengths and weaknesses of their child's learning profile.

See Chapter 4 on p. 51 for more information on recording attainments.

It is often hard to give parents difficult messages if their child is not performing well. This is an important part of your job, to communicate to parents the precise position in which their child lies in relation to other children in the class and indeed, then, in relation to other children nationally. It is not always easy to talk to parents but you have to learn how to give feedback honestly and you need to do that early. Many newly qualified teachers feel they have not had the opportunity to take this role in their training. This is not surprising given that parents are not willing to accept comments from trainee teachers but they will from qualified teachers. Therefore, this is something you have to learn, and learn the hard way, early in your career.

Negotiations with parents need to be learned but they can be a rewarding and profit-able experience. Just like children, parents feel flattered when you take interest in them and, particularly, if you take interest in their children. We all know that there are some youngsters who have behavioural problems, but we all know too that they are in a minority and that there is another minority who are withdrawn. Knowing the back-ground of children helps you understand behaviour. Make an effort to get to know families and when you see parents outside the school gate, talk to them. You need to recognise that the school is a world in which some parents have failed and they fear that their children may fail also. School is a world where some parents have not felt welcome in the past. It is a world where some parents do not have the self-esteem to feel able to talk to teachers. Some parents do carry a sense of guilt and feel they are responsible for the misdemeanours of their children and most parents want the opportunity to discuss, frankly and fully, the problems they perceive in their children.

Parents are as different as the children in your class and it is a mistake to think that all parents are the same. Spend time talking to them whenever possible and encourage them to trust you and know that you will tell them the truth while being fair. Some newly qualified teachers have felt ill prepared to deal with aggressive and abusive parents and, true, it is difficult to train anyone to be ready for rudeness and discourtesy. Never lose your temper with parents and never, ever respond in an aggressive or discourteous manner. If you encounter parents who shout and won't listen, keep your cool and wait until they calm down. If remarks become seriously abusive, them you will need to summon the help of the headteacher. Do not ever say anything to a parent, which you may later regret or which may get you into trouble.

Here are some of the encounters you may have to deal with:

- **A parent bursting in to school at the end of the day clearly high on something, insisting that their child has been misjudged over an incident.**
- **A parent insistent that their child has been overlooked in selection for a competition in, say, music.**
- **A parent of a high-achiever who learns that their son or daughter is not, currently, literate or numerate to their expected level.**

What will you do? How will you respond?

PARENTS' MEEETINGS

If parents' evenings are to be profitable both for the parent and for you, they need to be fully prepared for. Plan in advance what you are going to say about each child and make sure that you can begin with something positive and, hopefully, conclude with a small anecdote that places the child in a good light. This helps reassure parents that you do know their child very well. If you have negative things to say about a child, make sure that they are presented in a way that indicates to parents that you want them to help you overcome the problem. For example, in the case of repeated non-completion of work because a child is very easily distracted, emphasise that better progress will be made if work is completed and you want some assistance from the parents in ensuring that work is completed, and reward the completion of all work without concentrating on punishing distraction. Talk to parents about setting targets and rewarding successful achievement.

Writing reports for parents, every teacher knows, can be daunting. Nevertheless, theses are important documents for parents as well as for children. All of us can remember reports from school that told us very little because the style was too general and ambiguous. Make sure your reports are not like this. Identify very clearly what has been achieved and at what level and ensure that you have evidence to support what you are saying. Identify clearly also areas of weakness and how these must be improved to reach the desired level. Set targets that are achievable and indicate how you intend to involve the pupil in assessing their own progress. Indicate how parents might help the pupil improve on areas of concern, emphasising how parents can help motivate pupils by giving praise where appropriate. It is important that your report is businesslike and free from phrases that parents will not understand or are too 'airy-fairy'. Parents are also interested in where their child stands in relation to the rest of the class and they are entitled to have this information. Remember always that parents are, in a sense, your professional clients. You are accountable to them for the performance of their child and they are entitled to know what you are doing to support their child's learning.

The final point here is to treat with professionalism all staff and children and parents with whom you come into contact.

Your own professional development

In this final section you are asked to consider your future and where you expect to be in five years' time for example. At the beginning we identified specialist knowledge as a characteristic of a profession. As in other professions, knowledge and expertise about education is growing and changing all the time. It is up you to keep up to date both with your subject and new developments in primary education. It is impossible to judge and analyse new initiatives effectively if you don't fully understand them. Make sure that you are up to date with educational literature, that you read frequently educational journals and newspapers such as the *Times Educational Supplement* and/or *Primary Education*. Once you have completed your induction year that's not it! You will be a better teacher and a more self-fulfilled individual if you feel that you are constantly growing and developing as a teacher and as an educator. Teachers, quite justifiably, feel short of time and frequently hard-pressed. It is important that you manage your time efficiently and ensure that there is a balance in your working day and in your life outside school. You cannot do everything to perfection all the time, nor should you wish to. Appreciate that if you visit the doctor or solicitor, or a dentist, or the bank manager, your time with them is limited and an appointment has to be made which will finish on time. Too many teachers are over-generous with their time and feel unprofessional if they do not deal instantly with every request.

If you are planning on promotion within the next five years, think about it and think about how to organise your time so that you have space for further study and opportunities to attend courses and conferences.

The future is likely to be technology. Will you be able to develop your teaching so that both you and your pupils are familiar with e-mail and the internet and can capitalise on the technology to improve teacher effectiveness?

As you emerge as a professional and begin the task of becoming a fully qualified teacher, do remember to raise your head above the level of the classroom and school to look at the big picture and remind yourself why you are a teacher and why you are so proud to be one.

Further Reading

Davies, R, and Ferguson, J. (1997) 'Teachers' views of the role of Initial Teacher Education in developing their professionalism.' *Journal of Education for Teaching*. 23 (1) pp. 40-55. Provides authentic feedback from teachers about the ways in which they see working with trainees as helping develop reflection on their own practice and improving levels of personal behaviour.

GTCE (2001) *Professional Learning Framework*. London GTCE.

GTCE (2002) *Professional Code for Teachers*. London. GTCE.

Hayes, D (1997) *Success on your Teaching Experience*. London: Hodder & Stoughton. This book targets the trainee teacher and is full of useful and valuable advice about beginning teaching in school. In terms of professionalism, Chapter 1 'The student teacher in school' and Chapter 8 'Achieving Competence', give reliable guidance of orientation in school and professional behaviour and conduct.

Hoyle, E. (1980) 'Professionalism and de-professionalism in education' in Hoyle, E. and Hegarty, J (eds) (1980) *World Yearbook of Education: Professional Development of Teachers*. London Kogan Page.

Kyriacou, C. (1998) *Essential Teaching Skills*. Cheltenham: Stanley Thornes. This book is a classic and will assist you in a full range of the chapters dealt with in the book. In terms of professionalism, Chapter 8 on reflection and evaluation addresses the importance of managing your professional conduct and gives lots of useful tips on how to manage that.

Lawton, D. (1996) *Beyond the National Curriculum, Teacher Professionalism and Empowerment*. London: Hodder and Stoughton. This book has a more theoretical base and offers a sound analysis of teacher professionalism and empowerment for those who wish to consider the subject in more depth. Professor Lawton examines the tensions between the status of teachers as a profession and the problems such a professional group has in maintaining a positive public image. It contains a very useful appendix, which charts the growth of teacher professionalism across the twentieth century.

Hay/McBer (2000) *Research into Teacher Effectiveness, Phase II Report: A Model of Teacher Effectiveness*, DfEE Report. This report is a comprehensive consolidation of the characteristics and behaviours which go into making an effective teacher. While many teachers may argue there is nothing new in this report, the findings are of interest certainly to any new teacher entering the profession, if not to experienced teachers. Many references are made between professional characteristics of teachers and pupil progress. On Page 114 there is an interesting section on continuing professional development, career planning and performance management, which will be of interest to those with long-term career plans.

Stephen, P. and Crawley, T. (1994) *Becoming an Effective Teacher*. Cheltenham: Stanley Thornes. An easy to read book about the challenges of entering teaching and classrooms for the first time. Chapter 6 is particularly useful in providing guidance on relationships with colleagues and parents and on considering professional development issues.

Thody, A., Gray, D and Bowden, D. (2000) *The Teacher's Survival Guide*. London: Continuum. This book contains lots of tips in a very easy to read volume focusing on success. It gives guidance on success with pupils, colleagues and yourself. It addresses a number of professional matters about achieving professional matters, about achieving professional standing, working successfully and still finding time for yourself. For example, on p103 it gives advice on managing time to ensure that you have time for leisure. The final recommendation suggests marking Friday with a deep bubble bath, gin and tonic, aerobics class and a meal with friends! It contains many other very practical ways of maintaining professionalism, which sometimes means having to say no.

I PROFESSIONAL VALUES AND PRACTICE

Those awarded Qualified Teacher Status must understand and uphold the professional code of the General Teaching Council for England by demonstrating all of the following.

1.1   They have high expectations of all pupils; respect their social, cultural, linguistic, religious and ethnic backgrounds; and are committed to raising their educational achievement.

1.2   They treat pupils consistently, with respect and consideration, and are concerned for their development as learners.

1.3   They demonstrate and promote the positive values, attitudes and behaviour that they expect from their pupils.

1.4   They can communicate sensitively and effectively with parents and carers, recognising their roles in pupils' learning, and their rights, responsibilities and interests in this.

1.5   They can contribute to, and share responsibly in, the corporate life of schools.

1.6   They understand the contribution that support staff and other professionals make to teaching and learning.

1.7   They are able to improve their own teaching, by evaluating it, learning from the effective practice of others and from evidence. They are motivated and able to take increasing responsibility for their own professional development.

1.8   They are aware of, and work within, the statutory frameworks relating to teachers' responsibilities.

2 KNOWLEDGE AND UNDERSTANDING

Those awarded Qualified Teacher Status must demonstrate all of the following.

2.1   They have a secure knowledge and understanding of the subject(s) they are trained to teach. For those qualifying to teach secondary pupils this knowledge and understanding should be at a standard equivalent to degree level.

In relation to specific phases, this includes:

a. For the Foundation Stage, they know and understand the aims, principles, six areas of learning and early learning goals described in the QCA/DfEE Curriculum Guidance for the Foundation Stage and, for Reception children, the frameworks, methods and expectations set out in the National Numeracy and Literacy Strategies.

b. For Key Stage 1 and/or 2, they know and understand the curriculum for each of the National Curriculum core subjects, and the frameworks, methods and expectations set out in the National Literacy and Numeracy Strategies. They have sufficient understanding of a range of work across the following subjects:
    • history or geography
    • physical education
    • ICT
    • art and design or design and technology
    • performing arts, and
    • Religious Education

    to be able to teach them in the age range for which they are trained, with advice from an experienced colleague where necessary.

c. For Key Stage 3, they know and understand the relevant National Curriculum Programme(s) of Study, and for those qualifying to teach one or more of the core subjects, the relevant frameworks, methods and expectations set out in the National Strategy for Key Stage 3. All those qualifying to teach a subject at Key Stage 3 know and understand the cross-curricular expectations of the National Curriculum and are familiar with the guidance set out in the National Strategy for Key Stage 3.

d. For Key Stage 4 and post 16, they are aware of the pathways for progression through the 14-19 phase in school, college and work-based settings. They are familiar with the Key Skills as specified by QCA and the national qualifications framework, and they know the progression within and from their own subject and the range of qualifications to which their subject contributes. They understand how courses are combined in students' curricula.

2.2 They know and understand the Values, Aims and Purposes of the General Teaching Requirements set out in the National Curriculum Handbook. As relevant to the age range they are trained to teach, they are familiar with the Programme of Study for Citizenship and the National Curriculum Framework for Personal, Social and Heath Education.

2.3 They are aware of expectations, typical curricula and teaching arrangements in the Key Stages of phases before and after the ones they are trained to teach.

2.4 They understand how pupils' learning can be affected by their physical, intellectual, linguistic, social, cultural and emotional development.

2.5 They know how to use ICT effectively, both to teach their subject and to support their wider professional role.

2.6 They understand their responsiblities under the SEN Code of Practice, and know how to seek advice from specialists on less common types of special educational needs.

2.7 They know a range of strategies to promote good behaviour and establish a purposeful learning environment.

2.8 They have passed the Qualified Teacher Status skills tests in numeracy, literacy and ICT.

3 TEACHING

3.1 Planning, expectations and targets

Those awarded Qualified Teacher Status must demonstrate all of the following.

3.1.1 They set challenging teaching and learning objectives which are relevant to all pupils in their classes. They base them on their knowledge of:

- the pupils
- evidence of their past and current achievement
- the expected standards for pupils of the relevant age range
- the range and content of work relevant to pupils in that age range.

3.1.2 They use these teaching and learning objectives to plan lessons, and sequences of lessons, showing how they will assess pupils' learning. They take account of and support pupils' varying needs so that girls and boys, from all ethnic groups, can make good progress.

3.1.3 They select and prepare resources, and plan for their safe and effective organisation, taking account of pupils' interests and their language and cultural backgrounds, with the help of support staff where appropriate.

3.1.4 They take part in, and contribute to, teaching teams, as appropriate to the school. Where applicable, they plan for the deployment of additional adults who support pupils' learning.

3.1.5 As relevant to the age range they are trained to each, they are able to plan opportunities for pupils to learn in out-of-school contexts, such as school visits, museums, theatres, field-work and employment-based settings, with the help of others staff where appropriate.

3.2 Monitoring and Assessment

Those awarded Qualified Teacher Status must demonstrate all of the following.

3.2.1   They make appropriate use of a range of monitoring and assessment strategies to evaluate pupils' progress towards planned learning objectives, and use this information to improve their own planning and teaching.

3.2.2   They monitor and assess as they teach, giving immediate and constructive feedback to support pupils as they learn. They involve pupils in reflecting on, evaluating and improving their own performance.

3.2.3   They are able to assess pupils' progress accurately using, as relevant, the Early Learning Goals, National Curriculum level descriptors, criteria from national qualifications, the requirements of Awarding Bodies, National Curriculum and Foundation Stage assessment frameworks or objectives from the national strategies. They may have guidance from an experienced teacher where appropriate.

3.2.4   They identify and support more able pupils, those who are working below age-related expectations, those who are failing to achieve their potential in learning, and those who experience behavioural, emotional and social difficulties. They may have guidance from an experienced teacher where appropriate.

3.2.5   With the help of an experienced teacher, they can identify the levels of attainment of pupils learning English as an additional language. They begin to analyse the language demands and learning activities in order to provide cognitive challenge as well as language support.

3.2.6   They record pupils' progress and achievements systematically to provide evidence of the range of their work, progress and attainment over time. They use this to help pupils review their own progress and to inform planning.

3.2.7   They are able to use records as a basis for reporting on pupils' attainment and progress orally and in writing, concisely, informatively and accurately for parents, carers, other professionals and pupils.

3.3 Teaching and class management

Those awarded Qualified Teacher Status must demonstrate all of the following.

3.3.1   They have high expectations of pupils and build successful relationships, centred on teaching and learning. They establish a purposeful learning environment where diversity is valued and where pupils feel secure and confident.

3.3.2   They can teach the required or expected knowledge, understanding and skills relevant to the curriculum for pupils in the age range for which they are trained. In relation to specific phases:

a. those qualifying to teach Foundation Stage children teach all six areas of learning outlined in the QCA/DfEE Curriculum Guidance for the Foundation Stage and, for Reception children, the objectives in the National Literacy and Numeracy Strategy frameworks competently and independently;

b. those qualifying to teach pupils in Key Stage 1 and/or 2 teach the core subjects (English, including the National Literacy Strategy, mathematics through the National Numeracy Strategy, and science) competently and independently.
   They also teach, for either Key Stage 1 or Key Stage 2, a range of work across the following subjects:
   • history or geography
   • physical education

- ICT
  - art and design or design and technology, and
  - performing arts

  independently, with advice from an experienced colleague where appropriate;

  c. those qualifying to teach Key Stage 3 pupils teach their specialist subject(s) competently and independently using the National Curriculum Programmes of Study for Key Stage 3 and the relevant national frameworks and schemes of work. Those qualifying to teach the core subjects or ICT at Key Stage 3 must be able to use the cross-curricular elements, such as literacy and numeracy, set out in the National Strategy for Key Stage 3, in their teaching, as appropriate to their specialist subject;

  d. those qualifying to teach Key Stage 4 and post-16 pupils teach their specialist subject(s) competently and independently using, as relevant to the subject and age range, the National Curriculum Programmes of Study and related schemes of work, or programmes specified for national qualifications. They also provide opportunities for pupils to develop the key skills specified by QCA.

3.3.3 They teach clearly structured lessons or sequences of work which interest and motivate pupils and which:
- make learning objectives clear to pupils
- employ interactive teaching methods and collaborative group work
- promote active and independent learning that enables pupils to think for themselves, and to plan and manage their own learning.

3.3.4 They differentiate their teaching to meet the needs of pupils, including the more able and those with special educational needs. They may have guidance from an experienced teacher where appropriate.

3.3.5 They are able to support those who are learning English as an additional language, with the help of an experienced teacher where appropriate.

3.3.6 They take account of the varying interests, experiences and achievements of boys and girls, and pupils from different cultural and ethnic groups, to help pupils make good progress.

3.3.7 They organise and manage teaching and learning time effectively.

3.3.8 They organise and manage the physical teachings pace, tools, materials, texts and other resources safely and effectively with the help of support staff where appropriate.

3.3.9 They set high expectations for pupils' behaviour and establish a clear framework for classroom discipline to anticipate and manage pupils' behaviour constructively, and promote self-control and independence.

3.3.10 They use ICT effectively in their teaching.

3.3.11 They can take responsibility for teaching a class or classes over a sustained and substantial period of time. They are able to teach across the age and ability range for which they are trained.

3.3.12 They can provide homework and other out-of-class work which consolidates and extends work carried out in the class and encourages pupils to learn independently.

3.3.13 They work collaboratively with specialist teachers and other colleagues and, with the help of an experienced teacher as appropriate, manage the work of teaching assistants or other adults to enhance pupils' learning.

3.3.14 They recognise and respond effectively to equal opportunities issues as they arise in the classroom, including by challenging stereotyped views, bullying or harassment, following relevant policies and procedures.

Alexander, R. J. (1991) *Primary Education in Leeds: Report from the Primary Needs Independent Evaluation*. Leeds: University of Leeds School of Education.

Alexander, R. J. (1992) *Policy and Practice in Primary Education*. London: Routledge.

Alexander, R., Rose, J. and Woodhead, C. (1992) *Classroom Organisation and Classroom Practice in Primary Schools*. London: Department of Education and Science.

Alexander, R., Willcocks, J. and Kinder, K. (1989) *Changing Primary Practice*. London: Falmer.

Amabile, T. M. (1983) *The Social Psychology of Creativity*. New York: Springer Verlag.

Arnot, M., David, M. and Weiner, G. (1996) *Educational Reforms and Gender Equality in Schools*. Research Discussion Paper 17. Manchester: Equal Opportunities Commission.

Arnot, M., David, M. and Weiner, G. (1999) *Closing the Gender Gap: Postwar Education and Social Change*. Cambridge: Polity Press.

Arnot, M., Gray, J., James, M. and Rudduck, J. (1998) *Recent Research on Gender and Educational Performance*. London: Ofsted/The Stationery Office.

Ausubel, D. P. (1963) *The Psychology of Meaningful Learning: An Introduction to School Learning*. New York: Grune and Stratton.

Ausubel, D. P. (1968) *Educational Psychology: A Cognitive View*. New York: Holt, Rinehart and Winston.

Barthorpe, T. and Visser, J. (1991) *Differentiation: Your Responsibility*. Tamworth: National Association for Special Educational Needs.

Bassey, M. (1989) *Teaching Practice in the Primary School*. East Grinstead: Ward Lock Educational.

Bearne, E. (ed) (1996) *Differentiation and Diversity in the Primary School*. London: Routledge.

Bennett, N. and Dunne, E. (1992) *Managing Classroom Groups*. Hemel Hempstead: Simon and Schuster Education.

Black, P. and Wiliam, D. (1998) *Inside the Black Box: Raising Standards through Classroom Assessment*. London: King's College London, School of Education.

Blunkett, D. (1999) 'Social exclusion and the politics of opportunity: a mid-term progress check.' Speech to DEMOS /LSE's Centre for Analysis of Social Exclusion, 3rd November.

Bottery, M. (1993) 'The future of teachers' professionalism.' *Aspects of Education*. 48 pp. 158–169. Hull: University of Hull Institute of Education.

Braddy, S. (1988) 'Personal, social and moral education in the infants school: a practical approach' in Lang, P. C. (ed) *Thinking About Personal and Social Education in the Primary School*. Oxford: Blackwell.

Bryant, P. E. (1974) *Perception and Understanding in Young Children*. London: Methuen.

Child, D. (1997) *Psychology and the Teacher*. (6th edn). London: Cassell.

Cohen, L., Manion, L. and Morrison, K. (1996) *A Guide to Teaching Practice*. (4th edn). London: Routledge.

Cole, M., Hill, D. and Shan, S. (eds) (1997) *Promoting Equality in Primary Schools*. London: Cassell.

Collins, R. (1979) *The Credential Society: An Historical Sociology of Education and Stratification*. New York: Academic Press.

Convery, A. and Coyle, D. (1993) *Differentiation: Taking the Initiative*. London: Centre for Information on Language Teaching and Research.

Cooper, D. E. (1980) *Illusions of Equality*. London: Routledge and Kegan Paul.

CRE (1989) *Code of Practice for the Elimination of Racial Discrimination in Education*. London: Commission for Racial Equality.

CRE (1997) *Exclusion from School and Racial Equality*. London: Commission for Racial Equality.

CRE (1999) CRE's oral evidence to the Lawrence Inquiry. *http://www.cre.gov.uk/index.html*

Davies R. and Ferguson J. (1997) 'Teachers' views of the role of Initial Teacher Education in developing their professionalism.' *Journal of Education for Teaching*. 23 (1) pp. 40–55.

Davies, N. (1999) 'Poverty is the key.' *The Guardian*, 23 September.

Deboys, M. and Pitt, E. (1997) *Lines of Development in Primary Mathematics*. (3rd edn). Belfast: Blackstaff Press.

DES (1978) *Special Educational Needs: Report of the Committee of Enquiry into the Education of Handicapped and Young People* (the Warnock Report). London: HMSO.

DES (1985) *Education for All* (the Swann Report). London: HMSO.

DES (1988) *National Curriculum Task Group on Assessment and Testing. A Report*. London: Department of Education and Science.

DES (1989) *Discipline in Schools: Report of the Committee of Enquiry Chaired by Lord Elton* (The Elton Report). London: HMSO.

DES (1990) *Records of Achievement* (Circular 8/90). London: Department of Education and Science.

DFE (1992) *Reporting Pupils' Achievements to Parents* (Circular 5/92). London: Department for Education.

DfEE (1995) Protecting Children from Abuse: The Role of the Education Service (Circular 10/95). London: DfEE.

DfEE (1998) *Section 550A of the Education Act 1996: The Use of Force to Control or Restrain Pupils* (Circular 10/98). London: DfEE.

DfEE (1998) *The National Literacy Strategy*. London: DfEE.

DfEE (1998) *Teachers: Meeting the Challenge of Change* (Green Paper: Cm 4164). London: HMSO.

DfEE (1999) *National Curriculum Assessments of 7, 11 and 14 Year Olds by Local Education Authority, 1999* (DfEE SFR 29/1999). http://www.dfee.gov.uk/sfr.htm

DfEE (1999) *Social Inclusion: Pupil Support* (Circular 10/99). London: DfEE.

DfEE (1999) *The National Numeracy Strategy: Framework for Teaching Mathematics from Reception to Year 6*. London: DfEE.

DfES (2001) *SEN Tool Kit*. London: DfES.

DfES (2001) *Code of Practice for the Identification and Assessment of Special Educational Needs* (revised). London: DfES.

DfEE/QCA (1999) *The National Curriculum: Handbook for Primary Teachers in England: Key Stages 1 and 2*. London: DfEE.

DfES (2002) *School Teachers' Pay and Conditions* Document 2002 (Circular 12/99). London: DfES.

DfES (2002) *School Teachers' Pay and Conditions of Employment 2002: Guidance*. London: DfES.

DfES/TTA (2002) *Qualifying to Teach: Professional Standards for Qualified Teacher Status and Requirements for Initial Teacher Training*. London: DfES/TTA.

Dickinson, C. and Wright, J. (1993) *Differentiation: A Practical Handbook of Classroom Strategies*. Coventry: National Council for Educational Technology.

Donaldson, M. (1978) *Children's Minds*. London: Fontana.

Dunne, E. and Bennett, N. (1990) *Talking and Learning in Groups*. Basingstoke: Macmillan.

English Basketball Association (1989) *Basketball Curriculum Guide*. (2nd edn). Leeds: EBA.

Epstein, D. and Sealey, A. (1990) *Where it Really Matters… Developing Anti-Racist Education in Predominantly White Primary Schools*. Birmingham: Development Education Centre.

Epstein, D., Elwood, J., Hey, V. and Maw, J. (eds) (1999) *Failing Boys? Issues in Gender and Achievement*. Buckingham: Open University Press.

Ewens, T. (1998) 'Teacher education and PSMC: implications of the new requirements' in Richards, C., Simco, N. and Twiselton, S. (eds) *Primary Teacher Education: High Status? High Standards?* London: Falmer.

Farrell, M. (1998) *The Special Needs Handbook*. London: David Fulton.

Fisher, J. (1996) *Starting from the Child? Teaching and Learning from 4 to 8*. Buckingham: Open University Press.

Flavell, J. H. (1985) *Cognitive Development*. (2nd edn). Englewood Cliffs, N.J.: Prentice Hall.

Fontana, D. (1995) *Psychology for Teachers*. (3rd edn). Basingstoke: Macmillan.

Foster, P., Gomm, R., and Hammersley, M. (1996) *Constructing Educational Inequality*. London: Falmer.

Freeman, A. and Gray, H. (1989) *Organizing Special Educational Needs*. London: Paul Chapman.

Frost, D. (1997) *Reflective Action Planning for Teachers*. London: David Fulton.

Furlong, J. and Maynard, T. (1995) *Mentoring Student Teachers*. London: Routledge.

Gaine, C. (1988) *No Problem Here*. (revised edn). London: Hutchinson.

Gaine, C. (1995) *Still No Problem Here*. Stoke-on-Trent: Trentham Books.

Gaine, C. and George, R. (1999) *Gender, 'Race' and Class in Schooling: A New Introduction*. London: Falmer.

Gilborn, D. and Gipps, C. (1996) *Recent Research on the Achievements of Ethnic Minority Pupils*. London: Ofsted/HMSO.

Goleman, D. (1996) *Emotional Intelligence*. London: Bloomsbury.

Griffiths, M. and Davies, C. (1995) *In Fairness to Children*. London: David Fulton.

GTCE (2001) *Professional Learning Framework*. London: GTCE.

GTCE (2002) *Professional Code for Teachers*. London: GTCE.

Harlen, W. (1985) *Taking the Plunge*. London: Heinemann.

Hay/McBer (2000) *Research into Teacher Effectiveness: A Model of Teacher Effectiveness*. Report by Hay/McBer to the Department for Education and Employment, June 2000.

Hayes, D. (1997) *Success on Your Teaching Experience*. London: Hodder & Stoughton.

Hayes, D. (1999) *Foundations of Primary Teaching*. (2nd edn). London: David Fulton.

Hayes, D. (2000) *The Handbook for Newly Qualified Teachers*. London: David Fulton.

HMI (1989) *Personal and Social Education from 5-16: Curriculum Matters 14*. London: DES.

Hoyle, E. (1980) 'Professionalization and deprofessionalization in education' in Hoyle, E. and Hegarty, J. (eds) *World Yearbook of Education: Professional Development of Teachers*. London: Kogan Page.

Hughes, P. (1991) *Gender Issues in the Primary Classroom*. Leamington Spa: Scholastic.

Kagan, S. (1988) *Co-operative Learning: Resources for Teachers*. California: Riverside Books.

Kerry, T. and Kerry. C. (1997) 'Differentiation: teachers' views of the usefulness of recommended strategies in helping the more able pupils in primary and secondary classrooms'. *Educational Studies*, 23(3) pp. 439-457.

Kershner, R. and Miles, S. (1996) 'Thinking and talking about differentiation' in Bearne, E. (ed) *Differentiation and Diversity in the Primary School*. London: Routledge.

Klein, G. (1993) *Education Towards Race Equality*. London: Cassell.

Kyriacou, C. (1998) *Essential Teaching Skills*. (2nd edn). Cheltenham: Stanley Thornes.

Laslett, R. and Smith, C. (1984) 'Four rules of classroom management' in Pollard, A. (ed.) (1996) *Readings for Reflective Teaching in the Primary School*. London: Cassell Education.

Lefrançois, G. R. (1999) *Psychology for Teaching*. (10th edn). Belmont: Wadsworth.

Lepper, M. R. and Hodell, M. (1989) 'Intrinsic motivation in the classroom' in C. Ames and R. Ames (eds) *Research on Motivation in the Classroom*, vol. 3, pp. 73–105. San Diego: Academic Press.

Lewis, A. (1991) *Primary Special Needs and the National Curriculum*. London: Routledge.

MacPherson, W. (1999) *The Stephen Lawrence Inquiry*. London: The Stationery Office.

Maslow, A. H. (1968) *Towards a Psychology of Being*. New York: Harper and Row.

McGarvey, B., Morgan, V., Marriott, S. and Abbot, L. (1996) 'Differentiation and its problems: the views of primary teachers and curriculum support staff in Northern Ireland.' *Educational Studies*. 22(1) pp. 69–82.

McNamara, D. (1994) 'To group or not to group' in Pollard, A. (ed) (1996) *Readings for Reflective Teaching in the Primary School*. London: Cassell Education.

McNamara, S. (1999) *Differentiation: An Approach to Teaching and Learning*. Cambridge: Pearson.

McNamara, S. and Moreton, G. (1997) *Understanding Differentiation: A Teacher's Guide*. London: David Fulton.

Measor, L. and Sikes, P. J. (1992) *Gender and Schools*. London: Cassell.

Mitchell, C. and Koshy, V. (1995) *Effective Teacher Assessment: Looking at Children's Learning in the Primary Classroom*. (2nd edn). London: Hodder & Stoughton.

Mitsos, E. and Browne, K. (1998) 'Gender differences in education: the underachievement of boys'. *Sociology Review* 8 (1).

Morgan, C. and Morris, G. (1999) *Good Teaching and Learning*. Buckingham: Open University Press.

Morris, E. (1996) 'Labour's plans to give boys new hope.' *The Times*, 1 November.

Mortimore, P., Sammons, P., Stoll, L., Lewis, D. and Ecob R. (1988) *School Matters: The Junior Years*. Wells: Open Books.

Mosley, J. (1993) *Turn Your School Around*. Wisbech: LDA.

Moss, G. (1996) *A Strategy for Differentiation*. Birmingham: Questions Publishing Ltd.

NCC (1991) *Science and Pupils with Special Educational Needs*. York: National Curriculum Council.

NCC (1993) *Teaching Science at Key Stages 1 and 2*. York: National Curriculum Council.

NEOST/LGA/ATL/NAHT/NASUWT/NUT/PAT/SHA (2000) *Conditions of Service for School-teachers in England and Wales*. London: Employers' Organisation for Local Government.

Ofsted (1993) *Handbook for the Inspection of Schools*. London: Ofsted.

Ofsted (1995) *The Ofsted Handbook – Guidance on the Inspection of Nursery and Primary Schools*. London: HMSO.

Ofsted (1996) *Framework for the Inspection of Primary Schools*. London: Ofsted.

Ofsted (1996) *Raising Attainment of Minority Ethnic Pupils – School and LEA Responses*. London: Ofsted.

Ofsted (1999) *Inspecting Schools: The Framework*: Effective from January 2000. London: Ofsted.

Ofsted (1999) *Inspecting Schools: Handbook for Inspecting Primary and Nursery Schools*. London: The Stationery Office.

Peters, R. S. (1966) *Ethics and Education*. London: Allen and Unwin.

Pollard, A. (1997) *Reflective Teaching in the Primary School*. (3rd edn). London: Cassell.

Pollard, A. (ed) (1996) *Readings for Reflective Teaching in the Primary School*. London: Cassell.

Pollard, A. and Bourne, J. (eds) (1994) *Teaching and Learning in the Primary School*. London: Routledge.

Proctor, A., Entwhistle, M., Judge, B. and McKenzie-Murdoch, S. (1995) *Learning to Teach in the Primary Classroom*. London: Routledge.

QCA (1998) *Science: A Scheme of Work for Key Stages 1 and 2*. London: QCA.

QCA (2000) *Personal, Social and Health Education and Citizenship at Key Stages 1 and 2*. London: QCA.

Reading, H. F. (1977) *A Dictionary of the Social Sciences*. London: Routledge and Kegan Paul.

Reason, R. (1993) 'Good practice in groupwork' in Pollard, A. (ed) (1996) *Readings for Reflective Teaching in the Primary School*. London: Cassell Education.

Reid, J-A., Forrestal, P. and Cook, J. (1989) *Small Group Learning in the Classroom*. Scarborough: Chalkface Press.

Richards, C., Simco, N. and Twiselton, S. (eds) (1998) *Primary Teacher Education: High Status? High Standards?* London: Falmer.

Riley, K. A. (1994) *Quality and Equality: Promoting Opportunities in Schools.* London: Cassell.

Rogers, B. (1998) *You Know the Fair Rule.* London: Pitman.

Rogers, C. (1983) *Freedom to Learn for the 80's.* Columbus, Ohio: Merril.

Runnymede Trust (1993) *Equality Assurance in Schools: Quality, Identity, Society.* London: Runnymede Trust / Trentham Books.

SCAA (1995) *Planning the Curriculum at Key Stages 1 and 2.* London: SCAA.

Scott-Baumann, A., Bloomfield, A. and Roughton, L. (1997) *Becoming a Secondary School Teacher.* London: Hodder and Stoughton.

Skelton, C. (1989) *Whatever Happens to Little Women? Gender Issues and Primary Schooling.* Buckingham: Open University Press.

Skinner, B. F. (1968) *The Technology of Teaching.* New York: Appleton.

Smith, A. (1998) *Accelerated Learning in Practice.* Trowbridge: Redwood Books.

St Martin's College (2000) *Sample Lesson Plans for Mathematics Related to the National Numeracy Strategy.* Lancaster: St Martin's College.

Stanworth, M. (1983) *Gender and Schooling: A Study of Sexual Divisions in the Classroom.* London: Hutchinson.

Tattum, D. P. (1988) 'Social education in interaction' in Lang, P. C. (ed) *Thinking About Personal and Social Education in the Primary School.* Oxford: Blackwell.

Thody, A., Grey, B. and Bowden D. (2000) *The Teacher's Survival Guide.* London: Continuum.

Tizard, B. and Hughes, M. (1984) *Young Children Learning.* London: Fontana.

Tutchell, E. (1990) *Dolls and Dungarees: Gender Issues in the Primary School.* Buckingham: Open University Press.

Tyler, K. (1992) *Enhancing Children's Self-Concepts in the Primary School.* Loughborough: Loughborough University Department of Education.

Tyler, K. (1992) *Personal and Social Education in Primary Schools.* Loughborough: Loughborough University Department of Education.

Verma, G. (1994) 'Cultural diversity in primary schools: its nature, extent and cross-curricular implications' in Verma, G. K. and Pumfrey, P. (eds) *Cross Curricular Contexts, Themes and Dimension in Primary Schools.* London: Falmer.

Visser, J. (1993) *Differentiation: Making it Work.* Tamworth: National Association for Special Educational Needs.

Vygotsky, L. S. (1978) *Mind in Society.* M. Cole et al. (eds) Cambridge, Mass.: Harvard University Press.

Watkins, C. and Wagner, P. (1988) *School Discipline: A Whole School Approach.* Oxford: Blackwell.

Webster, A. (1995) 'Differentiation' in Moss, G. (ed) *The Basics of Special Needs: A Routledge/ Special Children Survival Guide for the Classroom Teacher.* London: Routledge.

Weiner, G. (ed) (1985) *Just a Bunch of Girls.* Milton Keynes: Open University Press.

Weston, P. (1992) 'A decade for differentiation'. *British Journal of Special Education.* 19(1) pp. 6–9.

Wiltshire County Council (1988) *Assessment in Physical Education.* Trowbridge: Wiltshire C.C.

Woodhead, C. (1998) 'Where do you stand?' *Times Educational Supplement,* 5 June.

Wragg, T. (1997) 'Oh boy!' *Times Educational Supplement,* 16 May.

Wragg, T. (1997) 'Support for boys need not hurt girls.' *Times Educational Supplement,* 30 May.

INDEX

Achieving QTS

The Achieving QTS series includes 20 titles, encompassing *Audit and Test*, *Knowledge and Understanding*, *Teaching Theory and Practice* and *Skills Tests* titles. As well as covering the core primary subject areas, the series addresses issues of teaching and learning across both primary curriculum and secondary phases. The Teacher Training Agency has identified books in this series as high quality resources for trainee teachers. You can find more information on each of these titles on our website: www.learningmatters.co.uk

Assessment for Learning and Teaching in Primary Schools
Mary Briggs, Peter Swatton, Cynthia Martin and Angela Woodfield
£15.00 176pp ISBN: 1 903300 74 6

Primary English
Audit and Test (second edition)
Doreen Challen
£8.00 64pp ISBN: 1 903300 86 X

Primary Mathematics
Audit and Test (second edition)
Claire Mooney and Mike Fletcher
£8.00 52pp ISBN: 1 903300 87 8

Primary Science
Audit and Test (second edition)
John Sharp and Jenny Byrne
£8.00 80pp ISBN: 1 903300 88 6

Learning and Teaching in Secondary Schools (second edition)
Edited by Viv Ellis
£15.00 176pp ISBN: 1 84445 004 X

Passing the ICT Skills Test
Clive Ferrigan
£6.99 80pp ISBN: 1 903300 13 4

Passing the Literacy Skills Test
Jim Johnson
£6.99 80pp ISBN: 1 903300 12 6

Passing the Numeracy Skills Test (third edition)
Mark Patmore
£8.00 64pp ISBN: 1 903300 94 0

Primary English: Knowledge and Understanding (second edition)
David Wray, Jane Medwell and George Moore
£15.00 224pp ISBN: 1 903300 53 3

Primary English: Teaching Theory and Practice (second edition)
David Wray, Jane Medwell, Hilary Minns, Elizabeth Coates and Vivienne Griffiths
£15.00 192pp ISBN: 1 903300 54 1

Primary ICT: Knowledge, Understanding and Practice (second edition)
Jane Sharp, Avril Loveless, John Potter and Jonathan Allen
£15.00 256pp ISBN: 1 903300 59 2

Primary Mathematics: Knowledge and Understanding (second edition)
Claire Mooney, Lindsey Ferrie, Sue Fox, Alice Hansen and Reg Wrathmell
£15.00 176pp ISBN: 1 903300 55 X

Primary Mathematics: Teaching Theory and Practice (second edition)
Claire Mooney, Mike Fletcher, Mary Briggs and Judith McCullouch
£15.00 192pp ISBN: 1 903300 56 8

Primary Science: Knowledge and Understanding (second edition)
Rob Johnsey, John Sharp, Graham Peacock and Debbie Wright
£15.00 232pp ISBN: 1 903300 57 6

Primary Science: Teaching Theory and Practice (second edition)
John Sharp, Graham Peacock, Rob Johnsey, Shirley Simon and Robin Smith
£15.00 140pp ISBN: 1 903300 58 4

Professional Studies: Primary Phase (second edition)
Kate Jacques and Rob Hyland
£15.00 224pp ISBN: 1 903300 60 6

Teaching Arts in Primary Schools
Stephanie Penny, Susan Young, Raywen Ford and Lawry Price
£15.00 192pp ISBN: 1 903300 35 5

Teaching Citizenship in Primary Schools
Hilary Claire
£15.00 160pp ISBN: 1 84445 010 4

Teaching Foundation Stage
Edited by Iris Keating
£15.00 200pp ISBN: 1 903300 33 9

Teaching Humanities in Primary Schools
Pat Hoodless, Sue Bermingham, Elaine McCreery and Paul Bowen
£15.00 192pp ISBN: 1 903300 36 3

To order please phone our order line 0845 230 9000 or send an official order or cheque to
BEBC, Albion Close, Parkstone, Poole, BH12 3LL
Order online at www.learningmatters.co.uk